An Alphabetical Guide to Wales and the Welsh

The People, the Places, the Traditions

By
Peter Williams

airleaf.com

ISBN: 1-59453-867-0

"In this work, when it shall be found that much is omitted, let it not be forgotten that much likewise is performed." (Dr. Samuel Johnson, *Preface* to *Dictionary of the English Language,* 1755).

Preface

While every effort has been made to ascertain the correctness of the information provided in this book, some of the dates, especially those of the medieval period, may be approximate. Birth dates are included for contemporary Welsh men and women whenever they have been provided.

Regrettably, it is impossible to include every person who has contributed in some way to the history, culture, language, or traditions of Wales, either at home or abroad, nor is it possible in the scope of this book to include every place, historical event or local tradition, but the most important are listed here in almost 2,500 entries. Places are included if they have played a role, no matter how small, in the development of the Welsh nation. Some people and places are included for their unusual character or special interest. Mythological personages or beasts are included if I believe they have helped create the Welsh character.

In the Welsh alphabet Ch, Dd, Ff, Ng, Ll, Rh, Th, and Ph are separate letters. To save confusion for non-Welsh readers, with two exceptions, entries follow the order of the English alphabet, so that words beginning with Ch are listed under C; words beginning with Th are listed under T. In the exceptions, following normal Welsh rules, words beginning with Ll are not listed under L, but under Ll (following L), words beginning with Th are found not under T, but under Th (following T).

The following letters do not appear in the Welsh alphabet: J, K, Q, V, X, Z (notwithstanding Catherine Zeta Jones and all the other Joneses).

A

The first letter of the Welsh Alphabet (pronounced as in the English word "cat," never as in "late."

A Oes Heddwch? (Is there Peace?) The stirring three-time cry of the Archdruid of Wales at the annual ceremony of the Gorsedd and on the National Eisteddfod stage, answered each time by "Heddwch" (Peace).

Abaty Cwm Hir (Abbey of the Long Valley): near Rhayader, Radnorshire, a former important Cistercian Abbey where the body of Prince Llywelyn ap Gruffudd was laid to rest in 1282.

Aberavon (S. Wales West Electoral Region): parliamentary constituency that sent Ramsey MacDonald to Westminster in 1922 (he became P.M. in 1924).

Aberconway, Lord (Henry MacLaren, 1914-2003): an industrialist with ship-building interests; President of the Royal Horticultural Society 1961-84, he gave his wonderful gardens at Bodnant (Conwy Valley) to the National Trust in 1948. In 1939 he had met Rudolph Hess in an unsuccessful attempt to avert war.

Aberconwy, Battle of (1194): in which Llywelyn the Great (Llywelyn Fawr) defeated Dafydd ap Owain Gwynedd to become sole ruler of Gwynedd.

Aberconwy, Treaty of (1277): punitive legislation that followed the victorious campaign of Edward 1st. by which Prince Llywelyn ap Gruffudd was forced to surrender territory east of the River Conwy and his people were forced to endure harsh conditions that soon led to rebellion.

Abercyfar, Carmarthen (2nd Century A.D.): site of the most westerly Roman villa in Britain.

Aberdare, Mid-Glmorgan: a former important center of the coal and iron industry, now the chief shopping and service centre for the Cynon Valley.

Aberdare Committee (1881): under Gladstone's government, chaired by Lord Aberdare, its report created university colleges at Bangor and Cardiff.

Aberdare, Henry, 1st Baron (1815-1895): Liberal M.P. for Merthyr. As Home Secretary, he was responsible for passage of the Liquor Licensing Act of 1872 that alienated brewers and publicans and led to the defeat of his party.

Aberdaron, Gwynedd: at the tip of the Llyn Peninsula, for centuries the gathering place for pilgrims on their way to Ynys Enlli (*Bardsey Island*) "the island of 20,00 saints."

Aberdyfi (Aberdovey), Mer: resort on Cardigan Bay made famous by "The Bells of Aberdovey" about the drowning of the town by the incoming tide.

Aberfan (*Aber Van*), Merthyr: on 21 October 1966, a mountain of coal waste, weakened by heavy rains, slid down onto the village school at Pant Glas, completely engulfing the building and killing 144 children and adults. The tragedy shook the whole nation and spurred efforts to clean up the coal tips in the Valleys left after more than a century and a half of mining and after repeated warnings about the unstable tip had been ignored.

Aberffraw, Anglesey: the chief court of the Princes of Gwynedd that came to an end with the death of Dafydd ap Gruffudd in 1283.

Abergavenny (Y Fenni): named for the Celtic god of smiths, Gofannon, the town was settled by Romans, then Normans; it is now a market town and dormitory for Newport and Cardiff. Nazi deputy-leader Rudolph Hess was imprisoned at nearby Maindiff Court in W.W. II.

Abergele Martyrs: in July 1969, William Jones and George Taylor were killed on the railway lines at Abergele by accidental detonation of explosives they were carrying to disrupt the Investiture ceremonies of Charles, the Prince of Wales at Caernarfon Castle.

Abergwaun (see Fishguard).

Abergwili, Carmarthen: in a former residence of the Bishops of St. David's is the Carmarthen County Musuem that displays the region's archeology, history and daily life.

Aberteifi (see Cardigan).

Aberystwyth, Ceredigion: principal center of Welsh culture, home of the University College, a Theological College and the Ceredigion Museum. The National Library of Wales on Penglais Hill holds the medieval *Black Book of Carmarthen*, the *Laws of Hywel Dda*, the *Book of Taliesin* and the earliest complete text of the *Mabinogion*. The town also has a rare Camera Obscura.

Aberystwyth: popular hymn tune by Dr. Joseph Parry, sung in English to the words of Charles Wesley, "Jesus, Lover of my soul."

Ablett, Noah (1883-1935): b. Rhondda Valley, an important miners' leader who inspired Labour leaders Aneurin Bevan, James Griffiths and Lewis Jones.

Abraham, William (*Mabon*, 1842-1922): popular, influential miners' leader who supported adoption of the sliding scale, gaining some concessions and a holiday on the first Monday of each month, "Mabon's Monday." Lib-lab M.P. for Rhondda in 1885, he became the first president of the South Wales Miners' Federation in 1989.

Abse, Dannie (b. 1923): b. Cardiff; dramatist, novelist, and medical doctor concerned with political and social events of the 1930's, and, in his seven volumes of poetry, the unusual.

Abse, Leo (b. 1917): lawyer; Labour M. P for Pontypool and Torfaen (1958-97, brother of Dannie.

Academi Gymreig, Yr *(the Welsh Academy,* f. 1959): a society that includes writers in English to promote literature in Wales and maintain standards.

Act for the Better Propagation and Preaching of the Gospel (1650): appointed commissioners in Wales to provide sufficient ministers to supplant the resident clergy, who had supported King Charles 1st. Puritan doctrines were to be officially enforced; it led to many congregations moving to the New World.

Acts of Union (1536 and 1543): abolished any legal distinction between the citizens of Wales and those of England, settled the border by the creation of new counties, and gave Wales seats in Parliament (its primary intention may have been to wipe out the Welsh language; this it failed to do).

Adam of Usk (1352-1430): historian whose *Chronicon Adae de Usk* details the Owain Glyndwr rebellion.

Adams, Sam (b. 1934): from Gilfach Goch, poet, critic and editor.

Aderyn Bee Y Llwyd: (see Mari Lwyd).

Adfer: translated as "to restore," a group founded in 1971 dedicated to the achievement of Welsh mono-lingualism in the heart lands of the language that still miraculously remain in north and west Wales.

Admiral Insurance (f. 1993): a Cardiff company guided by American born chief executive Henry Engelhardt that is the most valuable insurance company in Wales and its leader on the Stock Exchange.

Afallennau, Yr (*the Apple Trees*): stanzas in *The Black Book of Carmarthen* (1250) that contain the earliest nucleus of the Myrddin (Merlin) legend.

Age of Saints, the (5th-7th C.): the period when Wales became a national unity, Welsh in language and Christian in religion, with a great tradition of learning in its monasteries and religious houses.

Agricultural Societies (mid 18th C): formed to encourage the improvement of rural life, they brought much needed changes to Welsh agriculture.

Aizlewood, Mark (b. 1959): b. Newport; international footballer who learned Welsh as an adult to become a more successful commentator with BBC.

Alban Arthan: December 21, the Winter Solstice.

Alban Eilir: March 20, the Spring Equinox.

Alford, Jim (1914-2004): b. Cardiff, middle distance runner and first Welsh national athletics coach, winner of Olympic Gold in the mile in 1938 at Sydney, he introduced many techniques into Wales that later helped Steve Ovett, Herb Eelliot and Lynn Davies. During WWll, he was a squadron leader with RAF.

Alice Rowena (mid 5th C.): daughter of Hengist, encouraged Saxon rule over southern Britain, giving her name "Rowena's children" to the English. nation.

Almedha, St. (5-6 century): early Christian martyr, daughter of Brychan; celebrated August lst.

Alphabet, Welsh: (see Welsh Alphabet and Y Wyddor).

Ambrosius (*Emrys Wledig*, 5th C.): named by Gildas as a leader against the Saxons and by Nennius as a rival of Vortigern (Gwrtheyrn)

Amddiffynfa, Hen (*the Old Fort*, 1853): the home of the first Welsh settlers in Patagonia, Argentina.

Amerik, Richard (b. 1445): a Bristol merchant whose family came from Meryk Court, Glamorgan; the main investor in the second transatlantic voyage of John Cabot in 1498, and after whom, according to some, America may be named.

Amlwch, Anglesey: coastal resort, formerly the export outlet for copper from Parys Mountain that dominated the copper trade and set world prices in the 18th and 19th centuries.

Amserau, Yr (the Times, f. 1843): newspaper that merged with *Baner Cymru* in 1859 to form *Baner ac Amserau Cymru (*later *Y Faner).*

Anarawd (d. 916): eldest son of Rhodri Mawr who ruled the Kingdom of Gwynedd after defeating the Mercians.

Ancient Britons, the Most Honourable and Loyal Society of (f. 1715): first official Welsh society in London.

Andrews, Elizabeth (1882-1960): b. Rhondda; with a controversial letter writing career, she was an early suffragette, recruited by the new Labour Party as its first woman organizer; her evidence to the Sankey Commission led to the inception of pit head baths at the collieries; she campaigned for the first nursery school in Wales (opened in the Rhondda in 1938).

Aneirin (7th Century): poet from the Welsh-language area of Strathclyde, Scotland, composer of *Y Gododdin*, in which the name *Arthur* first appears.

Anerch I'r Cymru (*Greetings to the Welsh,* 1721): by Ellis Pugh; the first Welsh language book published in North America (at Philadelphia).

Angharad (1066-1162): wife of Gruffudd ap Cynan, King of Gwynedd, and mother of Owain Gwynedd and Gwenllian.

Anglesey (Ynys Mon): known as "Mam Cymru" (the Mother of Wales), an island county created by the Statute of Rhuddlan in 1284.

Anglesey eggs (Wyau Ynys Môn): a baked dish including eggs, potatoes, cheese, flour and butter.

Anglesey, 1st Marquess of (Henry William Paget, 1768-1854): of Plas Newydd (now owned by the National Trust), Viceroy of Ireland, commander of cavalry at Waterloo, where he lost a leg.

Anglo-Welsh: a term coined in the 1920's to describe Welsh authors who write in English, including Dylan Thomas, Richard Llewellyn and others.

Anglo-Welsh Review (f. 1957): begun as *Dock Leaves* in 1949 to close the gap between Welsh and Anglo-Welsh writers with translations and articles about Welsh literature in English.

Angor, Yr* (The Anchor, f. 1979):*** paper of the sizeable Liverpool Welsh community, also the name of the local paper (papur bro) for Aberystwyth.

Annales Cambriae: found in the Latin manuscript, *Brut y Tywysogion* (Chronicle of the Princes), it is a major source for medieval Welsh history. From three different historical periods, first edited in 1860.

Annwn (or Annawfn): the underworld; a place of permanent happiness and joy that under Christian influence became a place inhabited by fierce hellhounds whose barking foretells death.

Anterliwt (Interlude): a performance by traveling players throughout Wales in the late 18th century. The greatest writer was Twm O'r Nant (Thomas Edwards).

Antur (liberty): the dog that showed the starving Welsh settlers in Patagonia that the abundant guanaco and hares could be a source of food.

Antur Teifi: f. 1979, a southwest Wales community-based economic and social development company organized to promote prosperity by forging partnerships and providing tools for development. In 2004, with Cambrian Training Company, it spearheaded a three-year European project to secure the future and identity of regional food dishes and improve the visitor experience.

Anwyl, Sir Edward (1866-1914): b. Chester, Celtic scholar, university professor and notable leader of Welsh cultural life.

(Ap or Ab): "son of" in many instances the "ap" has transferred itself to the newer surname; thus ap Howell is now Powell, ap Rhys is now Pryce or Preece, ap Evan is now Bevan, and so on.

Ap Evan, Enoch (d. 1633): b. Clune, Shropshire, hanged for killing his mother and brother with an axe. London pamphlets that described his "barbarous and most cruel act" helped begin a thriving market in tabloid-style journalism that has never died.

Ap Gwilym, Gwynn (b. 1950): b. Bangor; editor, poet, translator, secretary of the Welsh section of Yr Academi Gymreig, co-editor of *Barn* and chairman of Cymdeithas Cerdd Dafod.

Ap Hywel, Elin (b. 1962): from Colwyn Bay, a leading Welsh-language poet whose work has been translated into many European languages.

Apperley, Charles J. (*Nimrod,* 1779-1843): Wrexham, author of ten books, including *Nimrod's Hunting Tours* (1835), *The life of a Sportsman* (1842).

Arcade (f. 1980-82): a fortnightly magazine covering life in Wales.

Archenfield (*Ergyng*): put in Herefordshire by Act of Union 1536; it remained mostly Welsh speaking into the 19th century, producing many notables.

***Archaeologia Britannica,* 1707:** one volume of a proposed survey of philology, antiquities, folklore natural history and geology of the Celtic countries; the first important work on Celtic philology.

Arddu: the dark Lord of the Dead, the spirit of winter and death.

Ardwyn Singers (Cantorion Ardwyn Caerdydd, f. 1964): Cardiff-based mixed choir that has become internationally known for its "Ardwyn Sound," performing in concerts and recordings.

Arfon: the heartland of the ancient kingdom of Gwynedd, centered at Caernarfon.

Arianrhod: sky goddess who guards the heavens, appearing as a human silhouette in a black sky blazing with stars.

Arloewswr, Yr **(The Pioneer, 1957-1960)**: a magazine published in Bangor for new Welsh poets that carried first chapters of contemporary Welsh novels and interviews with writers.

Ar *Lôg* (for Hire): a much-traveled popular folk music group in Wales during the 1970's and 80's with a high level of musicianship, making full use of the harp and including clog dancing.

Armes Prydein **(*The Prophecy of Britain c.* 930)**: a poem from *The Book of Taliesin* depicting an alliance between the Celts of Britain and Brittany with the Norsemen of Dublin to try to overthrow the Saxons under King Athelstan.

Armorica: a western peninsula of old Gaul, settled by Britons fleeing from Saxon invaders in the 5th century.

Armstrong-Jones, Anthony, Earl of Snowdon (b.1930): a society photographer born in England to a prominent Welsh family; once married to Princess Margaret.

Arthur (5-6th Century): warrior mentioned by Gildas and Nennius who first appears in the Welsh language poem *Y Gododdin*. The legends connected to Arthur are Wales's great contribution to the culture of Europe and to the world, with an International Arthurian Society and hundreds of scholarly books published each year (as well as movies, musicals and plays).

Arts Council of Wales: set up to administer government funding of the arts in Wales, it is accountable to the National Assembly and to Parliament through the Secretary of State for Culture, Media and Sport.

Ashley, Laura (1925-1985): home furnishings and fashion designer. The Laura Ashley Foundation began its Fellowship Awards in 1998.

Assembly, the Welsh: (see National Assembly for Wales).

Asser (9th Century A.D.): Welsh-born bishop of Sherborne, counselor to Alfred of Wessex, about whom he wrote his *Life of Alfred.*

Aubrey, William (the Great Civilian, 1529-95): Brecon; Fellow of Jesus and All Souls Colleges; Judge Advocate and Church reformer, Master of Requests at Court.

Awdl: a long poem in the traditional meters from the time of the Poets of the Gentry in the 15th Century.

Awst: eighth month of the year (August in English).

B

Second letter of the Welsh alphabet
(At the beginning of many words, b acts as a soft
mutation of the letter p (e.g. ben for pen, bont for pont,
and so on).

Bachegraig (Tremeirchion, Flints): reputed to be the first brick house in Wales. Built for Sir Richard Clough, second husband of Catrin of Berain in 1567, it was said to be the work of the Devil and was therefore demolished by new owner Hester Piozzi (Hester Thrale).

Bacon, Anthony (1717-1786): iron-master who helped develop the iron industry in Merthyr in the late 18th century, supplying most of the cannons during the War of American Independence (for both sides).

Bagillt, Flintshire: part of the Borough of Flint; site of Bettisfield Colliery where the Friendly Associated Coal Miners' Union in 1830 was the first trade union established in Wales.

Badon, Battle of (c 516): where Arthur "bore the Cross of Our Lord Jesus Christ on his shoulders for three days and three nights and the Britons were the victors" in *Annales Cambriae).*

Bailey, Crawshay (1789-1872): M.P., iron-master and railway pioneer at Cyfarthfa, Merthyr, commemorated with much sarcasm in the song "Y Mochyn Du" (*the Black Pig*).

Baker, David (Augustine Baker, 1575-1641): b. Abergavenny, Catholic writer on theology who had the temerity to suggest that spiritual guidance came to the soul directly from God and was to be sought and found in prayer. In 1624, he became spiritual director for the English Benedictine nuns at Cambrai, France.

Baker, Sir Stanley (1928-1976): Rhondda born actor of stage and screen, debuted in *The Druid's Rest* (1942). Starring in 55 films, he is most remembered for his roles as a tough guy and for his part as the Welsh captain in the Hollywood epic *Zulu.*

Bala, Merionethshire: famous in the 18th century for woolen stockings (a pair of which was worn by George III to help alleviate his rheumatism). *Bod Iwan* is the former home of Michael Jones, "father of Welsh nationalism," the founder of Welsh Patagonia. Local company "Cowbois" specializes in Welsh goods.

Bala Lake (Llyn Tegid): the largest natural lake in Wales. Source of the River Dee and the only home of the Gwyniad, a species of land-locked white fish, a survivor from the Ice Age.

Baldwin, Archbishop of Canterbury (d. 1191): he preached the Crusade in Wales in 1188 to emphasize his authority over the four Welsh cathedrals.

Bale, Christian (b. 1974): b. Haverford West; actor chosen as the next Batman; appeared at age 12 in *Empire of the Sun*; starred in Kenneth Branagh's *Henry V* and *American Psycho*.

Ballinger, John (1860-1933): b. Pontnewydd, Mont., the first librarian of the National Library of Wales (1908), with many texts on technical librarianship, he contributed much to the study of the literature and bibliography of Wales.

Bancroft, William John (1870-1959): great fullback in rugby union; Welsh captain in many matches, in two of which they won the Triple Crown.

Bando: a winter game formerly popular in the Valleys similar to hockey. The rules and number of players varied from parish to parish.

***Baner ac Amserau Cymru* (the Banner and Times of Wales, 1859-1992):** Welsh-language newspaper, a merger of two weeklies (*Amserau* and *Baner Cymru*). The paper had enormous influence on the religious, political and literary life of 19th and 20th century Wales with often-radical views. Re-launched as *Y Faner* in 1971, it became a weekly in 1977, under the auspices of the Welsh Arts Council, continuing to provide a forum for all kinds of public opinion.

Bangor, Gwynedd: the modest cathedral on the site of a monastic settlement begun in 525 by St. Deiniol, may be the oldest religious center in Britain in continuous use. Treasures include the *Anian Pontifical*, a service book for bishops, the "Mostyn Christ," and a tomb that may be Owain Gwynedd's.

Bangor Normal College (f.1858): teachers' training institution that joined the University of Wales in 1996.

Bangor on Dee (*Bangor Is-Coed*): site of a monastery destroyed in the 7th century by the Saxons, many of the monks escaping to Bardsey Island.

Bara Brith (speckled bread): wheat bread containing spices and currants, a favorite at Welsh teas.

Bara Ceirch: poor man's oatcakes (made with oats, water and bacon fat).

Bara Law: ("lava bread") a dish made of boiled seaweed and oatmeal, fried in bacon fat and known in the Swansea area as *Welshman's caviar*.

***Barbara Miltwn, Marwnad* (c. 1695):** an elegy by Huw Morys for Barbara, wife of Richard Middleton that is regarded as one of the finest in the Welsh language.

**Bard**: a member of the Gorsedd, which supervises the National Eisteddfod; members have distinguished themselves in many areas of public life in Wales or in the promulgation of Welsh culture outside Wales. The Bardic Order in Wales formed a privileged section of society; for more than 1000 years. By the late 1500's the Order was in decline, noble families having dispensed with bards. The present Gorsedd came out of the fertile mind of Iolo Morgannwg in the late 18th Century and has become an integral part of Welsh culture.

Bardd Gwlad (Country poet): a poet who writes in the traditional metres and in *cynghanedd* to celebrate communal life and events of his own locality.

Bardsey Island (Ynys Enlli): Llyn Peninsula, Gwynedd: a nature reserve formerly the site of an important religious settlement, dating from its founding by St. Cadfan in the 6th Century. Known as "the Isle of Twenty Thousand Saints," it is reached by boat over treacherous currents from Aberdaron.

Barlow, Roger (16th century): b. Pembrokeshire, a member of Sebastian Cabot's second voyage to the Americas in 1526. His translation of the Spanish *Suma de Geographi* was the first account of the New World in English.

Barmouth (*Aber Maw*), Merionethshire: a resort town where Dinas Oleu cliffs were the first property in Britain to be acquired by the National Trust in 1895.

Barn (Opinion, f. 1962): an influential monthly magazine of current affairs that became the mouthpiece for the successful Welsh Nationalist Movement in the 1960's by calling for Government reforms.

Barney (b. 1996): from Gwersyllt, near Wrexham, famous cat who alerted is owners to a fire in their kitchen in 2002, thus saving their lives and winning a national competition of the Cats' Protection League.

Barnie, John: from Abergavenny, assistant. editor of *Planet* and then editor. He has published collections of his own poetry, fiction and essays, winning Welsh Arts Council Book of the Year Award in 1990.

Barry (*Y Bari*), South Glamorganshire: a town that grew rapidly during the late 19th century when its extensive docks were built to handle the export of Welsh coal then monopolized by Cardiff. In 2001, the football team became the first Welsh side to win a Champions' League game, beating Shamkir, Azerbaijan.

Baseball: an old form of the game popular in the Valleys. There have been games against England since 1908, with Wales winning the great majority.

Basham, Johnny (1890-1947): born in Newport, he came to Wrexham with the Royal Welch Fusiliers, becoming famous as a boxer. Known as "The Happy Wanderer," he won Welterweight and Middle Weight European championships, with 91 professional fights.

Basingwerk Abbey, Flintshire: a Cistercian Abbey where a version of *Historia Regum Britanniae* and *Brut y Saeson* may have been composed (15th-16th C).

Bassey, Dame Shirley (b. 1937): Cardiff-born international entertainer. Her songs for the James Bond movies include "Goldfinger," "Diamonds are For Ever," and "Moonraker"; other hits include "Nobody Does it Like Me," and "Big Spender." Named *the Tigress of Tiger Bay,* Dame Shirley debuted on record with the "Banana Boat Song" in 1957. In 1977 she was chosen as the best female soloist in the past 50 years. In 2003, she was awarded France's Insignia de la Legion d'Honneur for her contributions to the music industry.

B.B.C. National Orchestra of Wales (f. 1935): begun under Director of Music, Idris Lewis; disbanded during W.W. II; reorganized in 1946 as a Welsh National Orchestra under such conductors as Mansel Thomas and Rae Jenkins. It moved to St. David's Hall, Cardiff in 1982 to become a full symphony orchestra and changed its name to BBC National Chorus of Wales in 1993.

B.B.C. Wales: began in 1923 as Station S.W.A. in Cardiff; became B.B.C. Wales as a separate radio station in 1978. Radio Cymru began in 1979.

Beaumaris (Biwmaris), Anglesey: home to a stunning Edward lst castle, courthouse of "Hanging" Judge Jeffries. The Parish Church has a stone coffin of Joan, wife of Prince Llywelyn and daughter of King John.

Beaumont, Hugh "Binkie"; (Hugh Griffiths Morgan (1908-1973); leading theatre impressario who began at Cardiff Playhouse and went on to London to manage Tallulah Bankhead in 1925.

Bebb, Dewi (1938-1996): b. Bangor, a rugby great; debuted for Swansea in 1958; began and ended his international career against England; he toured with the British Lions in S. Africa, N. Zealand, Australia and Canada.

Bebb, William Ambrose (1894-1955): from Cardiganshire; university lecturer and historian of Brittany and Wales who helped found *Y Mudiand Cymreig* in 1924 that grew into *Plaid Genedlaethol Cymru.*

Bedell, William: contemporary businessman from Llandrindod Wells who designed the Horse Weigh in 1992, a versatile mobile platform for weighing horses and cattle that is used worldwide.

Beddgelert, Gwynedd: mountain village where Gelert's Grave honors the dog who saved the life of the young son of Prince Llywelyn in a legend that is found other European countries and India.

Beirniad, Y (the Critic, 1859-1879): an influential periodical with articles on religion, history, literature, and geology that also supported women's emancipation and education, etc. A magazine of the same name appeared from 1911 to 1917 published under the auspices of the University of Wales to improve Welsh linguistics reform and literary standards.

Belenos: patron of fire and thermal springs; feast day is Beltaine, May lst.

Beli Mawr (c. 55 B.C.): mentioned by Nennius as King of the Britons (during the time of Caesar) from whom many prominent Welsh families claimed descent.

Bell, Sir Harold Idris (1879-1967): classical scholar, critic and translator, author of *The Development of Welsh Poetry; Dafydd ap Gwilym and Fifty Poems*; translator of *Hanes Llenyddiaeth Gymraeg Hyd* and much more.

Bellamy, Craig (b. 1979): b. Cardiff: feisty footballer with Newcastle United and Blackburn, who helped Wales defeat top European teams in 2002-3.

Belle, John (b. 1932): from Pontcanna, Cardiff; went to U.S. in 1959, an architect who has helped restore some of New York City's most famous landmarks, including the National Museum of Immigration on Ellis Island (named after Welshman from Flintshire), Grand Central Terminal, the Rockefeller Center, the Chrysler Building and many others. His most ambitious project is the rebuilding of Ground Zero, the site of the World Trade Center's Twin towers, demolished on September 11, 2001.

***Bells of Aberdovey* (Clychau Aberdyfi):** folk song first published in 1844.

Bennett, Hywel (b. 1944): b. Garnant, Amman Valley). A popular stage, radio, television and film actor.

Bennett, Elinor (b. 1945): internationally known, much sought-after harpist, for whom many distinguished composers have written works. With a law degree (Aberystwyth); trained under Osian Ellis at the Royal Academy of Music, has performed with such famous conductors as Barbirolli, Britten, Boult, Leinsdorf, and Colin Davies. She is undoubtedly the greatest harpist of contemporary Wales, with dozens of superb recordings and memorable concerts.

Bennett, Phil (b 1948): a rugby star with Llanelli; played 8 times for the British Lions, whom he captained in New Zealand (1977); his 29 caps for Wales helped win 3 Grand Slams and 4 Triple Crowns.

Bere, Cliff (1915-1997): one of a group of militant Welsh nationalists who founded the Republican Movement in the 1950's, publishing the bi-monthly *The Welsh Republican*, sold in the streets. In 1957, he joined Plaid Cymru.

Bere, Y (13th C.): ruined castle near Cadair Idris, Merioneth that may have been built by Llywelyn ap Iorwerth (Llywelyn Fawr); it was the center of resistance of Dafydd ap Gruffudd in the Second War of Welsh Independence (1282-83).

Bernard (12th century): chaplain to Matilda, the wife of Henry lst, in 1115 he was appointed Bishop of St. David's, where he vigorously opposed traditional Celtic monasteries in favor of closer ties with Rome. He popularized the cult of David, helping to spread his fame among Normans and Welsh.

Berry, Ron (b. 1920): Rhondda novelist; an ex-miner, soldier and merchant sailor who has written short stories and plays for radio and television.

Bersham, (Wrexham and Maelor): John "Iron-mad" Wilkinson set up shop here in 1761 to create one of the most important iron manufacturing centers in the world. The Davies Brothers also created their wrought-iron masterpieces here, including the gates at Chirk Castle, Denbighshire.

Bethesda (Gwynedd): a huge open cast mine, the Penrhyn slate quarry is a mile long and over 1200 feet deep.

Betws y Coed (Chapel in the Woods): popular mountain resort town where the Waterloo Bridge was designed by Thomas Telford in 1815.

Beuno, St. (7th Century): saint whose many miracles include healing Gwenffrewi (*Winefride*) at Holywell.

 **Bevan, Aneurin (1897-1960):** Labour M.P. for Ebbw Vale for 31 years (elected in 1929) "the father of the modern welfare state." An ex-miner and fiery, witty speaker, as Minister of Health in 1945, he helped created the National Health Service (that may have been modeled after a community health scheme at Tredegar). In a long, distinguished political career, Bevan fought hard for the rights of the common people. He was chairman of his local Miner's Lodge at age 19, becoming one of the leaders of the South Wales miners in the General Strike of 1926. Sadly ignoring an important part of his heritage, he wanted little to do with the Welsh language or with Welsh aspirations for independence but is revered for his socialist ideas, his concerns, and his social welfare accomplishments. In

2004, he won a *Western Mail* poll as the greatest Welsh hero.

Bevan, Derek (b. 1947): b. Clydach, Swansea Valley, internationally known rugby referee for 32 years, retiring in 1999-2000 season.

Bid Ale (Cwrw Bach): a singing and dancing gathering to raise money to help unfortunate neighbors by the sale of cakes and beer. Legally forbidden in 1534, it survived as the *pastai* of the Swansea Valley inns in the 19th century.

Bidgood, Ruth (b. 1922): a Swansea Valley poet and historian, with awards from the Welsh Arts Council.

Bielski, Alison (b. 1921): a poet from Newport, Gwent who draws on Welsh mythology and folklore.

Black Bart (see Roberts, Bartholemew).

Black Book of Carmarthen (*Lyfr Du Caerfyrddin*): 13th century manuscript that may be the oldest surviving in Welsh, with 10th, 11th, and 12th century poetry, many on Arthurian themes.

Black Book of Chirk: from the 13th Century, it includes the oldest text of the Laws of Hywel Dda.

Black Prince, the (1330-1376): Prince Edward, son of Edward III of England; he slew the King of Bohemia at the Battle of Crecy in 1346, taking his plume of three feathers with the German motto *Ich Dien* (I Serve) as his own to make it a badge of the English-born Princes of Wales ever since.

Blackborow, Perce (1895-1949): from Newport, Gwent, at age 19, he stowed away on the *Endurance* to become its steward on the 1914-1918 Shackleton Voyage to the South Pole.

Blackwell, John (Alun, 1797-1841): Mold, Flintshire poet remembered for his lyrical poems.

Blaenafon, Gwent: home of the Big Pit underground mine tour and museum, and the nearby Iron Works, designated a World Heritage Site by UNESCO.

Blaenau, Gwent: smallest of the Welsh local authorities (with the highest percentage of Welsh born residents and the lowest percentage of Welsh speakers).

Blaenau Ffestioniog, Gwynedd: former centre of the North Wales slate industry where tours explore the old workings and way of life of the quarrymen.

Blas Ar Gymru (a Taste of Wales): founded to promote Welsh produce and promote standards of excellence in the preparation, presentation and sale of Welsh produce in attractive surroundings, it was set up through a partnership with W.D.A, the Welsh Tourist Board, and Wales' regional tourism companies.

Bleddyn Fardd (d. 1283): one of the last of the Poets of the Princes; his poem on the death of Llywelyn ap Gruffudd compares the Welsh prince to King Priam.

Bledri ap Cydifor (early 12th century): Carmarthen; a master of romance, perhaps responsible for the ancient Welsh tales of *Tristan and Iseult* and the *Quest for the Holy Grail* entering medieval European literature.

Blind Irish Referees: the villains of Landsdowne Rd, Dublin, home of Irish Rugby (from a Max Boyce poem).

Blorenge (near Abergavenny): high on this 2,000 ft. mountain is a monument to the internationally known Olympic champion show jumper *Foxhunter*, buried near here in 1959.

**Bluebirds, the**: Cardiff's football team who have witnessed both victory and defeat in equal, epic proportions, In 1927 it took the F.A. Cup out of England for the only time in history by defeating Arsenal. In the season 2003-4, it was promoted to the First Division of the Football League (the Championship League).

***Blue Books, The* (1847):** a government report by three Anglican lawyers who blamed "the sad state of education" in Wales on Nonconformity and the Welsh language. The English-only Board Schools that resulted led to a precipitous decline in the use of Welsh (see *Brad y Llyfrau Gleision*).

Boadicea (Boudica, lst Century A.D.) Buddug, Queen of the Iceni, who led a revolt against the Romans, capturing Londinium and St. Albans, but was later defeated by Paulinus, her tribe and lands destroyed.

Board of Celtic Studies (f. 1919): following the Report of the Royal Commission of University Education in Wales, it set up three committees (language and literature, History and Law, Archaeology and Art) to encourage and organize Celtic studies in Wales (Social Science was added in 1969).

Bodelwyddan, Denbighshire: home of the Marble Church, where graves commemorate Canadian soldiers shot after a riot in 1919; the Castle has treasures from the National Portrait Gallery and the Victoria and Albert Museum.

Bodnant Gardens, Gwynedd: world famous gardens and terraces near Llanrwst, Conwy Valley, in care of the National Trust.

***Book of St. Chad, the* (early 8th century):** known also as the *Book of Teilo* or *The Lichfield Gospels*, now exiled at Lichfield, Staffordshire, a beautifully illustrated manuscript with the earliest surviving passage of written Welsh.

Book of Llandaff (1130 A.D.): an important source of early Welsh history.

***Book of Taliesin* (Llyfr Taliesin, 14th century):** a collection of poems written by Taliesin and others, it includes the prophecy, *Armes Prydein.*

***Book of Wales, A* (1953):** a popular anthology of prose and verse about Wales from all periods of Welsh literary history produced for the *Collins National Anthologies* by D. Myrddin and E.M. Lloyd.

Book of Wales, the (2004): published by Red Dragon Press (Newark, Delaware) it details Welsh traditions, symbols, and cultural icons.

Boston, Billy (b. 1934): b. Cardiff; rugby star. With Wigan's Rugby League side in 1954, he scored 36 tries in 36 games in a tour of Australia.

Bowen, David James (b. 1925): historian of medieval Welsh poetry, specifically that of Dafydd ap Gwilym and Gruffud Hiraethog.

Bowen, Edward George (1911-1991): from Swansea, a Fellow of the Royal Society, After his pioneer work in radar in the 1930's, he became head of the team that solved the problem of how to operate radar inside airplanes. Moving to Australia in 1944, he helped construct its first radio telescope.

Bowen, Emrys George (1900-93): historian, author of *Wales, A Study in Geography and History* (1941), *The Settlements of the Celtic Saints in Wales* (1954); and *Saints, Seaways, and Settlements* (1969).

Bowen, Euros (1904-1988): Rhondda-born classical scholar, priest and controversial poet, Crown winner, and translator of Latin and Greek into Welsh.

Bowen, Geraint (b. 1915): poet, patriot, educator, editor, former Archdruid of Wales, a master of traditional meters of Welsh poetry.

Bowen, Geraint (b. 1963): born London, from 1989 to 1995 organist at Hereford Cathedral where he founded the Hereford Bach Choir and helped organize the Three Choirs Festivals; went to St. David's in 1995 as master of choristers and artistic director of the Cathedral Festival; he founded the Cathedral Festival Choirs, has made many broadcasts on BBC and returned to Hereford in 2001.

Bowen, Robin Hugh (b. 1957): globe-trotting harpist born in Liverpool to Welsh speaking family, he specializes in Welsh folk and gypsy music. Won awards for the music he composed for the Welsh-language film *Eldra* in 2002. Plays with the group *Crasdant.*

Bowen, Jeremy (b. 1960): from Cardiff, the Middle East correspondent for the BBC, reporting on the front lines in many different areas of conflinct. In 1995 the won the Bayeux Award for reporting and in 1996, the award for best breaking news report for coverage of the assisintation of President Rabin of Israel.

Bower, Iris (b. 1915): from Cardigan, with the R.A.F. Nursing Service, Iris was the first woman to land on the Normandy beaches on D-Day, 1944. A widow at the time, she was awarded the MBE and many army medals.

Bowmen of Agincourt (1914: in "The Bowmen," *(The London Evening News,* 29 Sep, 1914), Arthur Machen used the historical fact of the Welsh archers' success at Agincourt (1415) to write a fictional account of the appearance of their ghosts helping a British company against the Germans at Mons in W.W.I. The story later came to be recorded as fact.

Boyce, Max (b. 1943): from Glynneath, near Swansea; former miner; singer and all-round entertainer. His first L.P. was *Live at Treorchy;* his most famous song is "Hymns and Arias." Max received the M.B.E. in the year 2000.

Brad y Llyfrau Gleision (*The Treachery of the Blue Books*): the title of a play by R.J. Derfel (1854). The satirical name was given to the Government Report of 1847 on the state of education in Wales.

Brain's Brewery, Cardiff: the largest independent brewer in Wales. In 1882, Samuel Brain bought the Old Brewery in Cardiff; it has remained in family ownership ever since. In 1997, Brain's purchased Crown Brewing (which had merged with Buckley's of Llanelli).

Brangwyn, Frank (1867-1956): painter born in Bruges to Welsh parents. His huge British Empire Panels, showing scenes from mythology, history and nature, rejected by Parliament, are found in the Guildhall, Swansea.

***Braslyn o Hanes Llenyddiaeth Gymraeg* (An Outline of the History of Welsh Literature, *1932*):** one of a projected series of monographs by Saunders Lewis placing medieval Welsh literature in the evolution of European thought.

Brecon Beacons National Park (Parc Cenedlaethol Bannau Brecheiniog): 519 sq. miles of mountain and moorland that includes Dan yr Ogof Caves and a steam railway.

Bredwardine (Brodorddyn): village in Herefordshire that was the home of the illustrious Vaughan family and a resort for itinerant poets. Francis Kilvert was vicar here for two years.

***Breuddwyd Rhonabwy (*Rhonabwy's Dream*):* mid-12th or 13th century text in the *Red Book of Hergest* containing many scenes and characters from different periods of Welsh history.

Bridgend (Pen y Bont Ar Ogwr): rapidly growing part of the South Wales corridor that became a parliamentary constituency in 1983.

Brithwe Dewi Sant (St. *David Tartan*): a national Welsh tartan (from 1997).

Brittonic (Brythonic): a branch of language that descended from Indo-European through p-Celtic into Welsh, Cornish and Breton. It was widely spoken in Britain at the time of the Roman invasions.

Bromwich, Rachel (b. 1915): scholar in Celtic languages and literature, editor of *Trioedd Ynys Prydein*, a dictionary of the characters of Welsh legend (1961), the Celtic sources of *Arthuriana,* the poetry of Dafydd ap Gwilym and others.

Broom, Sir Ivor Gordon (1921-2003): b. Cardiff; a W.W.II hero with the RAF. He later flew over the North Pole and set a trans-Atlantic flying record between Ottowa and London. In 1956, he helped set up the Bomber Command Development Unit.

Broughton, Rhoda (1840-1920): from Denbigh, poet and novelist with 25 novels and many short stories.

Brunt, Sir David (1886-1965): b. Abertillery; a Fellow of the Royal Society "the father of meteorology" began in the military in W.W.I to utilize his study of statistics to the new science of weather forecasting.

***Brut y Tywysogion* (The Chronicle of the Princes, *13th century*)**: begins in 682 with the translation of a lost Latin text that continues the *Historia Regum Britanniae* up to the death of Llywelyn ap Gruffudd in 1282.

Brute, Walter (1390-1402): cleric who affirmed the authority of the Gospel over that of the Church, believing that the Britons, the ancestors of the Welsh, had originally received Christianity from the East, and not from Rome.

Brutus (1170 B. C): the earliest Briton, according to Geoffrey of Monmouth, having fled Troy when the Greeks captured the city. His sons Locrinus, Camber, and Albanactus created the kingdoms of Lloegr (England), Cambria (Wales), and Alba (Scotland).

Brwes: a dish of crushed oatmeal steeped in meat stock that was a popular breakfast food for farm workers.

Brycheiniog: kingdom in the Usk Valley, founded by Brychan, an Irish chief; it was absorbed into Deheubarth in the 10th century and conquered by the Normans in 1093.

Brymbo Man (1600 B.C.): male skeleton discovered in a stone-lined grave near Wrexham in 1958.

Brynach, St. (5th-6th century): Brynach Wyddel (*the Irishman*) after whom some churches in South Wales are named (see entry for Nevern).

Bryn Calfaria: popular hymn tune said to have been written on a piece of slate by William Owen on his way to work at the Dorothea quarry.

Bryn Derwin, Battle of (1255): by which Llywelyn ap Gruffudd defeated his brothers Owain and Dafydd to restore Gwynedd to its former glory and receive the title of Prince of Wales.

Brython, Y **(The Briton, 1906-1939)**: newspaper for the large Welsh community in Liverpool; its influence extended throughout Wales.

Buckley's Brewery, Llanelli (f.1799): begun at the Falcon Inn by Henry Child, prominent Methodist and friend of John Wesley. In 1997, Crown Buckley merged with Brain's of Cardiff to cease brewing at Llanelli in 1998.

Buena Vista:, the ship that left Liverpool in 1849, captained by Dan Jones, taking newly converted Welsh Mormons to their promised land.

Bulkeley: an Anglesey family dominant in politics and social affairs for hundreds of years.

Bundling: an ancient custom in rural Wales by which young couples could lie together fully clothed or separated by a plank.

Burgess, Thomas (1756-1837): Bishop of St. David's (1803-1823, helped found St. David's College, Lampeter, in 1822.

Burrows, Stuart (b. 1933): b. Cilfynydd, world class lyric tenor at major opera houses; debuted at the Royal Opera House in 1967 and stayed for 35 years. His TV program *Stuart Burrows Sings* ran for eight years. He appeared in the S4C series *Gwlad y Gan* (land of Song) and adjudicated vocal contests.

 **Burton, Richard (Richard Jenkins, 1925-1984):** internationally known actor in theatre and movies. From Pontrhydyfen, Port Talbot, debuted in *The Last Days of Dolwen*, achieved stardom for his Shaekspeare roles, then *The Robe*, and many other Hollywood films, gained a reputation for his majestic theatrical voice, varied acting abilities, heavy drinking and for being married twice to Elizabeth Taylor.

Bute: family important in industry and politics. The 1st Marquis restored Cardiff Castle; the 2nd Marquis developed the Bute Dock in 1839 leading to Cardiff's phenomenal growth as a leading exporter of coal. The 3rd Marquis completed restoration of Cardiff castle.

Butler, Eleanor (1739-1829) and Ponsonby (1735-1831): "the Ladies of Llangollen" whose home Plas Newydd became a mecca for many distinguished visitors, including Shelley, Lord Byron, Sir Walter Scott, and the Duke of Wellington.

Button, Admiral Sir Thomas (d. 1634): from St. Lythans, sailed under Drake, Hawkins and Raleigh, commanded ships in 1609; a member of the Incorporated Discoverers to look for the North-West Passage, he was the first man to reach the west coast of American via Hudson's Straits; later appointed Admiral of the Irish Seas, he chased Barabary corsairs, Turkish and French ships.

Bwlchgwyn, Denbighshire: (near Wrexham), home of the fascinating Geological and Folk Museum of North Wales.

Bwrdd yr Iaith Gymraeg: (see Welsh Language Board).

C

Third letter of the Welsh alphabet
(always pronounced as in the English word *cat*; never
as in city)

Cadfan, St. (9th century): a missionary from Brittany
whose stone at Tywyn, Merionethshire contains the
oldest surviving example of Old Welsh.

Cadi Haf, a comic figure, dressed in old clothes, with
blackened face, carrying a version of the Maypole (or
an ash stave) that took part in May Day ceremonies in
Northeast Wales. Also known as *Yr Hen Gadi*, his
antics survived until the end of W.W.II; they have
recently been revived in Flintshire.

Cadog (5th Century): a saint associated with many
miracles and legends, after whom many churches are
named in Wales, Scotland, Cornwall, and Brittany.

Cadw (f. 1984): the Welsh Historic Monuments
Executive Agency, a part of the National Assembly for
Wales, responsible for the conservation, presentation,
and promotion of the built heritage of Wales.

Cadwaladr (7th century): a prince of whom poets
wrote would deliver Wales from the English. Known in

legend as "the last British King," his red dragon banner was carried by Henry Tudor at Bosworth.

Cadwaladr, Dilys (1902-1979): b. Four Crosses, Caernarfonshire; short story writer who once farmed on Ynys Enlli (Bardsey); the first woman to win the National Eisteddfod Crown (at Rhyl, 1953).

Cadwaladr (*Beti*) Elizabeth (Elizabeth Davies 1789-1860): b. Bala; worked as a domestic servant in Liverpool; served on ships, as a nurse, went to the Crimea as the real "Lady of the Lamp," doing the dirty work that haughty Florence Nightingale would not. A society for Welsh-speaking nurses is named for Beti, who inspired British Army hospital reforms.

Cadwallon: 7th Century King of Gwynedd who allied with Penda of Mercia to resist Northumbria and thus preserve Wales as a Celtic nation.

Cadwgan ap Bleddyn (d. 1111): prince with lands in Ceredigion and Powys; he fought against Rhys ap Tewdwer and the Normans, playing a prominent part in the Welsh campaigns against William Rufus.

Cadwr (5th Century): warrior who fought alongside Arthur whose wife Gwenhwyfar (Guinevere) he fostered. His son Custennin inherited the Crown of the Isle of Britain after Arthur's death in 539.

Caerleon, Gwent: known as *Isca Silurium*, one of the largest Roman strongholds in Northern Europe, with extensive remains of the amphitheatre, barracks and baths. According to Geoffrey of Monmouth, the town was also the capital of King Arthur (but see Chester).

Caernarfon, Gwynedd: the Roman military outpost of Segontium dominated by the stronghold of Edward 1st and the birthplace of Edward II, the first English Prince of Wales, the town today remains a bastion of the Welsh language.

***Caernarfon Herald* (f. 1831):** a weekly newspaper that first appeared as the *Caernarvon Herald and North Wales Advertiser.*

Caernarfonshire: one of the three North Wales counties created out of the old kingdom of Gwynedd by the Statute of Rhuddlan, 1284. From 1974 to 1996 it was part of the new county of Gwynedd.

Caerphilly (Caerffili): a County Borough with a Norman fortress, dating from 1268, second only in Europe to Windsor. Its water defenses make it practically impregnable. The town was famous for its production of white, crumbly cheese.

Caerwent, Gwent: the former town of *Venta Silurum*, where the local tribe of Silures was forcibly settled by a Roman army.

Caerwys, Flintshire: claims to be the smallest town in Britain. Eisteddfodau were held here in 1100, 1523 and in 1567 (the last by order of Elizabeth 1st, when bardic rules were formulated and licenses granted).

Caitrin (d. 1413): daughter of Owain Glyndwr captured at Harlech in 1409 and imprisoned in the Tower of London. Her memorial is at St. Swithin's Gardens, London.

Cale, John (b. 1942): b. Garnant, with over 40 years success as singer, composer, producer, and songwriter, made his name with the albums *Velvet Underground* and *Nic* and played with the Welsh Youth Orchestra before winning a Leonard Bernstein scholarship.

Caledfwlch: the mighty sword of Arthur (called *Caliburnus* by Geoffrey of Monmouth and *Excalibur* in English).

Calennig: a small gift given to children on New Year's Day in exchange for the recitation of a verse of poetry or song. It is also the name of a popular music group from South Wales.

Callaghan, James (1912-2005): b. Portsmouth, closely identified with Wales, following early career as union official and wartime service with the Royal Navy, Labour M.P. for Cardiff South in 1945; rose to become Chancellor of the Exchequer, Home Secretary, Foreign Secretary, then Prime Minister in 1976-9. As

Parliamentary Secretary to the Minister of Transport, he introduced Zebra Crossings and reflecting "Cat's Eyes" to Britain. Famous for his imperturbability in the Devaluation Crisis, the rioting in N. Ireland, and Britain's entry into the European Community, he became Baron Callaghan of Cardiff in 1987.

***Calon Lân (Pure Heart, 1869)*:** by John Hughes perhaps the most sung of all Welsh hymns, especially in pubs and rugby internationals by those who know only the first verse and chorus.

Calvin, Wyn (b. 1927): Pembrokeshire-born comedian and after-dinner speaker known as "The Welsh Prince of Laughter," awarded the Order of the British Empire for his charitable work.

Calzaghe, Joe ("The Terminator" b. 1972): from Blackwood, Gwent, a boxer with a string of successes; current W.B.O. super middleweight champion since defeating Chris Eubank in 1997.

Camber: a son of Brutus; with Locrinus and Albanactus, after whom Cambria is named; a founder of one of the three countries of the Isle of Britain.

Cambria: the Latinized form used by Giraldus Cambrensis from the name *Cymry* to denote the people of Wales (see entry for Cymru).

Cambria (f. Camarthen 1997): the National Magazine for Wales: a bi-monthly magazine featuring articles, poems, and photographs by some of Wales' best-known authors.

Cambrian, The (f. Swansea 1804): the first weekly newspaper in Wales, published mainly to foster commercial growth in Swansea. Published in English, it merged with *The Herald of Wales* in 1930.

Cambrian Archeological Society (f. 1864): it publishes *Archaeologia Cambrensis* with information on literature, genealogy, folklore, and archeology.

Cambrian Hall, Vancouver (f. 1929): home of the Welsh Society of Vancouver and focal point for the Welsh contribution to the cultural life of the city.

Cambrian Institute, The (1853-62): founded as the Historic Institute of Wales as a break away from the Cambrian Archeological Association to promote Celtic and Welsh literature and to advance the arts and sciences. It published *The Cambrian Journal* (1834-1864) with articles by many leading Welsh writers.

Cambrian Miners' Association (f. 1877): under the leadership of William Abraham (Mabon), it had enormous influence on the future of trade unionism.

Cambrian Company: the Welshpool company that was chosen, along with Antur Teifi, to spearhead a three-year project to secure the future and identity of regional food dishes and improve the visitor experience.

Cambriol, Newfoundland: three years before the *Mayflower* left Plymouth, a group of Welsh settlers arrived at the Avalon Peninsula encouraged by Sir William Vaughan of Golden Grove. Due to harsh conditions and lack of support, the colony failed.

***Cambro-Briton and General Celtic Repository, The* (1819-1822):** three volumes of a monthly magazine with articles on the Triads, the Welsh language, proverbs, music, English translations, etc.

Camlan: the battle in which, according to *Annales Cambriae*, Arthur was killed along with Medrod.

Campbell, Phil (b. 1961): from Treforest, rock guitarist originally with Persian Risk at Cardiff before joining *Motorhead* in 1984. Has toured the world many times and selected as a Welsh hero in a poll of 2003-4.

Camwy: river irrigated by Welsh settlers to help make a success of Wladfa (see Rachel Jenkins).

Candlemas Singing: a spring celebration of the Virgin Mary in which prayers were said to ensure successful harvests and verse contests took place.

Caniadau Cymru: **(the Songs of Wales)** an anthology of verses from mid-15th century to the end of the 19th, with selections from popular Welsh poets.

Canolbarth: the Welsh name for Mid-Wales, extending from southern Snowdonia to the eastern Valleys and Pembrokeshire.

Canon Laws of the Welsh (6-8th Century): a set of Church laws set down in Brittany that also governed religious practices in Wales.

Cantref: an administrative and territorial unit of medieval Wales.

Cantreír Gwaelod: in *The Black Book of Carmarthen*, the low-lying area drowned by Cardigan Bay.

Canwyll y Cymru **(The Candle of the Welsh, *1681*):** by Rhys Prichard, its verses and homilies were most influential in helping preserve the Welsh language and educating the common folk.

Cap Coch (1730-1820): infamous tavern keeper of Merthyr Mawr whose many murders were discovered after his death.

Caradoc: (Caratacus or Caractacus, lst Century): leader who resisted the Roman invaders. He was betrayed by the Queen of the Brigantes, paraded in

Rome by Emperor Claudius and condemned to death. His bravery and great dignity helped spare his life.

Caradog Freichfras: a hero in Welsh and French tales, cousin and chief counselor to Arthur.

Caradog of Llancarfan (12th C): author of several *Lives of the Saints,* referred to by Geoffrey of Monmouth and in *The Life of St. Cadog.*

Caradogion, Y (1790's): a society with weekly meetings at the Bull's Head in London that was an offshoot of the Gwyneddigion.

Carannog (6th C.): a saint commemorated in Wales, Ireland and Brittany.

Cardi: a native of Cardigan, where the natives may or may not deserve to be known as abnormally thrifty.

Cardiff County, Sir Caerdydd:
population, a little over 320,000 (only 7.6 percent

Welsh speaking). The county consists of Cardiff Central, Cardiff North, Cardiff South and Penarth, and Cardiff West). Selected as Wales' capital in 1955, the rapidly growing city is home to the Millenium Stadium, the National Assembly, the Welsh National

Opera, Cardiff Bay, a Norman and Victorian castle; an impressive Civic Centre; the National Museum of Wales and an international airport.

Cardiff Arms Park: home to Cardiff Rugby Club, and site of the retractable-roofed Millenium Stadium, completed in time for the Rugby World Cup of 1999.

Cardiff Devils: an ice-hockey team that defeated Sheffield Steelers 6-5 in February 2000 after being down 5-0 in the second period.

Cardiff Football Club: (see entry for Bluebirds).

Cardiff Rugby Club (f. 1876): one of the most successful Welsh rugby sides, having beaten South Africa, New Zealand and Australia and winners of the Welsh Cup on numerous occasions.

Cardigan (Ceredigion): county created out of the old Kingdom of Deheubarth in 1280 as part of Carmarthen and Cardigan to be administered by the King's Justice. From 1974 to 1996, it was part of the new county of Dyfed before reverting to its former name.

Cardigan (*Aberteifi*): former ship building center and point of departure for many emigrants to the New World and home of the national shrine of the Catholic Church in Wales. An eisteddfod was held here in 1176, hosted by the Lord Rhys in which small silver chairs were given as prizes for poetry. Irish settlers in the fifth century produced the *Sagranus Stone* with Ogham and Latin inscriptions that led to the deciphering of the Ogham script.

Cardigan, New Brunswick, Canada: settled by Welsh emigrants who arrived on the *Albion* in June, 1819.

Carew Castle, Pembrokeshire: a Norman fortress much rebuilt, home of Rhys ap Thomas in the early 15th century and a center of early Welsh literary life.

Carew Cross, Carms: nearly 14ft tall, decorated with elaborate Celtic and Scandinavian patterns; it was erected in 1035 A.D. to honor Maredydd, Prince of Deheubarth.

Carmarthen (Sir Caerfyrddin): county created out of the kingdom of Deheubarth in 1280; area 2,394 sq. km; population 169 thousand; 56.6 Welsh speaking. Associated with the magician Merlin (Myrddyn), the town is the home of the Ivy Bush Hotel, where the Gorsedd of Bards met in 1819.

***Carmarthen Journal* (f.1810):** Wales' oldest newspaper, mostly confined to local news.

Carreg Cennen, Carms: high on a limestone cliff, once held by the Lord Rhys, the castle was badly damaged during the Glyndwr rebellion.

Carreg Lafar (Echo Stone, f. 1993): a popular folk music group from Cardiff that has represented Wales in Celtic folk festivals and has many recordings.

Carter, Isaac (d. 1741): printer who established the first permanent printing press in Wales in 1718 at Trefhedyn, Newcastle Emlyn, Carmarthenshire.

Cartimandua (1st Century A. D): queen of the Brigantes who surrendered Caraticus to the Romans in AD 51.

Cassivellaunus (1st Century AD): British leader who led determined resistance to Julius Caesar.

Castell Dinas Bran, Llangollen: this 13th century castle was reputed to be the home of Myfanwy Fechan, immortalized in song by Dr. Joseph Parry.

Castell Henllys, Pembrokeshire: an Iron Age and Romano-British fort partly excavated and partly reconstructed to show the lifestyle of those times.

Castell Y Bere, Merionethshire: built by Llywelyn Fawr, in 1283 it was the last castle to fall to the English during the revolt of Prince Llywelyn ap Gruffudd.

Catatonia: popular Welsh rock group that began as street singers outside Debenham's store in Cardiff; first became a success with their *Mulder and Scully* in 1987.

***Cartrefi Cymru* (Welsh Homes, 1896):** a volume of essays by Owen M. Edwards in his magazine *Cymru* that describe his visits to the homes of major figures in Welsh history.

Casnodyn (1320-40): a Glamorgan poet whose work is the earliest to survive from that region.

Caswallon: a character in the *Mabinogi* who conquered the Island of the Mighty: and was crowned King in London.

Catrin of Berain (1534-1591): "The Mother of Wales," from Plas Penmynydd, seat of the Tudors in Anglesey, four times married, Catrin was the descendant of an illegitimate son of Henry VII.

Cawl Cennin: a national dish, a broth made of leeks, potatoes, carrots, cabbage and leftovers.

Cayw (Cymru ar Y We: Wales on the Web): led by the National Library of Wales, Cayw is a subject gateway on the World Wide Web offering dependable information relation to Wales and all aspects of Welsh life.

Ceffyl Pren (the Wooden Horse): a folk custom in which an accused felon was carried on a pole or leader in person or in effigy to a mock trial where the participants blackened their faces and wore motley or women's clothes.

Celt, Y (f. 1878): a weekly newspaper publiished in various towns that became *Y Celt Newydd* in 1903 and amalgamated with *Y Tyst* in 1906.

Ceiriog: (see John Ceiriog Hughes).

Celtec: a company based in St. Asaph to encourage indigenous economic growth through the development of the work force of North Wales.

Celtica, Machynlleth: an exhibition of the history of the Celtic peoples of Britain and Brittany housed in a beautiful country mansion.

Celtic Congress, The (f. 1901): a society for all six Celtic countries to foster their languages, their cultures and their national ideals (Wales, Ireland, Cornwall, Brittany, Scotland, the Isle of Man, and Galicia).

Celtic Fusion: a full-service destination management company based in Cardiff to produce incentive travel and conference programs and to encourage people worldwide to come to Wales.

Celtic Miscellany, A (1951): a volume of translations by Kenneth H. Jackson of prose and poetry from all seven Celtic countries. It is regarded as the first successful scholarly attempt to translate Celtic literature into modern English.

Celtic Studies, Board of (f.1919): a department of the University of Wales to stimulate studies in Welsh life, thought and culture and to encourage Celtic studies through its committees: Language and Literature; History and Law; Archaeology and Art; and (from 1969) Social Science.

Celts: the Greek historian Ephorus, 4th Century B.C., wrote of the *Keltoi* in parts of Europe who spoke various dialects of Indo-European sufficiently similar to be classified as a single language. Very few Celtic languages now survive, Welsh being one. Seven regions still claim to be Celtic: Wales, Ireland, Scotland, France, Brittany, the Isle of Man, and Galicia.

Cenarth Falls, Ceredigion: a village where a small museum documents the history of Welsh coracle fishing, now rapidly declining.

Cenhinen Bedr (Peter's Leek): a daffodil, with its green and white stem, it has become a national symbol for Wales.

Centre for Alternate Technology, Machynlleth: set up in 1974 by the Society for Environmental Improvement; its many attractions show different methods of energy generation, using water and wind power, bio-gas, wood gas and insulation and provide a great day out for a family.

Central Welsh Board (1896): following the Aberdare Commission of 1881 and the Welsh Intermediate Education Act of 1889, the Board was set up to provide county schools financed from public money.

Cerdd Dant: "the art of the strings" the singing of a counter-melody to a tune played on the harp. The Cymdeithas Cerdd Dant was founded in 1934.

Ceredigion: the Welsh name for the county of the ancient kingdom known in English as Cardiganshire.

Cerrigydrudion, Denbighshire: site of the hill fort where Caradog (*Caratacus*) was betrayed to Romans.

Cewydd ap Caw (6th C.): a saint associated with the belief that if it rained on July lst it would rain for the next forty days. (The belief was transferred later to St. Swithin's Day, 13 July).

Chairing of the Bard: an ancient and colourful ceremony at the National Eisteddfod of Wales in which a chair is awarded to the writer of the best *awdl*, a long poem in the traditional meters.

Chamberlain, Brenda (1912-1971): author of *Tide Race* (1962) about life on Bardsey (Ynys Enlli).

Charles, David (1762-1834): a Calvinistic Methodist, the brother of Thomas Charles; became famous as a writer of hymns and sermons.

Charles, John (b. 1931-2004): remembered in Italy as "Il buono gigante" (the gentle giant), Swansea-born Charles went to Leeds United in 1948, scored 42 goals in 1953-4 season, helping them get promoted. Great successes came with Juventus in Italy, where he scored 29 goals in his first season, winning three league titles and named Italian footballer of the year in 1958. His statue is outside the stadium. John's younger brother Mel also enjoyed a career with Swansea Town in the late 1950's, playing for Wales 31 times.

Charles, Thomas (1755-1814): joining the Methodist Movement in 1784, he set up the Sunday School Movement in North Wales that had enormous influence on the language and culture. Under his leadership, the British and Foreign Bible Society published a standardized text of their first Welsh Bible.

Charles y Telynor (mid-18th C): a harpist from Llanycil, Merioneth who is supposed to have ridiculed Nonconformists, sold his soul to the Devil, and perished in Llyn Tegid (Bala Lake).

Charter of Brecon (1409): after the rebellion of Owain Glyndwr, Henry IV enacted harsh punitive measures against Wales. The Charter stated "The liberties of Brecon shall be restricted to those whom we deem to be Englishmen and to such of their heirs as are English on both their mother's and their father's side."

Chepstow, Gwent: border town with famous racecourse and one of the first independent congregations in Wales at Llanfaches.

Cherry, Andrew: theatre manager at The New Theatre, Swansea (1801-1811) who engaged such distinguished actors as Edmund Kean.

Chilton, Irma (b. 1930): from Pengelli, a teacher and prize-winning writer, mainly of children's books.

Chirk Castle, (Castell y Waun) Denbighshire: inhabited by the Middleton family for four centuries (until 2004), reached through the incomparable Davies Brothers Gates and offering a glimpse of aristocratice border life.

Christ College, Llanfais: Brecon, a Dominican Friary re-founded by Henry VIII as a collegiate church and school in 1541.

Christopher Davies Ltd: formerly known as *Llyfrau'r Dryw (Books of the Wren)* it made an important contribution to Welsh letters with *Cyfres Crwydro Cymru* (Welsh Wanderer Series), *Barn* (Opinion), and *Poetry Wales* (1950's-70's).

Chubut. Patagonia: settled by Welsh immigrants in the latter part of the 19th century. Gaiman is an oasis of Welsh language and culture.

Church, Charlotte (b. 1986): b. Llandaff, the youngest artist ever to top the British classical music charts. Her *Voice of an Angel* earned a Gold in the U.S., and she performed for both the Pope and President Clinton in 1999. In May 2000, she received the Best British Artist Award.

Cilie family, the (Bois y Cilie): near Llangrannog, famous for their poets beginning with Jeremiah Jones (d. 1902); his son Fred Jones was an early member of Plaid Cymru and grandfather of Dafydd Iwan.

Cilmeri, Powys: a most sacred spot near Builth,

 Powys, where a monolith of Caernarfonshire granite was erected in 1956 to the memory of Prince Llywelyn ap Gruffudd slain nearby on the banks of the River Irfon on December, 1282 by an English knight unaware of the Welsh Prince's identity. An annual ceremony commemorates Llywelyn, "Ein Lliw Olaf." (Our last ruler).

Clancy, Joseph (b. 1928): b. New York City, influential poet, critic and translator of early Welsh poetry. His first volume of Welsh translations was *Medieval Welsh lyrics*, 1965; in 1970 he completed *The Earliest Welsh Poetry*, and in 2003, *Medieval Welsh Poems* (6th to 13th century).

Clark, Petula (b. 1932): born to a Welsh family in England, and most proud of her Welshness; debuted at age 9 in a radio program; became one of the Forces' Sweethearts of Britain during the War (with Vera Lynn and Gracie Fields). She was Girl Singer of the Year in France in 1961. This led to a new career in the U.S., selling over 70 million records.

Clarke, Gillian (b. 1937): poet and lecturer, free-lance broadcaster, editor of *The Anglo-Welsh Review* from 1979-1984. In 1978, Gwasg Gomer published her first full collection of poetry, *The Sundial.*

Cledwyn, Lord: see Hughes, Cledwyn.

Clough, Sir Richard (1530-1570): b. Denbigh, educated Chester Cathedral, became "Knight of the Holy Sepulchre" on a trip to Jerusalem, moved to Anmtwerp as manager for Sijr Thomas Gresham, was instrumental in the founding of the London Stock Exchange; married Kathryn of Berain, built Bachegragi at Tremeirchion, died at Hamburg.

Clowes, Dr. Carl: director of medical services for Powys who moved to Gwynedd; realizing that Wales needed a National Language Centre, he bought the deserted quarrying village of Nant Gwrtheyrn for that purpose.

Clwyd: county created in 1974 out of Flint and Denbigh when Colwyn, Glyndwr, and Wrexham

Maelor district councils were added to those of Delyn, Alun and Deeside, and Rhuddlan. It is also the name of the river and of its valley.

Clwyd, Ann (b.1937): Labour M.P. for Cynon Valley in 1984, after a career as BBC writer, manager and news correspondent. In 1979, she became Wales' only female Euro-MP (and only Welsh woman M.P. in 1984).

Clynnog, Morys (1525-81): Catholic author, Bishop of Bangor who renounced the 1539 Act of Supremacy and was exiled to Louvain under Elizabeth lst.

Cnapan: a game in which the men of whole villages took part to try to carry a small ball to a goal in the neighboring parish. It seemed to have no rules.

Coal: For two centuries the great southeast Wales coalfields fueled an iron industry that was the largest in the world. From the last quarter of the 18th Century, coal brought enormous changes to the economic, political, social and literary life of Wales. Welsh coal fueled the world's navies before the discovery of oil. Coal miners' unions led to the formation of the British Labour Party.

Cocos (Cockles): a seafood delicacy found in all Welsh River estuaries, especially at Penclawdd, Gower, gathered by the famous "webbed-foot cockle women" and sold at Swansea Market.

Coed Coch Bari: Welsh Mountain pony sold for a world record 22,050 pounds to an Australian breeder in 1978.

Coel Hen (5th century): a Roman-British leader transformed by medieval authors into Old King Cole.

Coffin, Walter (1784-1867): coal pioneer who opened the first coal-level in the Rhondda and directed the Taff Vale Railway; Liberal M.P. Cardiff, 1852-1857.

Coke, Thomas (1747-1814): from Brecon, he converted after hearing John Wesley, becoming his chief aide and superintendent of the Methodist Episcopal Church of America. He began the practice of having Welsh-speaking missioners at Ruthin, but died on his way to India to establish a Mission.

Coleg Glen Hafren (f. 1966): College of Technology set up to provide education and training to the business community, expanded and re-designated Coleg Hafren (Severn College) in 1989 as a further Education college.

Coleg Harlech, Merionethshire: "the College of the Second Chance," founded in 1927 to provide higher education for the working people of Wales who could not afford the universities or who had gone directly to work after leaving school.

Collen, St. (6th century), connected to the church settlement at Llangollen, his feast day is 21 May.

Conran, Anthony (b. 1931): India-born, educated in Wales, distinguished poet and translator, who writes poems in English on Welsh themes.

Conventicle Act (1664): legislation prohibiting groups of more than five persons from assembling for religious worship other than that prescribed by the Church and thus led to many Baptists and Quakers emigrating to the New World, where they became prominent in municipal government and the universities.

Conwy: dominated by the mighty castle of Edward 1st, the walled town is reached by Telford's suspension bridge of 1826; the Tubular Rail Bridge built by Stephenson in 1848, and the road bridge, completed in the late 1950's.

Cook, Arthur J. (1884-1931): came to the Rhondda in 1903 from Somerset; as national secretary of the Miners' Federation of Great Britain, he played a prominent role in the General Strike of 1926, with his slogan "Not a penny off the pay, not a second on the day."

Cooke, Nicole (b. 1983): b. Bridgend; world-beating cyclist and BBC Wales Sports Personality of the year in 2003 after winning the Gold at the Commonwealth

Games. In 2004, she won the Giro d'Italia, the women's version of Tour de France.

Coombes, Bert Lewis (1894-1974): Herefordshire-born author who worked as a miner in Resolven and learned Welsh. He published several essays and short stories on the lives of the miners between 1938 and 1942; became a frequent broadcaster on British society.

Cooper, Tommy (1922-1984): b. Caerphilly; one of Britain's funniest and best-loved comics. With his infectious laugh, wearing his red fez, Tommy starred on television and in many British films. He collapsed and died while performing.

Cor Meibion De Cymru (S. Wales Male Voice Choir): founded in 1984, brings together choirs from all parts of S. Wales to tour Britain and the world.

Coracle (*Cwrwgl*): mentioned by Roman historians, a little bowl-shaped boat, similar to the Irish curragh; a frame of saplings covered with hide (now replaced by canvas). Races are held on the Teifi at Cilgerran, where a small museum documents their long use.

Cordell, Alexander (1914-1997): Anglo-Welsh novelist George Graber, who wrote of the incessant struggles of the Welsh people. His trilogy *Rape of the Fair Country, The Hosts of Rebecca,* and *Song of the Earth,* has been made into a drama series. *Fire People* describes changes made by industry.

Corgi: the short-tailed Pembroke or the larger, long-tailed Cardigan, short-legged, rough-haired dogs used for herding cattle; good house pets.

Corwen, Denbighshire: a small town in the upper Dee Valley where Owain Glyndwr began his rebellion in 1400. In 1789 an eisteddfod was held here by a group of London Welsh to revive ancient bardic customs.

Cory: family who owned coal mines and shipping interests, influential in politics and philanthropy in 19th century Cardiff, and whose former home *Dyffryn*, near Cardiff, is famous for its gardens.

Cory Band (f. 1884): began in Ton Pentre as the Ton Temperance Band, later becoming the Cory Workmen's Band. The premier brass band in Wales, winning BBC Challenge competition in 1971, the National Championship in 1974, 1982, 83 and 84; European champions, 1980.

Cory Hall, Battle of (November, 1916): a fight between crowds who supported Britain's entry into the Great War and those who did not. The episode was quickly forgotten in the horrors of the War.

Cottingham, Cyril Morgan (1918-1943): from Comox, Aberystwyth, as a flying officer with the Royal Canadian Air Force he was shot down over the North Sea. The Comox Valley airport on Vancouver Island is named after him.

Council of the Marches: a court of law set up by Edward IV for the Prince of Wales in 1471 to supersede the lordships known as *Marchia Wallia.* Settled at Ludlow in 1473, it continued as Council of the King in the Dominion and Principality of Wales and the Marches until 1688.

Council of Museums in Wales, The: funded by the National Assembly to improve standards to preserve the Welsh heritage and to further educational purposes.

Country Quest:: a magazine for Wales and the Borders, published in Aberystwyth by Cambrian News.

Countryside Council for Wales (Cyngor Gwlad Cymru): the statutory adviser to the government appointed by the National Assembly to sustain natural beauty and wildlife and provide the opportunities for their enjoyment.

Court Poets, (12th century): poets who were encouraged by the flourishing of literature on mainland Europe (and by military successes of their Princes against the Normans). Noted in the art of the *awdl* were Llywarch ap Llywelyn and Gruffudd ap yr Ynad Coch.

Cradock, Walter (1610-59): Puritan preacher famous for his sermons who helped found the first Independent church in Wales at Llanfaches, Gwent.

Crasdant: an outstanding, much traveled contemporary folk music group.

Crawshay: a family that dominated iron working in South Wales, beginning with William at Cyfarthfa in 1786. On Robert Thompson Crawshay's tomb at Faenor, near Merthyr is enscribed "God Forgive Me."

Crawshay, Sir William R. (1920-1999): b. Abergavenny, served on the Boards of the National Museum of Wales, the Welsh Arts Council, the Council of the University of Wales, Cardiff and the N.W.A.F. In World War Two, he received the D.S.O. for gallantry as agent-saboteur with the French Resistance.

Crecy, Battle of (1346): a victory for the forces of  Edward lll and the Black Prince against the French army in which approx. 5.000 Welsh archers wore green and white coats and hats, perhaps the first military uniforms. They may have also worn the leek, the emblem of Wales ever since. The victory made the longbow famous. The Black Prince adopted the three feathers emblem of the King of Bohemia, slain in battle.

Crempog: a pancake, served with lemon and sugar or filled with raisins, consumed on Shrove Tuesday (Dydd Mawrth Ynyd, the day before Ash Wednesday).

Crockett, Anthony P. (b. 1946): archdeacon of Carmarthen, became Bishop of Bangor in 2004, the first divorced person in the U. K to be appointed bishop.

Croft, Robert (b. 1970): from Morriston, Swansea, a Glamorganshire cricketer; one of the very few Welsh speakers to represent England (Wales has no national cricket team).

Crogen, battle of (1165): a victory for Owain Glyndwr against Henry II at Dyffryn Ceiriog.

Cromlech: a prehistoric burial chamber (also called dolmen); greatly varying in size and purpose, found throughout Wales.

***Cronica de Wallia* (the Chronicle of Wales, 1190-1260)**: Latin text preserved at Exeter Cathedral.

***Cronica Glyndwr* (1422):** the earliest Welsh record of the Owain Glyndwr rebellion: and the source for his going into hiding on St. Matthew's Day in 1415.

***Cronicl Cymru* (Shrewsbury, 1866-1872)**: a weekly newspaper that attracted some leading Welsh writers.

Crowning of the Bard: a ceremony at the National Eisteddfod in which a crown is awarded to the winning composer of a poem in the free metres.

Crwth: a musical instrument of Wales (Middle Ages to about 1800), a lyre about the size of a violin.

Culhwch and Olwen (c. 1100): the earliest known Arthurian romance in *The Red Book of Hergest* with themes from history, mythology, and folk literature.

Cunedda (370-430 A.D.): chieftain from Celtic Scotland, who set up the kingdom of Gwynedd, defeating the Irish invaders (then known as the Scots) to preserve the language as Welsh rather than Gaelic. He was named "The father of the Welsh Nation" by Gwynfor Evans.

Curtis, Tony (b. 1945): poet, short-story writer, literary editor; elected chairman of the English-language section of *Yr Academi Gymreig*, 1984.

Cymreictod: a relatively recent word that denotes a feeling of, or asprations to, Welshness.

Cwm Hir (f. 12th C.): former Cistercian abbey near Rhayader devastated during the Glyndwr Rebellion. Llywelyn ap Gruffudd was secretly buried here.

Cwm Rhondda (1905): composed by John Hughes, Treorchy, for a Baptist Cymanfa at Pontypridd usually sung in English to words by William Williams, "Guide me, O, thou great Jehovah."

Cwn Annwn: the Dogs of Hell, portents of death.

Cwndid (16-18th C): a form of carol intended for moral instruction popular with Glamorgan minstrels.

Cwrs Wlpan: an intensive nine-week Welsh language course run each summer by the University of Waleas at St. David's College Lampeter, using the methods developed in Israel to teach Hebrew to recent immigrants (introduced in Wales by the late Chris Rees).

Cwta Cyfarwydd, Y **(The Short Guide):** a number of early 15th century manuscripts in the National Library of Wales containing poetry and prose in Latin, English and Welsh.

Cybi, St. (6th century): saint commemorated at Caergybi (Holyhead) and Llangybi, Llyn.

Cyfaill yr Aelwyd (1881-94): "the friend of the hearth" a monthly journal that carried articles on music, science, literature etc, that may have inspired O.M. Edwards to publish *Cymru* in 1891.

Cyfarthfa, Merthyr Tydfil: centre of the great ironworks established here in 1765; also the name of the home of the Crawshay family whose repressive measures precipitated the rebellion of 1831.

Cyfarwydd: the medieval bard who fulfilled the offices of chief poet and household poet.

Cyfres Crwydro Cymru (1952-1983): "Wandering through Wales "a series of travel books that dealt with the topography, history and culture of Wales (and later Cornwall, Brittany and even Patagonia).

Cyfres Gwyl Dewi **(The St. David's Day Series):** begun in 1928, a series of booklets containing biographies of prominent Welsh people and events.

Cyfres Pobun (Everyone's Series, 1940's): nineteen volumes of social, industrial and cultural issues. Editors included E. Tegla Davies.

Cyfres Brifysgol a'r Werin (1928-49): "The University and the Peoples' Series," 23 volumes by the University of Wales Press for adult education classes.

Cyfres y Fil (1901-1916): "The Thousand Series" published by O.M. Edwards about Welsh literary figures.

Cyfres y Werin (1920-1954): "the People's Series" Welsh translations to teach the ordinary people of Wales to beome familiar with European classics.

Cylch Cadwgan (Cadwgan Circle): a group of writers that met during W.W.II to discuss literary trends and to publish new works.

Cymanfa Ganu (Singing Meeting): in the 19th century Temperance Movement certain days were set aside for the singing of hymns, led by conductors to elicit the Welsh *hwyl* (deep-felt emotion). Such "singing gatherings" include those held the last Sunday of National Eisteddfod Week in Wales and the North American Festival of Wales each Labor Day Weekend.

Cymdeithas Bob Owen (f. 1976): society founded to published *Y Casglwr*, "the collector" dealing with the collecting of all kinds of printed materials.

Cymdeithas Cerdd Dafod ("the art of the tongue society"): formed 1976, holding competitions to stimulate interest in traditional Welsh poetry.

Cymdeithas Dafydd ap Gwilym (f. 1886): a society begun at. Oxford University to establish reforms for Welsh orthography.

Cymdeithas Emynau Cymru (f. 1967): "the hymn society of Wales" begun to foster interest in Welsh hymnody. Its *Bulletin* contains the annual lecture given at the National Eisteddfod.

Cymdeithas Madog (f. 1977): a non-profit organization begun in Poultney, Vermont, to help North Americans to learn and to use the Welsh language; it conducts an annual Welsh language course at various U.S. cities and Canada.

Cymdeithas yr Iaith Gymraeg (*the Society for the Welsh Language*): begun at Aberdare in 1885;

resurrected by Plaid Cymru at Pontarddulais, 1962. The Society attracted the youth of Wales in its ardent campaigns to create a bilingual Wales, to establish a Welsh television channel (S4C), and to gain official recognition of the Welsh language.

Cymmrodorion, the Honourable Society of: formed in London in 1751 to encourage interest in Welsh history and literature that later established the annual eisteddfod through the National Eisteddfod Association. It publishes scholarly studies, and awards the Society Medal for achievements in arts, science, and literature.

Cymraeg: a branch of Brythonic developed out of Celtic. In a poem of 633 A.D. the Welsh people came to be known as the *Cymry* and their language *Cymraeg.* The term *Welsh,* originally signifying a Germanic people, was used by the Saxon invaders to describe the Romanized native Britons.

Cymraeg Byw (*Living Welsh*): a spoken form taught throughout Wales as a second language since the raising of national consciousness in the 1960's.

Cymreigyddion, Y (*The Welsh Scholars*): a society of the London Welsh from 1794 until 1855 seeking to foster the Welsh language mainly through debates.

Cymreigyddion y Fenni (1831-1854): an Abergavenny society that held influential eisteddfodau;

that founded the Welsh Manuscripts Society in 1837. Its members including Augusta Hall and Thomas Price.

***Cymro, Y (The Welshman,* f.1932):** a weekly Welsh language newspaper of general interest now published in Mold, Flintshire.

Cymru (Wales): a term that came into being around the early 7th century to designate the land of the *Cymry*, later called *Welsh* by Anglo-Saxon invaders of Britain. A peninsula bounded in the north by the Irish Sea and in the South by the Bristol Channel, its maximum length is 140 miles and maximum width 100 miles. In the 8th century A.D., the Welsh to the West were separated from the Saxons to the East by Offa's Dyke. With a little over 8 percent of the area of the United Kingdom, Wales contains about 5 per cent of the total British population.

Cymru Fydd (*Future Wales):* founded in 1886 in London by Tom Ellis with a program of Home Rule for Wales that soon foundered on apathy of the Welsh people, especially its self-serving politicians in London.

Cynan: (see entry for Evans-Jones, Albert).

Cynan Meriadog: one of the founders of Brittany written of by Geoffrey of Monmouth. His supposed cutting out of women's tongues led to the Welsh name of Brittany as Llydaw (*Lled-taw, "silent gums"*).

Cynddelw Brydydd Mawr (Cynddelw the Great Poet): a most proficient and highly regarded Court poet of the 12th Century.

Cynefin: a sense of homeland, or belonging.

Cynfeirdd, Y (6-12th C.): "the early poets" most of whom wrote poems based on sagas and popular tales as well as nature poems and religious verse.

Cynghanedd (*harmony*): a popular verse form using internal rhyme and repetition of consonants.

Cyngor Cefn Gwlad: (see Welsh Countryside Council).

Cyngor y Disgwyr (CYD, pr. Keed): an organization founded in the 1970 to bring together Welsh speakers and learners to utilize the Welsh language.

Cynonfardd Eisteddfod (f. 1889): the oldest Eisteddfod in the US, it is named after Dr. T.C. Edwards (*Cynonfardd),* pastor at Dr. Edwards Memorial Congregational Church, Edwardsville, Pennsylvania.

Cynulliad Cenedlaethol Cymru (see National Assembly).

Cynwal, William (d. 1587): Ysbyty Ifan, Denbighshire, a prolific practitioner of traditional poetry.

Cywydd: a metrical form of poetry used by competitors for the Chair at the National Eisteddfod.

Ch

Fourth letter of the Welsh alphabet (pr. as Scottish *loch* or German *ach*, except when occurring in borrowings from English as in *Charles* or *Chirk*). It occurs as a mutation of C in initial position.

Chwefror: second month of the year (February in English).

D

Fifth letter of the Welsh alphabet; it is often mutated to "dd" in initial position.

Dab: a flat fish once common in Swansea Bay; "poor dab" is a common term of endearment and sympathy.

Dafis, Cynog (b. 1938): Plaid Cymru spokesman for education, elected M.P. for Ceredigion and Pembroke North in 1992, resigned to enter the National Assembly of Wales to work on education, environment, culture, language and Welsh rural affairs.

Daffodil: (*Cenhinen Bedr*, St Peter's Leek): a spring flower worn on St. David's Day often in preference to the more traditional, and more pungent, leek.

Dafydd ab Edmwnd (1450-80): innovative Flintshire poet who classified and defined the 24 Welsh bardic metres at the 1451 Carmarthen Eisteddfod.

Dafydd ab Owain Gwynedd (d. 1203): a son of Owain Gwynedd, he helped kill Hywel ab Owain to become ruler of Gwynedd, marrying Henry ll's half sister Emma of Anjou, but was forced out by Llywelyn Fawr.

Dafydd ap Gruffudd (d. 1283): younger brother of Llywelyn; he was the last Prince of Wales of the line of Gwynedd. After Llywelyn, he continued resistance to King Edward; was quickly captured and executed.

Dafydd ap Gwilym (1320-80): from Llanbadarn Fawr, a world-class Welsh-language poet much influenced by Ovid and contemporary French literature, bringing innovations to the language, subject matter, and techniques of poetry, Dafydd's command of language is unparalleled among Welsh poets. Most of the 150 of the poems that survive are love poems set in a world of nature.

Dafydd ap Llywelyn (d. 1246): Prince of Gwynedd, son of Llywelyn ap Iorwerth and Joan (daughter of King John of England). After his brother Gruffudd died escaping from the Tower of London, Dafydd rebelled against Henry III but died fighting.

Dafydd Ddu Meddyg (*Black David the Doctor*: David Samwell): Captain Cook's surgeon who made the first written record of the Maori language.

Dafydd, Edward (1600-1678): the last professional household poet, he wrote for prominent Glamorgan families.

Dafydd Gam (d. 1415): skilful soldier who fought against Owain Glyndwr but was killed at Agincourt in the service of Henry V. Possibly the model for Shakespeare's Fluellen.

Dafydd y Garreg Wen (David Owen, 1711-41): b. harpist from Ynyscynhaearn, Caerns, who composed the eponymous tune published in Edward Jones' *Musical and Poetical Relicks of the Welsh Bards* in 1784.

Dafydd, Marged (Meg Ellis, b. 1950): Aberystwyth, assistant editor of *Y Faner* in 1982, has published poetry, a novel and short stories.

Dafydd Nanmor (1450-80): from Nanmor, Caerns; one of the greatest Poets of the Gentry who eulogized Edmund and Jasper Tudor and wrote of the world of men and the civilized life in the dignified style of a master cywyddwr.

Dahl, Roald (1916-1990): b. Llandaff to Norwegian parents, following service as an RAF pilot in WWII, he became a most successful author of children's stories including *Willie Wonka and the Chocolate Factory.*

Dai: short form of David, a popular usage often used as a nickname such as *Dai Bananas* (Sir David Maxwell Fyfe, Secretary for Wales in the 1950's). *Dai Bread* is a character in Dylan Thomas' *Under Milk Wood.*

Dai Bandito: (see Williams, Orig).

Dai Lossin: a likeable rogue, the name for a cartoon character who captained the Cwmsgwt team in *The South Wales Football Echo* between the Wars.

Dalton, Hugh (1887-1962): Neath-born, After service in W.W.I, he entered Parliament in 1924; taught at London School of Economics; re-entered Parliament in 1935 to become Minister of Economic Warfare, Minister of Board of Trade, and Chancellor of the Exchequer in the Labour Government in 1945; made a Life Peer (1960).

Dalton, Timothy (1940): Wrexham-born actor, seen as the new Laurence Olivier for Heathcliffe; he appeared as *Agent 007* (James Bond) in two Hollywood movies and has made many movies for British television.

Dame Wales **(Dame Vendotia alias Modryb Gwen, mid-19th century):** a mid-19th century caricature of  North Wales, as an old woman in what was considered a traditional dress with tall hat carrying a large bundle on her back. The original drawing, by Hugh Hughes was titled, *Dame Venedotia, alias Modryb Gwen* (Aunt Gwen). Vendotia is the Latin name for the old Kingdom of Gwynedd. The drawing was first published in *Beauties of Cambria,* 1820 and reproduced by engraver J.J. Dodd and many others.

Daniel, Glyn Edmund (1914-1986): distinguished archeologist, writer, and Cambridge University professor, whose wit, personality and erudition made him a most popular television personality in the 1950's in programs such as *The Brain's Trust.*

Daniel, Sir Goronwy (1914-2003): b. Ystradgynlais; Chief Statistician in the Ministry of Fuel and Power, The first Permanent Under-Secretary of the Welsh Office. Principal at Aberystwyth from 1969 to 79. A Fellow of the University of Wales, in 1982 he became the first Chairman of the Welsh Fourth Channel. During the second half of the 20th century, he was powerful in Welsh educational, cultural and commercial circles, and influential in Whitehall. He was one of the "Three Wise Men" who convinced the Tory Government to establish a Welsh language television channel in 1982.

David, Dennis (1918-2000): b. Tongwynlais, Glam; only 21 years old during the Battle of Britain, he shot down eleven enemy planes and defended a field hospital by helping bring down another fourteen.

David, Elizabeth (1913-1992): proud of her Welsh ancestry, through her cook books, Elizabeth Gwynne (her real name) introduced the war-weary British public to foods then considered exotic, including olive oil, garlic, and pasta.

David, St. (Dewi Sant, 6th century): the son of King Sant of Ceredigion and Non of Brittany. After studying under Paulinus at Llanddeusant, he built a monastery at Glyn Rhosyn, Dyfed. Known as *David the Waterman*, he lived a frugal existence preaching the gospel and establishing churches in many parts of Wales and beyond. His tomb became an important site for pilgrims including William lst, Henry II, and Edward lst. He was cannonized by Calixtus II in 1120, and celebrated as the patron saint of Wales on March lst.

David, Tania (b. 1966): b Bridgend; a top scientist with the Forensic Science Service helping Customs and Excise Office and the Police solve crimes.

David, Sir T.W. Edgeworth (1858-1935); Cardiff-born Australian geologist who helped survey the geology of New South Wales 1882-91; he was also on Shackleton's Second Antarctic Expedition, 1907-9 which located the South Magnetic Pole.

Davidson, Jane (b. 1957): Assembly Cabinet Member for Education and Lifelong Learning; former Head of Social Affairs Welsh Local Government and Secretary to Rhodri Morgan, leader of the Assembly.

Davies, Aled Wyn: b, Llanbrynmair: tenor, winner of the Soloist of the Year at the National Eisteddfod in 2001 after having won lst prize in folk singing at Llangollen. He toured Australasia with Cor Codre'r Arian in 2002.

Davies, Sir Alun Talfan (1913-2001): from Gorseinon, Swansea; recorder of Merthyr, 1963-8; Swansea 1968-9; Cardiff 1969-84: President of the National Eisteddfod 1977-80; Board Member of Welsh National Opera 1978-86: Chairman Bank of Wales 1951-96, and much more in a distinguished career.

Davies, Andrew Wynford (b. 1936): Cardiff; author, winner of many awards, inc. *Guardian* Children's Fiction, 1979; Boston Globe Horn Award 1979; TV programs include *Moll Flanders, Pride and Prejudice.* His children's books include *Educating Marmalade.*

Davies, Aneirin Talfan (1909-1980): b. Felindre, Cards; critic, poet and radio broadcaster who became Head of Programs at BBC Wales in 1966. A prolific author with a wide range of interests, a patron of Welsh writers, he also helped found the publishing company now known as Christopher Davies.

Davies, Arthur Bowen (1862-1928): Welsh-American romantic painter who organized an exhibition of the Ashcan School, and who was a major influence at the Armory Show in New York City in 1913.

Davies Brothers, Robert and John (early 18th century): iron workers at Bersham, near Wrexham, who produced the magnificent gates at Chirk Castle, and St. Giles Church Wrexham among others.

Davies, Bryan Martin (b. 1933): from Brynamman, teacher, translator of Welsh, and Crown winning poet.

Davies, Clara Novello (1861-1943): Cardiff-born musician and choir leader, mother of composer Ivor Novello.

Davies, Clement (1884-1962): lawyer; Liberal M.P. for Montgomeryshire (1929-62) and popular, influential leader of his party 1945-56. As Chairman of the All-Party Action Group, he helped force Chamberlain to resign in May, 1940. Davies was also President of the Parliamentary Association of World Government.

Davies, Dai (b. 1948): Amman Valley, one of Wales' greatest goalkeepers with Swansea, Everton, and Wrexham. Played for Wales 52 times.

Davies, Dan Isaac (1839-87): Llandovery, a teacher and headmaster at Aberdare, he proposed the use of Welsh in the classroom to the Royal Commission on Elementary Education in Wales; he was one of the founders of Cymdeithas yr Iaith Gymraeg, and author of many articles.

Davies, David (Dai'r Cantwr, 1812-74): from Llancarfan, Glamorgan; sent to Van Dieman's Land after the Rebecca Riots, returned to Wales as a vagrant (his pipe set fire to the barn in which he was sleeping and he was burnt to death).

Davies, David (Tom Sawyer, 1818-90): from Llandinam, railway pioneer who also began the Parc and Maerdy pits in the Rhondda to form the Ocean Coal Company in 1887 and a dock at Barry to compete with Cardiff. He became Liberal MP for Cardigan; his son Lord Davies established *The Welsh Outlook* in 1914. His grandson was lst Baron.

Davies, David, lst Baron, of Llandinam (1880-1944): Labour M.P., private secretary to Lloyd George in 1916, promoted the League of Nations; worked to improve university education in Wales; daughters Gwendoline Elizabeth and Margaret Sydney, collected the French Impressionist paintings now at the National Museum of Wales. They bought Gregynog Hall to make it a center for Welsh music and the famous private press.

Davies, David Ivor (Ivor Novello, 1893-1951): Cardiff-born composer, actor and playwright, son of singer Dame Clara Anastasia Novello, his songs were popular in World War I and after; his musical comedies had great success.

Davies, David James (1893-1956): b. Llandebie, Carmarthenshire; went to Pennsylvania at age 19 after working underground in the Gwendraeth Valley; miner, boxer, prospector and sailor, writer on politics and economics who returned to Wales and joined Plaid Cymru at its formation, greatly influencing its early socialist and nationalist policies.

Davies, David P. (1920-2004): Neath-born chief test pilot of the Civil Aviation Authority's flight department for 33 years. During World War Two he flew off the fighter catapult ship *Patia,* the carriers *Unicorn* and *Illustrious.* When Britain pioneered in the new age of jet and turboprop airliners, David originated the fundamentally new pilot handling requirements for the jet age, including those for the *Concorde* supersonic airliner.

Davies, Donald (1924-2000): b. Treorchy; a pioneer computer scientist whose work is fundamental to the Internet. During W W ll, he worked with Alan Turing on the Enigma solution. In 1965, he developed a system that allowed computers to send information back and forth over public telecommunication networks, called "pocket switching," the basis of today's Internet.

Davies, Edward Tegla (1880-1967): minister and prolific prose author whose children's books were very popular as were his delightfully satiric weekly columns for *Yr Herald Cymraeg.*

Davies, Elizabeth: (see entry for Cadwaladr, Beti).

Davies, Evan (Myfyr Morganwg, 1801-88): yet another eccentric from Pontypridd; affected by druidic fever, he claimed to be Archdruid of the Bards of Britain; conducted mystic ceremonies and wrote of druidism.

Davies, Gareth Alban (b. 1926): from Ton Pentre, Rhondda, former coal miner, educated at Oxford; became Chair of Spanish at Leeds University in 1975, but has published Welsh works, including verse and essays.

Davies, George Maitland Ll. (1880-1949): b. Liverpool to Welsh parents, he served in the Royal Welsh Fusiliers before becoming deeply opposed to WW 1. Secretary to the Housing Trust set up by David Davies of Llandinam, he worked for the Fellowship of Reconciliation at Cambridge before moving back to Wales, meeting with De Valera of Ireland, Lloyd George, the Archbishop of Canterbury, and Lord Salisbury to try to alleviate the dire situation in post war Germany. In 1923, he won the University of Wales Parliament seat (its only pacifist). He spent the rest of his life helping the poor and unemployed.

Davies, Geraint Talfan (b. 1943): journalist and television director who was Controller of BBC Wales from 1990 until 1999, steering it through years of momentous change brought about by the resurgence of things Welsh.

Davies, Geraint Wyn (b. 1957): Swansea born actor, veteran of stage and screen (son of Cerwyn Davies).

Davies, Gerald (b. 1945): b. Cydweli, Carms; rugby winger who helped the British Lions defeat New Zealand in 1971. He began a new career as an after-dinner speaker. Inducted into International Rugby Hall of Fame in 1999.

Davies, Glyn (1919-2003):, from Aberbeeg, Mon., he won first place in the Royal Society of Arts Exam in economics in 1938, before serving in the army during W.W.II, including the Battle of El Alamein. In 1968, he became chief economics advisor to George Thomas, Secretary of State for Wales, and Sir Julian Hodge. Professor of Banking and Finance at the University of Wales Institute of Science and Technology (1970 to 1985); the author of the definitive work: *A History of Money from Ancient Times to the Present Day.*

Davies, Gwen Frangcon (1891-1992): renowned stage actress named after a valley in Snowdonia; in 1924 she played *Juliet* to Gielgud's *Romeo.* She became Dame of the British Empire in 1991, the year of her last TV appearance, 80 years after her debut.

Davies, Gwilym (1879-1955): Baptist minister, Honorary Director of the League of Nations Union, whose draft plans for international cop-operation in education were adopted as the constitution of UNESCO. On St. David's Day, 1923, he gave the first radio broadcast in the Welsh language one year after inaugurating the annual Goodwill Message of the Children of Wales.

Davies, Sir Henry Walford (1869-1941): composer, music professor at Aberystwyth, fostered musical education mainly through popular radio talks.

Davies, Captain Hywel (1680-1719): Milford Haven, 'the Cavalier Prince of Pirates": he was the master of and inspiration for the infamous Black Bart.

Davies, (David), Hywel (b.1929): Cardiff-born, Deputy-General, Science, Research and Development, E.U.C. Brussels, 1982-6: former head of Airborne Radar Group; prominent writer on electronics, radar and remote sensing.

Davies, Idris (1905-53): b. Rhymney, ex-miner and teacher in London, the Rhondda and Rhymney, whose *Gwalia Deserta* (1938) followed by *The Angry Summer* (1943) deal with the desert created by unemployment in South Wales.

Davies, Islwyn (1928-2002): Sarn, Powys, "the Honourable Islwyn," chaired the Royal Welsh Agricultural Society for 15 years, making it one of the most successful in Britain. Son of Lord Davies of Llandinam, he served with the Royal Navy during W.W.II and later established champion herds of Welsh Black and Hereford Cattle.

Davies, James John (1873-1947): b. Tredegar; iron worker who went to the U.S. in 1881 (his grandfather had built an iron furnace in Maryland) becoming an important figure in the government of Harding and Coolidge as Secretary of Labor, and U.S. Senator from Pennsylvania. A promoter, organizer, and financier of Welsh-American cultural activities, co-owner of Welsh American newspaper *The Druid*, he helped incresse membership of the Loyal Order of Mooose to one and a half million (from just 250) and established the lodge in Britain (at Tredegar in 1926).

Davies, James Conway (1891-1971): b. Llanelli, Custodian of Manuscripts at Durham Cathedral and Reader at University of Durham; published books on legal and administrative aspects of medieval Britain.

Davies, James Kitchener (1902-1952): Cardiganshire-born poet, an early advocate of Plaid Cymru; his *Cwm Glo* (Valley of Coal) deals with the effects of the Great Depression in the Rhondda. His autobiographical *Swn y Gwynt syn Chwythu* (Sound of the Wind that is Blowing) is one of the finest Welsh-language poems of the 20th Century.

Davies, Jocelyn (b. 1959): from Newbridge; one of the first lay inspectors of schools in 1994; Member of the National Assembly of Wales for Plaid Cymru.

Davies, John (b. 1937): b. Rhondda; raised in Bwlch Llan, Ceredigion: prolific, accomplished historian, lecturer, and broadcaster on history and politics. His works include the masterful *Hanes Cymru* of 1990 re-published *as A History of Wales* (1993), *The Making of*

Wales (1996), and many more important works of Welsh history and culture, including. *100 Welsh Heroes* (2004).

Davies, John (John Davies of Hereford) 1565-1618: "the Welsh Poet," wrote of the superiority of Wales in the Union to Henry Stuart, son of James lst; a teacher to royalty, he published several collections of verse.

Davies, John of Mallwyd, 1567-1644): a distinguished scholar who revised the Welsh Bible for the popular new version of 1610, published a Welsh grammar, a Latin-Welsh dictionary, and collected and copied ancient texts.

Davies, John Cadvan (Cadvan, 1846-1921): scholar, hymn-writer, eisteddfod adjudicator, writer, and Archdruid of the Gorsedd.

Davies, John F. (dates unknown): from Tredegar, he played a vital part in the Welsh settlement at Scranton, Pa., where he had been invited to set up a hot blast furnace to smelt iron with anthracite. Followed by foreman Evan Williams He helped make 19th Century Scranton the largest Welsh settlement in the US.

Davies, John Glyn (1870-1953): b. Liverpool, scholar, Head of Department at Liverpool University, tireless worker for the establishment of the National Library of Wales, and author of popular verses for children.

Davies, John Humphreys (1871-1926): b. Llangeitho; Principal at University of Wales, Aberystwyth in 1919. Published many articles and books on Welsh literature and Ballads.

Davies, John Tudor: from Rhosllanerchrugog; distinguished contemporary conductor and musical director of the Rhos Male Voice Choir organist, composer of hymn tunes, adjudicator; awarded the MBE in 2002.

Davies, Jonathan (b.1962): captain of Wales, who switched to Rugby League. In 1990, he scored 34 points in one game for Widnes. In 1995, he returned to Rugby Union with Cardiff. He then began a career with BBC.

Davies, Jonathan Ceredig (1859-1932): Llangunillo, Cards, traveler and writer especially of Wladfa, Patagonia.

Davies, Lewis (1863-1931): from Hirwaun, teacher and author of adventure books for children and romantic stories based on Welsh history.

Davies, Lynn (*Lynn the Leap*): b. Nantymoel; Gold Medal winner at the 1964 Olympics, first with Olympic, Commonwealth and European Long Jump titles at the same time; the first Briton to win an Olympic field event.

Davies, Mervyn (*Merv the Swerve*, b. 1946): with Llanelli, debuted against Scotland in 1969: played 31 times for Wales; retired through injury; elected to International Rugby Hall of Fame in 1999.

Davies, Neal (b. 1966): Newport, leading operatic bass, studied under the patronage of Dame Gwyneth Jones at Zurich after graduating from the Royal Academy of Music. He won the 1991 Lieder Prize at the Cardiff Singer of the World Contest.

Davies, Pennar (Davies Aberpennar, 1911-1996): from Mountain Ash, poet, scholar, and novelist. After a distinguished academic career at Cardiff, Oxford, and Yale, he became a minister of religion and a professor at Bala-Bangor Theological Collect; Principal of Memorial College, Brecon (1952-1981); wrote poetry in English and Welsh. A member of Cylch Cadwgan, he was a leader in the campaign for Welsh language rights and broadcasting in the 1960's.

Davies, Philip. (b. 1943): from Carmarthen, former executive with Novartis Pharmaceuticals, N J. and architect with HOK International New York; has a Ph.D. from the Welsh National School of Medicine. A permanent member of the scientific staff at Medical Research Council London, and Executive Director of Research at Merck Laboratories, Rahway, N. J, a director of the National Welsh American Foundation and treasurer and president of the Welsh Society of

Central New Jersey., he became president of NWAF in May, 2005.

Davies, R. (19th century): deserving of mention is this butcher slated to play the lead in *Romeo and Juliet* at a Wrexham Theatre on December 13, 1806. He came on stage inebriated, landed up sprawled in the gallery, and staggered into the street, his part having to be read by a member of the company. The theatre later became a Temperance Hall.

Davies, Rev. R. Cerwyn (b. 1928) from Pembrokeshire, left Wales in 1963 for Canada; he was minister at Toronto Welsh United Church for 14 years. From 1996-8 he was President of WNGGA; and is also a member of the Gorsedd for his services to the North American Welsh.

Davies, Rees (dates unknown): from Tredegar, he began the Tredegar iron works at Richmond, Virginia that played an important part in the Civil War, producing 50 percnet of all the canon used by the Confederacy.

Davies, Sir Rees (1938-2005): born near Llandderfel, Merionydd, an outstanding and influential teacher of history who championed Welsh identity, professor of history at universities of Swansea, Aberystwyth, University College, London, and finally Chichele Professor of Medieval History at Oxford. With his advice much in demand; he received some to f the highest awards available in the humanities and knighted in 1996.

Davies, Rhys (1903-1978): Anglo-Welsh novelist and short-story writer who emphasized the grit and daily humor of the coal miners. His most famous novel is *The Black Venus* (1944); he also wrote novels based on Ivor Novello and Dylan Thomas.

Davies, Richard (1501-81): helped persuade Parliament to pass the 1563 Act that ordered the translation of the Bible and Book of Common Prayer into Welsh.

Davies, Robert (b. 1977): from Llanelli, Robert caught a 9 ft long sturgeon in Swansea Bay in June, 2004 weighing 264 lbs (in the Natural History Museum).

Davies, Robert (Bardd Nantglyn, 1769-1825): from Nantglyn, Denbigh, known for his humorous verses, won at Caerwys Eisteddfod 1798, moved to London to work with the Gwyneddigion Society; his *Grammar* of 1808 greatly influenced Welsh poetry during the 19th century.

Davies, Robert Rees: (b. 1938): from Bala: historian and professor, Chair of Modern History at University of Oxford and former President of the Royal Historical Society; winner of the First Modern British Book Prize.

Davies, Ron (b. 1946): elected Labour M.P. for Caerphilly in 1983, Secretary of State for Wales In 1997, leading his party's successful campaign in favor of a Welsh Assembly, his greatest triumph. A member of the Gorsedd, Despite personal problems, he continued to faithfully serve Wales in the Assembly until March 2003, when he was forced to resign, but has remained active, serving Wales in various capacities.

Davies, Russell T. (b. 1963): Swansea-born, award-winning BBC producer, writer, and presenter, chief writer and producer of the revival of "Dr. Who."

Davies, Ryan (1937-77): from Carmarthenshire, much-loved entertainer of stage, radio and television. With Ronnie Williams he formed *Ryan a Ronnie*, a popular Welsh TV series. He died suddenly in New York City.

Davies, Samuel (1723-1761): Welsh American Presbyterian minister from Delaware; helped found Princeton University, fought for religious rights against the established church; he was the first successful American hymn writer.

Davies, S.O. (1886-1972): Labour M.P. from Merthyr Tydfil, known as a fiery radical socialist, who presented his Parliament for Wales Bill in 1955. In 1970, he was elected as Independent Labour M.P. for Methyr.

Davies, Thomas Glynne (b. 1926): BBC news reporter, producer, and broadcaster who won the

Eisteddfod Crown in 1951 and whose novel *Marged* and his short stories contribute to modern Welsh literature.

Davies, Tony (b. 1938): from Groesgoch, Pemb; became managing director of ERF South Africa in 1975 as well as a director of several companies: with the OBE for services to the British Commercial vehicle industry, he is President of the Witwatersrand Cambrian Society and Cor Meibion Cymru De Afffica.

Davies, Walford (1869-1941): b. Oswestry; organist, and composer. Prof. of Music at Aberystwyth, succeeded Elgar as Master of the King's Music in 1934; renowned for his oratorios and choral suites. He was Director of Music during the War for the R.A.F.

Davies, Walford ((b. 1940): from Pontyberem, lectured at University of Wales, Aberystwyth, and at St. Anne's College, Oxford, Director of Extra-Mural studies at Aberystwyth; essayist and critic.

Davies Walter Haydn (1903-1984): from Bedlinog, Glamorgan, collier, then headmaster at Bargoed Grammar Technical School, who published three volumes of autobiography shedding light on local customs.

Davies, Wilfred Mitford (1895-1966): from Menai Bridge, a commercial artist who illustrated many childrens' books associated with *Urdd Gobaith Cymru.*

Davies, William (d. 1593): Catholic martyr; from Caernarfonshire, he helped re-print *Y Drych Cristianogawl* at Llandudo but was later executed.

Davis, Hywel (1680-1719): known as "the cavalier prince of pirates," from Milford Haven, he looted ships of all nationalities and raided ports everywhere.

Davies, W.H. (William Henry, 1871-1940): Newport-born "tramp" poet who lost a foot riding the rails in the US, prospected in the Klondyke ("What is this world, if full of care/We have no time to stand and stare?").

Davies, W. Tudor: from Rhos, near Wrexham: distinguished, prominent musician, former bandmaster of Rhos Silver Band, appointed conductor of the world-renowned Rhos Male Voioice Chior in 1992, bringing it many honors.

***De Excidio Britanniae* (The Destruction of Britain, c. 547):** by Gildas, who castigates the Britons for God's punishment, blames Vortigern for inviting the Saxons, but mentions the British victory at Mount Badon.

Deceangli: a tribe living between the rivers Dee and the Clwyd at the time of the Roman occupation.

Deck the Halls (with boughs of holly): one of the world's best-known carols, sung to one of 12 untitled tunes arranged by John Parry of Ruabon for a collection of Welsh, Scottish and English airs in 1780.

Declaimer or Datgeiniad (Middle Ages): a low class of poet who could play the crwth and declaim the poetry of others in his capacity as servant.

Dee, John (1527-1608): London Welshman, alchemist, astrologer and mathematician. His promotion of Prince Madog's supposed 12th Century discovery of the New World was used by Queen Elizabeth's Court officials to justify their war against Spain and British involvement in the Americas.

Deganwy, Gwynedd: a small resort town; the remains of the court of Maelgwyn Gwynedd, rebuilt as a Norman castle, have almost completely disappeared.

Deheubarth: one of the three kingdoms of Wales in the 12th century, a center of literary activity; divided up after the death of Rhys ap Gruffudd in 1197.

Deiniol, St. (mid-6th century): the first Bishop of Bangor. St. Deiniol's Library at Hawarden, Flintshire, attracts scholars to study mainly theological works.

Deio ab Ieuan Du (1450-80): from Llangynfelyn, Cardigan, a poet responsible for the line *Y Ddraig Goch ddyry cychwyn* (the Red Dragon shows the way) now used on the royal badge of Wales.

Delaney, Mark (b. 1976): Haverfordwest, international footballer with Aston Villa; the only

Premier league club player who began in the League of Wales.

Demetae: the leading tribe in southwest Wales during the Roman occupation.

Derfel, Robert Jones (1824-1915): radical author whose play *Brad y Llyfrau Gleision* (Treachery of the Blue Books, 1854) satirizes the 1847 government report on the state of education in Wales.

***Decriptio Kambriae* (1193):** by Giraldus Cambrensis, a description of a journey through Wales with Archbishop Baldwin in 1181 contains the "Prophecy of the Old Man of Pencader"(see separate entry).

***Description of Wales* (1584):** from many sources, an important book by scholar and antiquary Humphrey Llwyd making known the history of medieval Wales.

Dewi Sant (see St. David).

Dial-a-Poem (f. 1970) begun by the Welsh Arts Council, each week for four years a poet recorded a poem on the radio. It was taken over by the South East Wales Arts Association from 1975-79).

Dic Aberdaron (1780-1843): Richard Roberts Jones, unemployed self-educated linguist, master of many different languages, whose Welsh, Greek, and Hebrew dictionary is kept at St. Asaph (Llanelwy) Cathedral.

Dici Bach Dwl: a character from the plays of John Oswald Francis (1882-1956), a term now used for a dull-witted, country person.

Dic Penderyn (Richard Lewis, d. 1831): after the Merthyr Riots of 1831, was hanged for the crime of wounding a soldier; he vigorously protested his innocence. It is recorded that the last words Lewis spoke on the scaffold were "O Arglwydd, dyma gamwedd "(Oh Lord, what an injustice) making the poor man a martyr to the people of the Valleys (forty years later, Ieuan Parker, of Cwmafan, who lived in the United States, confessed to the crime).

Dic Sion Dafydd: a 19th-century expression, found in a poem by John Jones (*Jac Glan y Gors,* 1766-1821): a person who pretends to have forgotten his Welsh or who affects the loss of his national identity in order to succeed in English society ("an Uncle Tom").

Diffiniad: a contemporary Welsh pop group that started with dance music whose big break came with the release of *Digon* in 1998.

Dillwyn, Amy Elizabeth (1845-1935): novelist and literary critic, daughter of Lewis Llewellyn, industrial magnate and M.P. for Swansea, she pioneered women's rights in industrial and public life. Her novel *The Rebecca Rioters* was published in 1880.

Dillwyn, Mary (1816-1906): b. Swansea; pioneer who created the world's first portrait of a smile (on her nephew William Mansel Llewelyn) sold for 48,225 pounds in 2003 to the National library of Wales. She was related to Henry Fox Talbot who announced the discovery of photography in 1839.

Dinas Dinorwig, Caerns: site of the very first meeting of the Gorsedd in 1799 presided over by Iolo Morganwg.

Dinesydd, Y **(the Citizen):** begun in Cardiff in 1973, the first of what soon became a torrent of Welsh-language community newspapers (*papurau bro*).

Dinorwig Quarry, Gwynedd: the largest slate quarry in Wales that employed more than 3,000 men 1850-1910: it closed in 1959.

Dirwest Y: a Welsh temperance society begun in Clwyd in 1832, following meetings among Welsh populations in Lancashire that spread rapidly, publishing *Y Dirwestydd (*the tea-totaller) in 1836. Many of its activities ltransferred to the Cymanfa Ganu (Singing Meeting) that gave voice to the annual temperance processions in in mid-19th century Wales.

Disestablishment of the Church in Wales (1920): a Bill that finally deprived the Anglican Church of its status as the state church in Wales.

Disley, John (b. 1928): a mountaineering instructor from Corris, Snowdonia, he broke the official World and Olympic 3,000 steeplechase record at the Dynamo Stadium, Moscow in September 1955.

***Doctors' Papers*:** according to Max Boyce, these are the very popular letters from your local physician testifying to the sudden appearance of a mysterious illness during weekends of the Welsh rugby season.

Dodd, Arthur Herbert (1891-1975): from Wrexham, professor at Bangor University, author and historian, especially of Stuart Wales. He is the author of *The Industrial Revolution in North Wales* (1933) and *Life in Wales* (1972).

Dodd, Stephen (b. 1967): internationally known Welsh golfer who won the British Amateur championship in 1989, the Chinese Open in 2004, and the Irish Open in 2005.

Dodd, Charles Harold (1884-1973): b. Wrexham "the most influential British New Testament scholar of the 20th century." In 1930, he became Rylands Professor of Biblical Criticism at Manchester, then Norris Hulse Chair of Divinity at Cambridge (the first non-Anglican Professor of Divinity). A fellow of Jesus College, he received numerous fellowships and honorary degrees, and published countless books and articles on biblical study. He was the General Director of the translation of the New English Bible, 1970.

Dolbadarn Castle, Llanberis: a former stronghold of the Princes of Gwynedd.

Dolaucothi, Carmarthenshire: site of Roman gold mines, worked again in the 19th and early 20th Century, finally closing in 1936. There is a visitor's centre.

Dolgellau, Merioncthshire: site of Owain Glyndwr's last parliament in 1404, an 18th C. Welsh flannel industry; and gold mines once run by the Vaughan family, living in isolated splendor at Nannau, surrounded by 50 miles of stone walls.

Dolwyddelan Castle, Gwynedd: reputedly the birthplace of Llywelyn the Great; the lonely square keep is all that remains of the castle destroyed by Edward Ist.

Donaldson, Jessie (1799-1867): b. Swansea, she moved to Cincinnati at age 57 after marrying an American cousin. A friend of Frederick Douglass and William Lloyd Garrison, she up "safe houses" (with Welsh names) on the banks of the Ohio to shelter runaway slaves, playing a crucial role in the fight to free the U.S. from the scourge of slavery.

Dowlais: the site of the great iron works of Guest Lewis at Merthyr Tydfil, supplying the rails for the U.S. in the early 19th century as well as a high percentage of rails for Russia and other countries.

***Drafod, Y* (the Discourse, f. 1891):** quarterly newspaper (in Welsh and Spanish) begun by Lewis Jones for the Welsh community of Patagonia.

***Dragon, The* (Y Ddraig, f. 1878):** magazine of the University of Wales, Aberystwyth that has attracted many of Wales' finest writers.

***Dramau'r Byd* (Plays of the World, f. 1969):** published for the Welsh Arts Council; a series of plays translated into Welsh from other languages.

***Dream of Macsen Wledig*:** in the *Mabinogion*, it deals with Maximus (*Macsen*) Roman leader in Britain who withdrew his legions in the 5th century, and from whom most of the Royal dynasties of North Wales traced their descent.

Drefach Felindre (Ceredigion): site of the Cambrian Woolen Mills, now a Museum, where a factory trail shows the history of the woolen industry.

Driscoll, Jim (1880-1925): b. Cardiff: featherweight champion. In 1909, he boxed world champion, Abe Attell to a draw. A return bout was promised, but Jim had already promised a charity match to aid an orphanage in Cardiff. Regarded by Nat Fleischer as one of the greatest ever, Peerless Jim died of tuberculosis. His statue is in Cardiff.

Drover (15-19th C.): one who drove cattle and sheep (or even geese) from Wales to English markets by regular routes. One prosperous drover, David Jones founded Banc yr Eidion Du (*The Bank of the Black Ox*) at Llandovery in 1799 (now Lloyd's Bank).

Druid: a ancient Celtic priest-philosopher, guardian of traditions and learning, controlling the calendar and the planting of crops, and presiding over the religious festivals before the coming of the Roman armies to Britain when the order was destroyed. Modern day druids are not connected to their ancient namesakes, nor are the druid-bards of the National Eisteddfod.

Drych, Y (The Mirror, f. 1851): a valuable source for the history of Welsh Americans, *Y Drych* followed *Y Cymro America* (1832, and *Haul Gomer* (Jan-Sep, 1851). In 2004 it merged with *Ninnau* to form a single newspaper.

Drych Cristianogawl, Y. (*The Christian Mirror*, 1585): secretly printed at a cave at Llandudno, perhaps the first book published in Wales.

Dwynwen, St. (5th century): patron saint of Welsh lovers; her feast day, *Gwyl Ffolant*, is 25 January. Her ancient church and magic well are at Llanddwyn, Anglesey.

Dydd, Y (the Day, 1868): newspaper launched by Samuel Roberts of Llanbrynmair, merged with *Y Tyst*

Cymreig in 1871; became *Y Dydd a'r Corwen Chronicle* in 1914.

Dyer, John (1699-1757): b. Llanfynydd, Carms, the author of *Grongar Hill*, lived at nearby Aberglasne where the famed gardens have been restored.

Dyfed: the region of West Wales whose royal dynasty became extinct in the 10th century when it became part of the kingdom of Deheubarth.

Dyfrig, St. (Dubricius, 5th century): an important religious leader connected with Archenfield, in Herefordshire, Bishop of Llanilltud Fawr and Caldey; and also Llandaf (the first Bishop and Primate of Wales).

Dydd Mawrth Crempog (Pancake Day): a day of feasting before the start of Lent; also see Dyddd Mawrth Ynyd (Shrove Tuesday).

Dyffryn Nantlle, Gwynedd: the center of the Welsh slate industry in the 18C with more than 40 quarries, the last one closing in 2002.

Dynevor Castle (*Dynefwr*), Carms: one of three major royal residences of Wales, home of Rhys ap Gruffudd of Deheubarth.

Dyn Hysbys (*Wise man*): a Welsh wizard who could break the power of evil spells and who could protect both humans and animals from harm.

Dd

Sixth letter of the Welsh alphabet (pronounced as the th in the English words *seethe, the, them.* In many Welsh words the letter appears initially as a mutation of d).

E

Seventh letter of the Welsh alphabet (pronounced as in English *egg,* or echo, never as in *eve*).

Eagle and the Dragon, The: quarterly newsletter of the North American Welsh Foundation.

Eagles of Snowdonia: an ancient Welsh tradition in which the flight of the eagles predicted war or peace.

Eames, Aled (1921-1996): author of books on the maritime history of Anglesey and Porthmadog.

Eames, Marion (b. 1921): b. Birkenhead; former librarian and regional organizer for Plaid Cymru, worked as radio producer in Cardiff with BBC; her historical novels make her a major literary figure.

Earnshaw, Robert (b. 1981): b. Zambia, footballer with Cardiff City, now West Bromwich Albion, played for Wales under 21 and then full international in May 2002; scored the winning goal against Germany on his debut for Wales; scored three goals "a hat track" against Scotland in Feb, 2004.

Eating the Leek: a ceremony indulged in by the youngest member in each company of the Royal Welch Fusiliers and Welsh Guards each St. David's Day.

Eben Fardd (Ebenezer Thomas, 1802-1863): Llanarmon, Caernarfonshire; a poet and hymn writer who contributed much to late 19th century eisteddfodau;

Ebrill: fourth month of the year (April in English).

Ebbw Vale (Cwm Ebw, Gwent): former iron, steel and tinplate manufacturing center that was the constituency of Aneurin Bevan; site of the 1992 Garden Festival, lost 10, 000 jobs with the closure of the steel mills in 1974.

Edelman, Maurice (1911-75): b. Cardiff; politician and novelist; War correspondent; Labour M.P. for Coventry West and later Coventry North West, was delegate to the Consultative Assembly of the Council of Europe.

Edinburgh: now the capital city of Scotland, but formerly *Din Eidyn* in Brythonic-speaking Strathclyde.

Ednyfed Fychan ap Cynwrig (d. 1246): chief counselor and envoy of Llywelyn Fawr, he founded a dynasty that gave rise to many landed North Wales families, including the Tudors.

Edwards, Arthur Trystan (1884-1973): b. Merthyr Tydfil, served in the Royal Navy; a pioneer of town planning and author of books on architectural topics.

Edwards, Brian Morgan (1934-2003): Swansea-born businessman and nationalist central to the setting up of *Sain*, the recording company and the first rural housing association in Wales, Cymdeithas Tai Gwynedd. He left the Conservatives for Plaid Cymru.

Edwards, Charles (1628-91): clergyman, writer, translator, and editor; his most important work is *Y Ffydd Ddi-ffuant* (The Sincere Faith), the general history of Christianity and its growth in Wales.

Edwards, David Miall (1873-1941): from Llanfyllin, Montgomeryshire, Professor of Theology and Philosophy of Religion at Brecon, a prolific writer in Welsh and English on religion.

Edwards, Dorothy (1903-34): from Ogmore Vale, a Nationalist and Socialist, wrote a collection of short stories and an outstanding novel (*Winter Sonata*, 1928), but committed suicide.

Edwards, Fanny (1876-1959); b. Penrhyndeudraeth; poet, dramatists, children's short story writer and the first woman to publish a novel in Welsh (1908).

Edwards, Francis (1852-1927): b. Llangollen, Liberal MP for Radnorshire (1892-1918): his *Translations from the Welsh* (1913) made modern contemporary Welsh poetry available to English readers.

Edwards, Gareth (b. 1947): b. Pontardawe; voted the greatest rugby player of all time; first capped for Wales in 1967. Gareth won 53 caps for Wales, toured three times with British Lions. In 1997, he was inducted into the International Rugby Hall of Fame.

Edwards, Henry Morgan (1844-1925): from Ebbw Valee; an active and indfluiential Welsh community leader, he became one of Pennsylvania's foremost jurists; *Harri Ddu* in the Gorsedd of Wales, a bard and orator.

Edwards, Huw (b. 1962): from Llangenech, Llanelli; a household name in Wales as the anchorman of flagship BBC news program: *The Ten O'clock News*. Huw began his career with *Swansea Sound Radio*, later becoming chief parliamentary reporter for BBC News. His TV series *The Story of Welsh* attracted an enormous audience.

Edwards, Huw T. (1892-1970): from Penmaenmawr; influential secretary of the Transport and General Workers Union in the north of England and Secretary of the Council of Wales, he defected from Labour to Plaid Cymru in 1959. Hugh worked as a miner in the Rhondda, fought in France in W.W.I, became a secretary of T.G.U. to begin a public career with Flintshire County Council, Welsh Advisory Council; he refused a knighthood in his deep commitment to Wales. He returned to the Labour Party a few years before his death.

Edwards, Ifan ab Owen (1895-1970): b. Llanuwchllyn, Mer; began as editor of *Cymru'r Plant* (Wales for Children), he founded Urdd Gobaith Cymru (Welsh League of Youth). Son of famed "O. M," he started the first Welsh-medium primary school at Aberystwyth in 1939.

Edwards, Jane (b. 1938): distinguished novelist and short-story writer in Welsh, and a radio and television broadcaster.

Edwards, Janice B: from Vermont's slate region, founder and Director of the Welsh American Genealogical Society, and founder and current President of the Poultney Area St. David's Society, she is recognized throughout Welsh America for her dedication to Welsh heritage programs.

Edwards, Jenkin Morgan (1903-78): poet who expressed deep concern over the loss of spiritual values to industry and modern technology.

Edwards, John Goronwy (1891-1976): a leading historian of the period of the Welsh princes; director of the Institute of Historical Research and History Professor at University of London.

Edwards, John Hugh (1869-1945): biographer of David Lloyd George, editor and publisher of the magazine *Wales*. A regular contributor to English newspapers, he was Liberal M.P. for Mid-Glamorgan 1910-1922.

Edwards, Lewis (1809-1887): minister and essayist, brother-in-law of David Charles, with whom he opened the Bala Calvinistic Methodist College.

Edwards, Rev. Morgan (1722-95): from Pontypool, went to Pennepek, Philadelphia as a minister in 1761, he later helped found Brown University, Providence, Rhode Island and wrote the history of American Baptists.

Edwards, Ness (1897-1968): former miner, elected Labour M.P. for Caerphilly in 1939, worked closely with Aneurin Bevan and James Griffiths during WWII; Postmaster General (1950-51); helped Czech miners escape Sudetenland in 1939; Parliamentary Secretary to the Ministry of Labour and National Service 1945-50; spoke vigorously on Welsh affairs; wrote *A History of the South Wales Miners'* Federation and a History of the South Wales Miners.

Edwards, Nicholas (Lord Crickhowell): Conservative MP for Pembrokeshire in 1970; Secretary of State for Wales in 1979, and Life Peer in 1987.

Edwards, Owen (b. 1933): director S4C (Welsh television channel); program organizer on BBC Wales, Program Head (1970-74); won many awards for his TV work; chaired National Eisteddfod, 1986-89.

Edwards, Sir Owen Morgan (1858-1920): Llanuwchlyn, Bala. An Oxford scholar and influential teacher known as "O.M.," he published Welsh books and magazines to counteract the rapid spread of English publications. In 1890 he started *Cymru,* followed by *Cymry'r Plant*, successful children's magazines.

Edwards, Roger (1811-86): Bala hymn writer, prominent Calvinistic Methodist and magazine editor who helped found *Y Traethodydd* (Essayist) in 1843.

Edwards, Thomas (*Twm o'r Nant*, 1738-1810): writer of interludes and ballads and a significant figure in Welsh drama.

Edwards, Thomas (Caerfallwch, 1779-1858): b. Northop, Flintshire, completed the dictionary of William Owen Pughe and coined many acceptable Welsh words including *Cyngerdd* (concert) *nwy* (gas) and *safon* (standard).

Edwards, Thomas Charles (1837-1900): the first principal of the University College of Wales, Aberystwyth that opened in October, 1872.

Edwards, Tracy (b. 1962): b. raised on the Gower, she completed the 1985 race Whitbread Round the World Yacht Race for an all-woman crew on *Maiden, Great Britain,* to become Sportswoman of the Year.

Edwards, Trebor (b. 1937): born Denbigh; farmer at Corwen and nationally known tenor with 5 Gold discs who has travelled the world with his voice.

Edwards, Maudie (1906-1991): comedienne, stage and television actress She spoke the first words on the popular British soap opera *Coronation Street.*

Edwards, Meredith (1917-1999): b. Rhosllanerchrugog; stage, television and screen actor famous for his roles as a policeman, he starred in the successful film comedy *A Run for your Money.*

Edwards, Richey (1967-95): lyricist and founder member of the Manic Street Preachers Rock Band.

Edwards, Sara: fluent Welsh speaker who was brought up in London but lives in Carmarthenshire and works in Cardiff with the BBC where she present the BBC Wales nightly news program. she is one of tv's best loved personalities andf is deeply involved with a number of Welsh charities.

Edwards, Wayne (1975-1993): b. Cefn Mawr, Nr. Wrexham, with the Royal Welch Fusiliers, the first British soldier to be killed in Bosnia.

Edwards, William (1719-89): stonemason, designer of the Pontypridd Bridge in 1755 that was the longest and most beautiful single-span bridge in the world.

Edwards, William: in 1841, as Chartist candidate for Monmouth Boroughs, he did not receive a single vote in the General Election, not even his own.

Edworth, Sir T. W: b. Cardiff, scientific officer of the Shackleton Antarctic Expedition of 1907-09 that first reached the southern magnetic pole.

***Efrydiau Athronyddol (Philosophical Studies,* f. 1938):** published by Univ. of Wales Press carries a wide range of articles and book reviews.

Eifionydd, Gwynedd: area renowned for its poets and prose-writers.

Einion Offeiriad (Einion the Priest, 14th C.): writer of a bardic grammar important in the study of metrics and esthetics.

Eirion, Sion (b. 1954): from Hirwaun, Cynon Valley; a leading dramatist in both Welsh and English whose plays have been performed by the Welsh College of Music and Drama and other companies.

Eisteddfod: a session or "chairing". The competition had its beginnings in the year 1176 when the Lord Rhys ap Gruffudd held court in at Cardigan (Aberteifi). Eisteddfodau (pl) were held during the reign of Queen Elizabeth 1st, mainly to license the activities of the Welsh bards, but they lapsed into obscurity until the latter part of the 18th Century. A Glamorgan stone mason, Edward Williams, known to posterity as Iolo Morganwg, helped create the elaborate, colorful ceremonies that eventually led to those of today's National Eisteddfod of Wales. In the 1860's the National Eisteddfod Society was founded and the modern era of the competitions began. The chief poetry contests are for the Chair and for the Crown. The Eisteddfod now includes arts and crafts, country dancing, folk singing, choral competitions, and drama and prose contests, all providing a tremendous impetus to the fostering of Welsh as a living language. No English is allowed on stage.

Eisteddfod Mawr (*the great Eisteddfod*): begun at Beti Huws' farm in 1876 at Chubut; a major part of the social life of the Patagonia Welsh ever since.

El Bandito (b. 1928); from Ysbyty Ifan, professional name of Orig Williams, who became a wrester after playing football in the Welsh League in the late 1940's. After retiring from the ring, he took up acting. His autobiography is *Cario'r Ddraig* (Carrying the Dragon).

Elen of the Hosts (Elen Luyddog, 4th C.): a heroine in *The Dream of Macsen* based on the daughter of Eudaf, a Briton who held Segontium for the Romans. She married Maximu and gave her name to the road Sarn Helen.

Elias, John (1774-1841): the "Methodist Pope," uncompromising in his belief in the literal truth of the Bible, famous for his preaching as the first Calvinistic Methodist Minister.

Eliot, George (1819-1880): pen-name of Mary Ann Evans, regarded as the quintessential English novelist, but who was born in Warwickshire where her Welsh father had her attend Welsh Methodist Chapel as a child.

Eliseg's Pillar, Llangollen: much eroded stone pillar, adjacent to Valle Crucis Abbey; deciphered in 1696, it was erected in the Ninth Century by Cyngen in memory of his great grandfather Eliseg, who freed Powys from English rule.

Elis-Thomas, Lord Dafydd (b. 1946): b. Carmarthen; Presiding Officer to the National Assembly for Wales, Chair of the House Committee, former college teacher, M.P. for Meirionnydd 1974-83 and M.P. for Merionnydd Nant Conwy since 1983: President of the University of Wales, Bangor, former Chairman of the Welsh Language Board (1994-99): member of Welsh Arts Council, Wales Film Council and Welsh Film Board.

Elizabeth lst (1533-1603): Queen of England, sometimes proud of her Welsh heritage as a Tudor, is included here by virtue of her description by English historian A.L. Rowse as "that red-headed Welsh harridan."

El Malacara: (d. 1909): the horse that carried Welsh settler John Evans to safety after his companions had been killed by Patagonian natives.

Ellis, Osian (b. 1928): b. Ffynongroew, Flints; a village that supplied many of the miners for the Point of Ayr Colliery, Ellis studied at the Royal Academy of Music (London) where he became a professor in 1959 until retirement in 1980. Ellis is highly regarded as one of the world's great harpists as a recitalist and orchestra member. Many composers have written concertos and pieces written for him, including Benjamin Britten.

Ellis, Richard Salisbury (b. 1950): from Colywn Bay, Ph. D in Astrophysics (Oxford University, 1974). Professor of Astronomy, California Institute of Technology, Deputy Director, Palomar Observatory, Professor of Observational Astrophysics at University of Cambridge with a host of honors and medals in astrophysics.

Ellis, Rowland (1650-1731): Methodist leader from Merioneth, a leading figure in Pennsylvania after whose old home Bryn Mawr College is named.

Ellis, Ruth (1927-1955): b. Rhyl, Denbs; the last female executed in Britain, for killing her racing driver lover, Donald Blakey (see Timothy Evans).

Ellis, Samuel: b. Ewloe, Flintshire; owner of Ellis Island in the 1770's. From 1892 to 1943, it was the major immigration station in the U.S.

Ellis, Thomas Edward (1859-1899): his election in 1886 for Merioneth broke the monopoly of the landlord classes at Westminster. He supported land reform, education and church disestablishment, founding Cymru Fydd to campaign for Home Rule; lack of support and his early death delayed the movement for almost 50 years.

Ellis, Thomas Iorwerth (1899-1970) b. London, headmaster of Rhyl County School, a prolific contributor to Welsh periodicals; served on many committees including the University of Wales, the National Library and the Church in Wales as well as serving as secretary of Undeb Cymru Fydd (1941-67).

Elwy Valley, Clwyd: site of the Pontnewydd Cave, where the remains of the earliest human occupation of Wales (early Neanderthal Man) were disovered.

Emanuel, David (b. 1952): a most sought-after couturier, much-favored by Europe's royal families; creator of Princess Diana's wedding gown in 1981 and Catherine Zeta Jones's gown in 2000; he also designed for ballet, the theatre and television.

Emmanuel, Ivor (b. 1926): famed tenor who debuted with the musical *Oklahoma* in London, then joined

D'Oyley Carte Opera before returning to the show stage; starred on Welsh radio and appeared in the film *Zulu.*

Emrys ap Iwan (1851-1906): b. Abergele, fighter for Wales and the Welsh language his volume of sermons (*Homiliau)* is a prose classic. His call for a form of self-government for Wales was to take fifty years to bear fruit.

Emrys Wledig (Ambrosius, 5th C): named by Gildas as a leader against the Saxon invaders of Britain, In Geoffrey of Monmouth, he is called *Merlin*, responsible for the prophecy of the red dragon triumphing over the white.

Enfys, Yr (the Rainbow): newspaper of Cymru ar Byd (formerly Cymru ar Wasgar). It grew out of *Seren y Dwyrain* (Star of the East) published in Egypt for Welsh soldiers in the Middle East during W.W.II.

England, Mike (b. 1941): b. Holywell; a footballer with Blackburn; went to Tottenham Hotspur for a British record fee in 1966; played for Wales 44 times.

Englefield (*Tegeingl)*: inhabited by the Deceangli, claimed by the Norman Earls of Chester, reconquered by Llywelyn Fawr and Llywelyn ap Gruffudd, became part of the county of Flint in 1284.

Englyn: a form of poetic used since the ninth century. Originally a verse in a long poem but is more commonly a single stanza, brief and intense.

Environment Agency Wales: a public body sponsored by the National Assembly to regulate, monitor and manage the land, air, and water.

Erging, Herefordshire: one of the original lordships of Wales known for the skill of its bowmen, its Welsh tongue, and its adherence to Roman Catholicism.

Eryri: (*the home of Eagles*): the Snowdon mountain massif in Gwynedd, the highest peak of which is *Yr Wyddfa* at 3,560 ft.

Etheridge, Ken (1911-81): b. Ammanford, influential teacher, poet, playwright and painter who taught at St. Elizabeth's Grammar School, Carmarthen.

Evans, Alice Catherine (1881-1975): b. Neath, Pennsylvania, to a Welsh family. Working with the Dairy Division of the U.S. Dept of Agriculture in 1910, she showed that raw milk could cause human diseases. Pasteurization thus became mandatory in the U.S. Dairy industry, preventing brucella, a national scourge. In 1928, she was the first woman president of the Society of American bacteriologists. A posthumous member of the National Women's Hall of Fame, her story is told in *Gentle Hunter*, by Virginia Law Burns.

Evans, Beriah Gwynfe (1848-1927): from Nant y Glo, a schoolmaster who launched the periodical *Cyfaill y Aelwyd* (1881), secretary of Cymru Fydd and the first secretary of Cymdeithas Yr Iaith Gymraeg in 1885. Wrote several books, including one of Lloyd George and *Dafydd Davis* about a Welshman in London.

Evans, Caradoc (David Evans, 1878-1945): Anglo-Welsh author whose satirical, unflattering portrayals of the Welsh people gave him much notoriety; regarded as a founding father of modern Anglo-Welsh literature.

Evans, Chris (b. 1957): from Port Talbot, one of the world's most successful biotech industry entrepreneurs. With a Ph. D trom the University of Michigan, he became involived in the fast-growing American biotech industry and the founder of Chiroscience, and Toad PLC car alarm system. An advisor to the British government on biotech matters, he lives in Crickhowell, near Brecon.

Evans, Christmas (1776-1838): preacher and hymn-writer from Llandysul, Carmarthenshire, whose dramatic presentations made him popular in Wales (and scared the living daylights out of his congregations).

Evans, Clifford (1912-1985): actor and stage-director, worked with some greats of the British theatre, later becoming popular on British television and movies.

Evans, Daniel Silvan (1818-1903); B. Llanarth, Cardigan, parish priest, lexicographer and Professor of Welsh at Aberystwyth (1875-1883).

Evans, Dick (b. 1905): f. Moelfre, Anglesey, lifeboat coxwain who twice won the Royal National Lifeboat Institution Gold Medal for bravery rescuing the crews of the *Hindlea* in 48 ft waves in 1959, and the *Nafsiporos* in a cyclone in 1976.

Evans, Donald (b. 1940): from Cardiganshire, a poet who won both the Chair and the Crown in 1977 and 1980; a prolific poet and master of Cerdd Dafod.

Evans, Edgar (1876-1912): explorer from Gower who died with Robert Falcon Scott on the ill-fated return journey from the South Pole.

Evans, Ellis Humphrey (*Hedd Wyn*, 1887-1917): a farmer-poet from Trawsfynydd, Merioneth, posthumously awarded the Chair at the National Eisteddfod, Birkenhead, Cheshire (the Eisteddfod of the Black Chair) after his death in World War One. The Welsh-language film *Hedd Wyn,* about his life, was nominated for a Hollywood Academy Award in 1992.

Evans, Elwyn (1902-2004): former head of BBC training dept, worked for BBC in Nigeria in the 1950's publishing his recollections as *Cyfarfod ag Affrica* (1995).

Evans, (William) Emrys (1924-2004): b. Llanfair Careinion, Montgomeryshire; Chairman and founder trustee of *Sefydliad Addysg Menter Busnes*, Member of Council for Welsh Language, and University of Wales. Chairman of the Royal Welsh Agricultural Society, he was one of the first speakers of Welsh in a commercial (on TV Channel S4C in 1982). As executive director of the Midland Bank in Wales, he successfully campaigned for Welsh cheques and bilingual signs in his bank, forcing others to follow.

Evans, Evan (Ieuan *Brydydd Hir*, 1731-1788): b. Lledrod, Ceredigion; scholar and poet, principal figure in the mid-18th century revival of Welsh classical poetry. He helped preserve many priceless Welsh manuscripts. His *Some Specimens of the Poetry of the Ancient Welsh Bards* (1764) satisfied a thirst in English literary circles for Celtic literature.

Evans, Evan (*Ieuan Glan Geirionydd*, 1795 -1855): the most versatile Welsh poet of the 19th century and an outstanding hymn writer; a pioneer of the Welsh lyric.

Evans, Sir Geraint (1922-92): Cilfynydd-born; an all-time favorite in international opera, began as a teenager on *Welsh Rarebit*, joining Covent Garden Opera in 1947 after service in the R.A.F. Famous for his interpretation of *Figaro* and *Falstaff*, he appeared in the world's leading opera houses; he was the principal baritone at Covent Garden Opera from 1948 to 1992.

Evans, Gwyndaf (b. 1959): Machynlleth, one of Britain's top Road Rally champions with many victories.

Evans, Gwynfil (1898-1938): writer of boys' fiction and one of the creators of Sexton Blake, hero of a hundred stories, one of the most popular characters in all British juvenile fiction.

Evans, Gwynfor (1912-2005)): from Barry, with a law

 degree from Oxford University, the Grand Old Man of Welsh politics, patriot, nationalist, and author of books on Welsh history and Welsh heroes. Elected to Carmarthen County Council in 1949 for Plaid. President of Plaid Cymru from 1945-81; M.P. for Carmarthen in 1966 and 1979, and later Honorary President, Gwynfor's promise to go on a hunger strike influenced the government's approval of the Welsh language TV channel). For his intense patriotism, He is generally regarded as one of the most influential Welshmen of all time.

Evans, Handel Cromwell (1932-99): b. Pontypridd licentiate of the Royal Academy of Music and the London College of Music. Found fame as an artist with many commissioned works worldwide.

Evans, Harold Meurig (b. 1911): Pontarddulais headmaster and author helped complete *Y Geiriadur Mawr* (1958) and *The Dictionary of Modern Welsh* (1981).

Evans Howell Thomas (1877-1930): from Cwmbwrla, Swansea, headmaster at Aberaeron who published several books on the history of Wales.

Evans Hugh (1854-1934): author from Llangwm, Denbigh whose most popular work is *Cwm Eithin*, (1931) trans: as *Gorse Glen,* 1948, a thesaurus of rural life.

Evans, Ieuan (b. 1964): rugby player, "the Carmarthen Cowboy" scored 33 tries in 72 games for Wales and the British Lions (captain on 13 occasions). With Llanelli, he scored more tries for Wales than any other player.

Evans, Jack (1889-1971): b. Bala, footballer with Wrexham. Moving to Cardiff as a printer, he became the very first professional signed by City, and scored their very first goal (a friendly against Aston Villa in 1910). Nickmamed "Bala Bang" he returned home from the W.W.I to continue playing for Cardiff City.

Evans, Jill (b. 1959): from the Rhondda, former County Councilor, Chair of Plaid Cymru 1994-96: leader of the Plaid Cymru European Parliamentary Party and member of many important committees. In

November, 2004, Jill became the first person to give a speech in Welsh at the European Parliament, Brussels.

Evans, John (1814-1897): b. Ohio to parents from Porthmadog; a medical doctor in Chicago, teaching at Northwestern University, founded the Illinois Republican Party; as Governor of Colorado, got the intercontinental railroad to run through Denver. Proud of his Welsh background, he helped found the University of Colorado and played an active part in many Welsh cultural affairs in the state. Evanston, Illinois and Mount Evans (Colorado) are named for him.

Evans, John (1770-1799): explorer from Waunfawr, Gwynedd, who searched for descendants from Prince Madog's supposed expedition of 1169. Evans worked for the Spanish Missouri Company looking for the way to the Pacific; he found no Welsh links with the Mandans, with whom he lived for six months. He later traveled over 2000 miles exploring the Missouri. Some of his maps were later used by Lewis and Clark, sent out to find a route to the Pacific by Thomas Jefferson, himself of Welsh descent.

Evans, John (b. 1958): from Pontypridd, author who began with a punk rock band. His books *Industria, G.B.H.* and *How Real is My Valley* show nightmare images of a decaying South Wales Valleys landscape.

Evans, John (Y Bardd Cocos, 1827-88): from Menai Bridge, sold cockles, wrote ingenious doggerel, earning him the local title of *Archfardd Cocysdaidd Tywysogol* (Royal Cockle Poet).

Evans, John (Gwenogvryn, 1852-1930): editor, whose reports on Welsh manuscripts form the foundation of modern studies of medieval Welsh literature.

Evans, John Albert (b. 1937): b. Tregaron; former Welsh Language Organizer for Mid-Glamorgan; a schools inspector and Welsh Language officer for Rhondda Cynon Taf County Council; until 2005, he organized Welsh language courses at the annual North American Welsh Heritage Week.

Evans, John Roberts (1914-82): b. Lampeter, after service in the Royal Navy, taught in Cardiganshire; published many plays, novels, and short stories.

Evans, Prof. (Henry) John (b. 1930): b. Llanelli, Director of Medical Research Council on Human Genetics at Edinburgh 1969-94. Professor of Genetics at Aberdeen, member of Scientific Advisory Council, distinguished science writer.

Evans, Julian Cayo (1937-1995): b. England, lived in Carmarthenshire; he led the Free Wales Army, a shadowy group with revolutionary aims and was imprisoned for conspiracy relating to the 1969 Investiture of Prince Charles.

Evans (William), Lindsay (b. 1933): TV actor lecturer; member of Wales Arts Council, author of numerous radio and TV plays and documentaries.

Evans Lyn (b. 1945): from Aberdare, director of The European Organization for Nuclear Research (CERN) at Geneva, responsible for the world's biggest particle accelerator, to be completed in 2007. Lyn has to coordinate all the organization's building components for the accelerator and supervise another 200-300 scientists and engineers worldwide.

Evans, Margaret (*Marged uch Ifan*, 1695-1801): from Penllyn, Llanberis, praised by Thomas Pennant for her prodigious feats in hunting, fishing, shooting, wrestling and skill in music.

Evans, (Arthur) Mostyn (b.1925): b. Cefn Coed, General Secretary of Transport and General Workers' Union (1978-85); General Council of T.U.C. (1977-85); with a distinguished career in engineering, chemicals, and rubber.

Evans, Myron Wyn (b. 1950): from Craigcefnparc; scientist and engineer who came to the U.S. in 1986 to continue his research in Sci-Tech. He is a former science advisor to Plaid Cymru with numerous awards for his work in science and engineering, including a Distinguished American Science Award.

Evans, Nigel (b. 1957): Swansea; joined Conservative Party in 1974; M.P. for Ribble Valley in 1992 after serving on West Glamorgan County Council; currently the Shadow Secretary of State for Wales.

Evans, Oliver (1755-1819): Welsh-American inventor and pioneer of the high-pressure steam engine and improvements in milling. In 1805, in Philadelphia, Oliver Evans drove his *Orukter Amphibolos* (Amphibious digger), using his own high-pressure steam engine (the world's first automobile).

Evans, Philip (1645-79): Monmouth-born Catholic martyr executed during the "Popish Plot" of 1678; canonized by Pope Paul VI in 1970. Said to have praised the gallows as being a fine pulpit.

Evans, Rebecca: born Pontrhydyfen, regarded as one of the world's leading sopranos, has sung for the Santa Fe Opera), the Chicago Lyric Opera; San Franciso Opera; and the Metropolitan Opera, New York. In Europe, her roles have included Welsh National Opera; English National Opera and the Royal Opera House, Covent Garden. Her concert experience includes appearances at the BBC Proms and Edinburgh International Festival; Gala Concerts with Andrea Bocelli in Germany and with Luciano Pavarotti in Britain; and a Gala Concert to celebrate the opening of the Welsh Assembly in the presence of Her Majesty the Queen and HRH The Prince of Wales. Rebecca hosted her own television series 'A Touch of Classics' with the BBC National Orchestra of Wales on BBC1 Wales.

Evans, Richard (1905-2001): from Moelfre, Anglesey, where he earned two gold medals as coxwain of the lifeboat for saving the crews of the *Hindlea* in a storm off Moelfre Rocks in 1959 and that of the *Nafsipourous* in an even fiercer storm off the Skerries in 1968. In 50 years of service the lifeboat was launched 179 times, saving 281 lives.

Evans, Prof. (Hubert) Roy (b. 1942): from Llandysul, Vice Chancellor of University of Wales, Bangor since 1995, a leading expert in field of structural energy and plate structures; has awards from Britain and Czech Republic.

Evans, Stuart (b. 1934): Swansea-born, served in the Navy, taught at Brunel College of Advanced Technology, then for BBC Radio with the Schools Broadcasting Dept. Has written poetry, but is better known as a novelist.

Evans, Theophilus (1693-1767): Anglican priest whose prose classic *Drych y Prif Oesoedd* (Mirror of the First Ages, 1716) recounts the history of the Welsh people from the Tower of Babel to Llywelyn ap Gruffudd.

Evans, Thomas (Tomos Glyn Cothi, 1764-1833); b. Gwernogle, Carmarthen, minister at Cwm Cothi, the first Unitarian chapel in Wales; pastor at Aberdare, where he edited hymns for Unitarians and wrote the first Unitarian sermon to be published in Welsh.

Evans, Timothy (1924-1950): from Merthyr Vale, was hanged on a charge of strangling his wife at 10 Rillington Place, North Kensington, the home of John Reginald Christie, who later confessed to murdering poor Mr. Evans's wife. After Christie's execution on July 15, 1953, two fierce debates in the House of Commons. abolished the Death Penalty; it has never been restored.

Evans, Trabor Lloyd (1909-79): from Bala, independent minister who became Secretary of the Union of Welsh Independents in 1904; wrote many books on religious subjects.

Evans William (Wil Ifan, 1882-1968): playwright and poet, three-time Crown winner; Archdruid 1947-50.

Evans-Jones, Albert, the Rev. (*Cynan,* 1895-1970): ex army chaplain, Calvinistic Methodist minister and college tutor, poet, playwright and Archdruid of Wales. A three-time Crown winner, he played a leading role in the investiture of Prince Charles; he created many of the colorful ceremonies of the modern Eisteddfod.

***Evening Leader, the* (f. 1973):** a newspaper for Wrexham, with separate editions for Flintshire, Cheshire, and the North Wales Coast.

Everest, Sir George (1790-1866): Brecon-born Surveyor General of India; gave his name to the world's highest mountain.

F

Eighth letter of the Welsh alphabet (pr. as v as in English word *Avon)*.

Faggots and Peas: a dish made mainly of chopped liver set in a bowl of mushy peas, popular in such fine culinary establishments as the Neath Indoor Market.

Fairbourne and Barmouth Steam Railway: narrow-gauge railway that changed from horse-drawn trams to steam in 1916, lovingly preserved.

Fan, Y: a mansion at Caerphilly that entertained many itinerant poets during the 16th and 17th centuries.

Farr, Thomas George (Tommy "The Tonypandy Terror" 1914-1986): born in Clydach Vale. He began boxing in 1926 and had his last fight in 1953. He defeated Max Baer in 1937, but gallantly lost to the world champion Joe Louis in New York. City in a fight broadcast around the world.

Feat Stone: a heavy stone used in ancient games to determine a gentleman's status in society.

Felinfoel Ale: (Llanelli), a good Welsh ale. In December, 1935 it was the first beer in Europe to be sold in cans (using tin made at St. David's Tinplate works, Bynea). The brewery began in 1878 following 40 years of home brewing at the Union Inn (formerly the King's Head).

Fellten, Y (The Lightning): a radical weekly published in Merthyr, 1860-1876.

Fenton, Richard (1747-1821): b. St. David's; author of *A Historical Tour through Pembrokeshire* (1810) and *Tours in Wales 1804-13*.

Ferris, Paul (b. 1929): from Swansea, journalist and author writing for television and *The Observer,* with biographies of Dylan Thomas and Richard Burton as well as many investigative novels.

Festivals of Wales (*Gwyliau Cymru*): Important are the International Eisteddfod, Llangollen (July); the National Eisteddfod of Wales (August); the Urdd National Eisteddfod (June): the Welsh Proms at St. David's Hall, Cardiff (July); the Fishguard International Music Festival (July); the Swansea Festival of Music and the Arts (October); and the St. David's Cathedral Festival (late May to early June).

Finch, Catrin (b. 1981): b. Aberystwyth, one of her nation's top harpists. Trained by Elinor Bennett, and at the Royal Academy of Music, she was chosen by Prince Charles to be Royal Harpist, a position established especially for Catrin after a lapse of 125 years. Catrin has won many awards for her skills; at age ten, she performed in the BBC Promenade Concert at the Royal Albert Hall.

Firbank, Thomas (b. 1910): Canadian-born author of the enormously popular book of life during the late 1930's on a Welsh farm: *I Bought a Mountain (1940)*.

First Account in English of the newly discovered Americas, 1526: (see Barlow, Roger).

First Book Published in Welsh (1585): *Y Llyvyr Hwnn* (*This book*), religious texts by John Prys, Brecon.

First Brick Houses in Wales: Bachegraig, Tremeirchion; and Plas Clough, nr Denbigh both ordered built by Sir ichard Clough (1530-70).

First British Soldier killed in Bosnia Conflict, 1993: Wayne Edwards from Cefn Mawr nr Wrexham, aged 18 yrs.

First Christmas Carol (surviving) in Welsh: "Geni Crist" written by Madog ap Gwallter in the 13th C.

First Distillery in the U.S.: opened by American Welshman Evan Williams in Louisville, Ky., 1783 to make Bourbon.

First English book to be printed in Wales: *First Map of Wales (1573)* published by Humphrey Lhuyd.

First Airplane flight from Wales to Ireland: on April 16, 1912, Vivian Hewitt, pioneer aviator from Rhyl flew from Holyhead to Dublin in his Bleriot monoplane.

First Miss World from Wales, 1961: Rosemarie Frankland, born 1943 in Rhosllanerchrugog, Wrexham; she toured Alaska with Bob Hope.

First Permanent Printing Press in Wales (see Carter, Isaac).

First Photograph taken in Wales: Margam Caslte, March, 1851 (see Calvert Richard Jones).

First Welsh Bible (1588): the incomparable work of translation by a team of scholars, headed by Bishop William Morgan, following the Government Act of 1563 that ordered the Bible to be translated into Welsh (to further the cause of Protestantism in the kingdom), it is seen by historians as saving the Welsh language from perhaps becoming nothing more than a mere country dialect and ensuring the continuance of the iiterary tradition of Wales.

First Welsh Book printed in North America: *Anerch I'r Cymru* (Greetings to the Welsh) by Ellis Pugh at Philadadelphia in 1721 and translated in 1727 by Rowland Ellis.

First Welsh Book Printed in Wales: *Y Drych Gristianogdawl* (The Christian Mirror 1585), reputedly printed in Llandudno cave.

First Welsh Language Speech at the European Parliament: November 17, 2004 by Plaid Cymruy Euro M.P. Jill Evans, from the Rhondda.

First Welsh Language Programs: began 1927 on *Radio Eireann*, the voice of the Irish Republic. One million Welsh speakers had been ignored by BBC—a major factor in the rapid decline of the language.

First Welsh Language Weekly for Women: *Y Gymraes* (the Welsh Woman) begun by Ieuan Gwynedd in 1850, to encourage Welsh women to become readers and writers. as a response to the "Blue Books" controversy.

First Welsh Passage in a Book: (see Book of St. Chad).

First Welsh Pop Group to top the British national charts: *Amen Corner* with "If Paradise was half as nice" in 1969.

First Welsh Setlement in South America: led by Evan Evans of Nanty Glo, a group of almost 200 Welsh people settled in in Rio Grande do Sul in Brazil in 1850, but moved to another province when coal was discovered there.

First Welsh Words heard on Radio (13 Feb 1923): "Cariwch medd Dafydd" from *Dafydd Y Garreg Wen,* sung by Mostyn Thomas on Station 5WA, Cardiff.

First Quaker Evangelical in Wales (see John ap John).

Fisher, George (1909-70): dramatist whose work with Theatr Fach Llangefni (1950's) contributed a great deal to the development of modern drama in Wales.

Fishguard (Abergwaun), Pembrokeshire: at the Royal Oak Inn, a copy of the 1797 treaty and a 1999 tapestry commemorate the surrender of a French force to the local militia (augmented by Jemima Nicholas and local Welsh women).

Fitzwarine, Fulk (d. 1256): outlaw whose exploits are recounted in folklore and contemporary poetry.

Flame Bearers of Welsh History (*The Sons of Cunedd, 1905)* written by Robert Scourfield Mills to give Welsh children a favorable account of the history of their nation from the earliest times to 1485.

Flint (Y Fflint): site of the castle built by Edward I on the banks of the Dee as the first link in the chain of castles to strangle

Wales, the town received a charter in 1284. The remains of the masterpiece of James of St. George include a unique circular tower or *Dongeon,* where Richard II met his favorite Piers Gaveston and where he also was forced to surrend to Bolingbroke (later Henry IV) in 1399.

Flowering Sunday (Sul y Blodau): Palm Sunday, the Sunday before Easter, when an ancient custom has graves decorated with flowers, usually daffodils.

Fluellen: a Welsh character in Shakespeare's *Henry V,* who remarks on the ancient custom of wearing a leek on St. David's Day (March lst) probably a misspelling of the name Llywelyn or an English approximation.

Ford Gron, Y (the Round Table): monthly magazine published by Hughes a'i Fab 1930-1935 with poetry, short stories, literary articles, travel, the eisteddfod etc, mainly for Welsh "exiles."

Ford, Trevor: (b. 1923): forward with Cardiff and Wales, banned from British football for writing his controversial *I Lead the Attack.* He was converted from fullback after scoring six games for an army team during W.W.II.

Forward Wales 2000 (f. 1995): a quarterly magazine published by the *Western Mail* to sell Wales to its own people, but also to the UK, Europe and the world as a dynamic place in which to invest.

Foster, Idris Llewelyn (1911-1984): b. Bethesda, distinguished professor of Celtic at Liverpool 1936-47; he served with British Intelligence during W.W.II; Chaired Celtic Studies at Oxford: researched early Welsh poetry, medieval Welsh prose, the *Mabinogian,* and religious manuscripts. Five distinguished professors of Welsh language and literature studied under him at Jesus College, Oxford.

Fothergill family: influential iron-masters at Abernant, Penydarren, and Sirhowy (1794 to the 1870's).

Foulkes, Isaac (Llyfrbryf, 1836-1904): from Llandwrog, Denbigh; publisher, biographer, and editor who gave Welsh literature a wide audience.

Fowkes, Robert A (1913-1999): b. New York State, a master of languages. Bob was Head of the Intelligence Division of the U.S. Army Corps of Engineers in W.W. II. President of the St. David's Society of New York from 1955-1958, he wrote a beginner's guide to the Welsh dictionary, numerous scholarly articles on linguistics, Celtic, and Welsh studies, helped create Welsh language courses: admitted to the Gorsedd for his contributions to Welsh culture.

Francis, Dai (Dai o'r Onllwyn, 1911-1980): from Blaendulais; influential miners' leader, and fervent supporter of Welsh nationalism and Welsh culture. As chief administrative officer of the S. Wales area of the

National Union of Mineworkers, he helped establish the Welsh Council of Trade Unions.

Francis, John Oswald (1882-1956): playwright whose one-act comedy *The Poacher* (1914) introduced *Dici Bach Dwl* as an ignorant, country bumpkin.

Free Wales Army, the (1965-9): a quasi-military organization led by Julian "Cayo" Evans, mostly harmless but played up by the daily newspapers.

Freeman, Kathleen (Mary Fitt, 1897-1959): Cardiff born classical scholar and novelist.

French, Dawn (1957): the Holyhead-born half of the TV duo French and Saunders, Dawn taught drama in London where she met Jennifer with whom she later starred in *Absolutely Fabulous* before becoming the Vicar of Dibley in the TV series.

Frere, Sir Bartle (1815-1884): Breconshire-born, colonial administrator in India and S. Africa; helped suppress the Indian Mutiny of 1857; served as governor of Bombay for five years. In South Africa, he provoked a war with the Zulus leading to the Isandhlwana disaster and his recall to Britain.

Fro Gymraeg, Y (the "bro"): the areas of Wales considered the strongholds of language and culture.

Frongoch, Merionethshire: prison camp set up 1916 to house many Irish Republican leaders, thus ensuring that their prison became a Gaelic college, "Sinn Fein University". The government of a future independent Irish Republic was planned here by Michael Collins, Arthur Griffith and others.

Frost, Bill (1850-1935): from Pembs, he designed a flyning machine that he claimed to have flown at Stammer Hill, Saundersfoot, on September, 1895. The machine hit a tree after take off; documentary proof is missing.

Frost, John (1784-1877): in January, 1840, following the Newport Rising, former town councilor, magistrate, and mayor, he was found guilty of high treason, along with William Jones, and Rees (Jack the Fifer). Death sentences were reduced to penal servitude in Van Dieman's Land (Tasmania). Frost returned in 1856 to a hero's welcome. Still denouncing the Government, he spoke at a public meeting in Merthyr in 1857.

Fyfe, Sir David Maxwell (1st Earl of Kilmuir): The 1st Minister of State for Welsh Affairs in 1951. Called *Dai Bananas* (after the Fyfe fruit company), he was British Deputy Chief Prosecutor at the Nuremberg Trials of Nazi leaders following the Second World War.

Ff

Ninth letter of the Welsh alphabet (pronounced as English F). Sometimes used to represent the English ph as in ffôn (phone).

Ffestiniog Railway: a narrow gauge line that operated 1832-1946 to carry slate from the quarries down to Porthmadog. Restored and opened for passengers in 1954, it is the oldest independent railway company in the world.

Fflach Trad: Cardigan based folk music company with three different recording labels that began in 1978 as a band, setting up a studio in 1983.

***Fflam, Y* (the Flame):** a literary magazine of the late 1940's in which articles in Welsh and English gave voice to many young, provocative writers.

***Fflat Huw Puw* (Huw Puw's Deck):** a popular sea-shanty first published in 1848, re-introduced to Welsh audiences by modern folk-singer Dafydd Iwan.

Ffôn Wen: (a white stick): an old custom by which a stripped hazel rod was sent anonymously to a rejected swain the day of his sweetheart's wedding.

Ffordd yng Nghymru (The Road in Wales): a children's history book by R.T. Jenkins, published in 1933 that is regarded as a minor classic.

Ffowc Elis, Islwyn (1924-2004): minister, radio producer, popular novelist, editor and translator. His novels, dealing with contemporary issues in Wales, began with *Cysgod y Cryman* (Shadow of the Sickle), 1953. He was politically active with Plaid Cymru.

***Ffydd Ddi-ffuant, Y* (The Sincere Faith, 1667):** prose classic by Charles Edwards that outlined the Christian faith of Wales and the world to give an account of Welsh history.

G

Tenth letter of the Welsh alphabet, pronounced as in English word *goat*, never as in *George*.

Gaiman: a small town in the Chubut Valley, Patagonia, Argentina, where the Welsh language remains strong, and where teashops offer a taste of Wales.

Gallie, Menna (b. 1920): Ystradgynlais-born novelist whose *Full Moon* (1973) is a translation of Caradog Pritchard's *Un Nos Ola Leuad*. She has written about life in the mining valleys of Wales.

Gambold, William (1672-1728): a grammarian who published one of the first English books to be printed in Wales: *Grammar of the Welsh Language* (1727).

Gardd Foteneg Genedlaethol Cymru (see National Botanic Garden of Wales).

Garlick, Raymond (b. 1926): b. London, poet, critic and important essayist in Anglo-Welsh literature.

Garmon (Germanus, 378-448): Bishop of Auxerre who led the Britons against the Saxons at Maes Garmon, Clwyd in 480. As a Christian champion, he is the hero of Sanders Lewis' play *Buchedd Garmon* (1937).

Gavelkind: the method of bequeathing land equally to the owner's sons. Practiced in Wales until the Act of Union, it did much to undermine the stability of Welsh society.

Gee, Thomas (1815-1889): publisher of Gwasg Gee, turning out books of poetry, grammar, dictionaries, newspapers etc., including *Baner ac Amserau Cymru.* His opinions greatly influenced Welsh politics in the later 19th century. Gwasg Gee ended in 2001.

***Genedl Gymreig, Y (The Welsh Nation,* 1897-37):** a radical weekly published in Caernarfon that merged with *Yr Herald Cymraeg* in 1937.

***Geninen, Y (The Leek,* 1883-1928):** a quarterly magazine revived by Gomer Press in 1951 to become a lively periodical of traditional Welsh rural culture.

Geoffrey of Monmouth (c. 1090-1155): Norman-Welsh writer who began a whole new European literature of *Arthuriana* in which a benevolent king presided over a chivalric court in a Golden Age of Britain. His most important work is *Historia Regum Britanniae.*

George, William R. P (b. 1912): b. Criccieth, Caerns; poet and biographer, has written two books about his uncle Lloyd George, a collection of the Eluned Morgan letters, and verse and plays for radio.

Gibbs, Scott (b. 1971): rugby player with Swansea; scored a last minute try to help defeat England 32-31 in 1999; he played in over 50 internationals.

Giggs, Ryan (b. 1974): skilled footballer, signed for Manchester United as a teenager, made his debut for Wales v. Germany at age of seventeen; helped United win many Premier League championships.

Gilchrist Thomas, Sidney (1850-85): London born son of a Welsh civil servant, as a chemist working with his cousin Percy, he succeeded in eliminating phosphorus from the Bessemer converter to produce high quality steel—a process bought by Andrew Carnegi in the U.S. and used world wide.

Gildas (495-570): Latin scholar educated at St. Illtud's school, Glamorgan, who established monasteries in Wales. His *De Excidio Britannia* presents Wales as a nation deserving of punishment; blames Vortigern for inviting the Saxons to Britain; praises Emrys Wledig; and refers to the victory of Arthur at the battle of Mount Badon.

Giraldus Cambrensis, (Gerald of Wales, c. 1146-1223): important medieval writer whose important works include *The Conquest of Ireland, The Topography of Ireland, The Journey through Wales,* and *A Description of Wales.* Failing to become Bishop of St. David's to make it independent of Canterbury, Giraldus stressed that Wales was a distinct unit in terms of culture and customs, thus fulfilled the definition of a nation.

Gittins Report (1967): headed by Professor Gittins, of Swansea University, a government committee report on education in Wales that recommended every child should be given sufficient opportunity to be reasonably bilingual by the end of the primary stage.

Glamorgan (Morgannwg): a county created in 1536; it was divided into West Glamorgan, Mid Glamorgan, and South Glamorgan in 1974.

Glamorgan Canal (b.1794): bringing coal and iron products from Merthyr, it led to the rapid growth of Cardiff and was quickly followed by others linking Swansea and Newport to the coalfields.

Glamorgan Cricket Club: the only County cricket club in Wales, begun at the Angel Hotel, Cardiff on July 6, 1888 (an earlier club, had begun 1869 at Neath).

Glamorgan Sausage: a vegetarian dish of eggs, herbs, and breadcrumbs.

Gloddfa Ganol, Blaenau Ffestiniog: once the world's largest slate mine, with workers' cottages and tours. Paintings from London's National Galleryl were stored here for safekeeping during World War II.

Glover, Roger (b. 1956): from Bwlch, nr. Brecon; began at local eisteddfodau; regarded as one of the world's great rock stars, the leader of the group *Deep Purple*.

Glyn, Gareth (b. 1961): from Machynlleth; a music composer with numerous awards whose works are performed world wide, Gareth is a member of the Gorsedd with an Honorary Doctorate, University. of Wales.

Glyndwr, Catrin (1380-1413): daughter of Owain, in 1402 she married Edmund Mortimer. He died at Harlech in 1409, and Catrin was imprisoned in London.

Glyn Vivian, the: Swansea's prestigious art gallery, named for the Vivian family, whose 19th C. copper smelting works brought them untold wealth and caused untold harm to the health of the people of the area.

***Gododdin, Y* (c.600 A. D):** a long poem, attributed to Strrathclyde poet Aneirin that commemorates a band of warriors who died fighting the hated Saxons at the battle of Catraeth. *Arthur* is first mentioned in this poem.

Gogerddan, Cardiganshire: home of the Welsh Plant Breeding Station, it was formerly a mansion important for its bardic patronage for many generations.

***Gogynfeirdd, Y* (The early poets):** professional poets (early 12th C to late 14th C.) who wrote in a style distinct from that of the Poets of the Princes.

Goleuad, Y (the Torch, f. 1869): newspaper of the Calvinistic Methodists.

Goodman, Gabriel (1528-1601): b. Ruthin, where he established Christ's Hospital and a grammar school; he became Dean of Westminster, helped translate the Bishop's Bible of 1568 and William Morgan's Bible.

Goodwin, Geraint (1903-41): short-story writer and novelist who wrote *The Heyday in the Blood* (1936).

***Gorchestion Beirdd Cymru* (The Triumphs of the Welsh Poets, 1773):** compilation by Rice Jones; a standard anthology of Welsh poetry for a century.

***Gorsedd Beirdd Ynys Prydain* (f. 1792, The Assembly of Bards of the Isle of Britain:** begun in London by Iolo Morganwg. It presides over the National Eisteddfod. Members may not all be poets, but all have contributed greatly to Welsh life and culture. Members can belong to one of three orders: The Ovate Order (Green Robe) obtained by examination or by recommendaton of the Gorsedd Board; the Order of Bards, Musicians and Literati (Blue Robe) the second step, obtained by passing the final Examination; and the Druidic Order (White Robe): restricted to those having made a substantial contribution of recognised national standard to Literature, Music, Scholarship or Art in Wales (or overseas).

Gorffenaf: seventh month of the year, July in English.

Gough, Mathew (Mathau Goch, 1386-1430): from Hanmer, Dee Valley, a solder with a distinguished service in France, where he was known as Mathago; ambassador of Henry Vl, captain of the Tower of London, he was killed defending it in Jack Cade's rebellion.

Gould, Arthur (1864-1919): Welsh athlete, excelling in sprints, hurdles, and the high jump, and captain of the Welsh rugby side 18 times, including the 1893 season when they first beat England in England.

Gower (Gwyr), West Glamorgan: a peninsula west of Swansea with numerous bays, cliffs and beaches designated at the first Area of Outstanding Beauty in Britain. Paleolithic Age remains have been discovered here, including the "Red Lady of Paviland" (see separate entry) and many prehistoric burial chambers. Worm's Head was named by Viking explorers.

Graber, George Alexander: (see Cordell, Alexander).

Granger, Clive W.J. (b. 1934): b. Swansea, Nobel Prize winnng economist and statistician; Professor, of Economics, University of San Diego. With a host of major publications in economics and statistics, he introduced and helped develop concepts such as causality testing and the combination of forecasts.

Great Revival, the: led by Evan Roberts in Cardiganshire in 1904, it shaped Welsh character for much of the 20th century, hastening the decline of the established church (and much traditional folk music) to create the severe Welsh Sabbath (now almost extinct).

Great Sessions of Wales, 1543: a Tudor method of providing a cheap and efficient form of justice for Wales that somehow lasted until 1830.

Great Strike, The (Nov 1900-Nov 1903): a stoppage of work at the Penrhyn quarries in North Wales, which became the longest strike in British history, pitting the quarrymen against Lord Penrhyn in an attempt to preserve the "bargain" system and the right to form an effective union. The workers' defeat caused bitterness in the area for 50 years.

Greville, Charles Francis (1749-1809): nephew of Sir William Hamilton, he created the port of Milford Haven by attracting New England whalers, and by obtaining a ship building contract from the navy (he also passed on his mistress Emma to his uncle).

***Green Horse* (1978):** an anthology of verse by young Anglo-Welsh and English poets, some later famous.

Gregynog Press, the (f. 1923): near Newtown, Mid-Wales that has become justifiably world famous for the superb quality of its publications. In 1974, it became Gwasg Gregynog, publishing the best of Welsh authors.

Gresford, near Wrexham, Denbighshire: In 1934 an explosion took the lives of 266 miners. Over 160 widows were left to provide for over 200 children. Seventeen hundred men were unemployed as a result of the disaster.

Grey-Thompson, Tanni (b 1969): top wheelchair athlete; Welsh female athlete of the past 25 years; won five London marathons; and at Sydney in 2000 repeated the winning of four gold medals won at Barcelona in 1992. Tanni, who has the O.B.E, won another two Golds at Athens in 2004. Her autobiography is *Seize the Day.*

Griffith, Hugh (1913-1980): Anglesey character actor who played many lovable scoundrels, famous for his part as Squire Western in the movie *Tom Jones*, he won an Oscar for his role in *Ben Hur.* He appeared in many Hollywood movies.

Griffith, J. Griffith (1850-1919): from Glamorganshire, left Wales to become a prominent and controversial character in Los Angeles, where he worked as a journalist before joining a mining syndicate and becoming a millionaire. His donation of over 3000 acres to the city became the largest city park in the

Unites States; he financed the building of the Griffith Observatory on Grffith Peak, named for him.

Griffith, John (*Y Gohebydd*, "the Correspondent," 1821-77): journalist who helped establish the Cymmrodorion; he was a keen supporter of the Eisteddfod and advocate of higher education.

Griffith, Kenncth (b. 1921): actor, Welsh nationalist who began his long film career in 1941; seen in *Four Weddings and a Funeral* and *The Englishman who Went up a hill and Came down a Mountain* and many others.

Griffith, Llewelyn Wyn (1890-1977): novelist, poet and translator; a popular broadcaster in Welsh and English; a major contributor to Welsh culture.

Griffith, Samuel Walker (1845-1920): b. Merthyr, he became Prime Minister and Chief Justice of Queensland, with enormous influence on the legal profession and administration of law. He helped draft Australia's Commonwealth Constitution in 1900.

Griffiths, Ann (1776-1805): b. Dolwar Fach, whose intense hymns, recited to her maid on the long walks to chapel each week are some of the most rhythmic and melodious in the Welsh language. Ann's poems and hymns reflect her profound spiritual experiences and her poetic mastery, including "Wele'n sefyll rhwng y myrtwydd" sung to the tune *Cwm Rhondda*.

Griffiths, Elwyn (b. 1940): b. Denbigh, scientist working on the quality and safety of biologicals at the World Health Organization, Geneva, involved with the Pan American Health Organization's study of the threat of bio-terrorism.

Griffiths, Ernest Howard (1851-1932): from Brecon, Fellow of the Royal Society who brought much needed discipline to experimental data, thus furthering the progress of science by linking theoretical and experimental studies.

Griffiths, James (1890-1975): b. Ammanford, popular miners' leader, he was elected president of the South Wales Miners' Federation in 1934; Labour M.P. for Llanelli (1936-1970), Minister for National Insurance under Attlee in 1945; Secretary of State for the Colonies in 1950, and the first Secretary of State for Wales in 1964. "Jim" was a much loved and respected Labour leader who helped Aneurin Bevan with the National Health Plan; he was a strong supporter of Welsh autonomy and the survival of its language and culture.

Griffiths, Jemma (b. 1976)): from Cardiff, now making a name for herself as a soul singer in the US as Jem, with a host of tv appearances.

Griffiths, J. Gwyn (1911-2004): Rhondda-born poet and scholar; helped found Cylch Cadwgan; translator of Aristotle's essay on poetry, publisher of many scholarly works, political pamphlets; edited Plaid's newspaper *Y Ddraig Goch*. A classicist and Egyptologist, he taught at Cairo and Oxford Universities; Professor Emeritus of Classics and Egyptology at the University of Wales, Swansea; his works include *Triads and Trinity* (1996).

Griffiths, Lydia (b. 1981): Wrexham star of West End musicals and British television who has soloed alongdide some famous names in show business.

Griffiths, Ralph (b. 1937): author of a number of important works on medieval Welsh history.

Griffiths, Tawe (b. 1900): from Cwmbwrla, a Baptist minister who led the informal hymn singing for many years at National Eisteddfodau and at Hyde Park Corner, London.

Griffiths, Terry (b. 1949): world-class snooker player from Llanelli, who won the Embassy World Championship in 1979 at his first attempt.

Griffiths, T. Elwyn: Honorary President and founder of *Cymru a'r Byd* that began in Cairo with *Seren y Dwyrain* (Star of the East) at the end of World War Two distributed to Welsh soldiers serving in the Middle East.

Griffiths, Thomas D. (1837-1914): Cardiganshire born, distinguished surgeon and President of the British Medical Association, practiced in Swansea where. he was recognized as the foremost consulting medical practitioner in South Wales. He founded the Swansea Nursing Institute and brought much needed reforms to the Swansea Hospital.

Grimes, William Francis (1905-1988): Director of the Institute of Archeology and professor, University of London, author of many scholarly books and articles, including *The Prehistory of Wales*.

Grove, Sir William Robert (1811-1896): Swansea-born, Justice of Britain's High Court. Professor of Physics at the London Institution, he enunciated the conservation of energy a year before von Helmholt and developed the two-fluid electric cell.

Gruffudd ap Cynan (1055-1137): b. Dublin; eventually established himself as King of Gwynedd, resisting rival Welsh and Normans to create a climate where arts could flourish and independence fostered.

Gruffudd ap Llywelyn (1007-1063): King of Gwynedd and Powys who became the only Welsh leader to unite Wales into a single kingdom. He recovered much of northeast Wales from English rule, defended the boundaries of Wales for a quarter of a century, and created a sense of national unity that endured for centuries despite later assimilation into England.

Gruffudd ap Maredudd ap Dafydd (1352-1382): one of the great poets after the death of Llywelyn ap Gruffudd in 1282. (His poem to Gwenhwyfar is considered his masterpiece).

Gruffuddd, Elis (1490-1552): b. Llanasa, Flints; chronicler and translator; a soldier in Calais, he copied many manuscripts of Welsh prose and poetry.

Gruffudd Hiraethog (d. 1564): a poet who worked closely with William Salesbury in their efforts to preserve Welsh as a medium for salvation.

Gruffudd, Ioan (b. 1974): b. Cardiff; increasingly popular actor who debuted at age of 14 on the popular, long-running Welsh language soap opera *Pobol y Cwm*, and went on to star in BBC television series as Poldark, later as Captain Horatio Hornblower, and in *Great Expectations*. His many Hollywood films include *Titanic, 102 Dalmations, Very Annie Mary, King Arthur, and Fantastic Four.*

Gruffydd, Robert Geraint (b. 1928): from Tal y Bont, Merioneth; Professor of Welsh at Aberystwyth; Librarian at the National Library of Welsh, 1980; Director of the Institute of Advanced Welsh and Celtic Studies in 1985.

Gruffydd, William John (1881-1954): poet and scholar, appointed Professor of Celtic at Cardiff University in 1918; for 30 years edited *Y Llenor* (the Literateur). In response to the Archbishop of Wales' statement "There is no room in the world for small and snarling nations," Gruffydd replied, "There is no room in Wales for small and snarling prelates."

Gruffydd, William John (Elerydd, 1916-): Cardiganshire poet, novelist and short story writer, Crown winner in 1955 and 1960, Archdruid in 1983.

Guest family: in 1763, John began the iron works that under his son Thomas was to become the largest in the world in mid-19th Century. Sir Josiah John Guest was M.P. for Merthyr.

Guest, Lady Charlotte (1812-95): wife of Josiah Guest, Merthyr ironmaster; she is best known as the translator (with John Jones) of the eleven medieval Welsh tales known as the *Mabinogion* into English, published 1846-1877.

Guest, Dr. George (*Sior Hirael*, 1924-2002): Bangor-born, educated at King's School, Chester; choirmaster at St. John's College, Cambridge; director of the National Welsh Youth Choir. In 1986, appointed director of Cardiff's Llandaf Festival. He was an esteemed member of the Cymmrodorion and the Gorsedd.

Guinevere **(Gwenhwyfar, 6th Century):** wife of King Arthur; first mentioned in the *Mabinogion*.

Guto'r Glyn (1440-93): from Glyn Ceiriog, one of the first "poets of the gentry" to show feelings of Welsh nationhood inspired by the revolt of Glyndwr.

Guto Nyth Bran (Griffith Morgan, 1700-1737): b. Llwyncelyn; legendary runner "able to catch birds in flight, outrun race horses, and run seven miles from home and back before the kettle boiled." He is remembered by Nos Galan Races (New Year's Eve Races) begun in 1958.

Gwalchmai fab Gwyr: Gawain or Gauvain, one of Arthur's knights, the essence of courtesy and bravery.

Gwalia: a name for Wales used in the later Middle Ages (from *Wallia*).

Gwasanaeth Mair (Mary's Service. **15th C):** the only Middle Welsh translation of an ecclesiastical service.

Gwenhwyfar: (see Guinevere).

Gwenffrewi: (see Winefride).

Gwenllian (12th century): daughter of Gruffudd ap Cynan and sister of Owain Gwynedd, she led an army against the Normans at Cydweli Castle in 1136, but was killed at Maes Gwenllian. Her death was avenged by her two sons at the Battle of Crug Mawr that freed Ceredigion of Norman influence.

Gwenllian (Princess of Wales, 1282-1337): b. Abergwyngregrin, near Bangor; only daughter of Eleanor and Llywelyn ap Gruffydd; heir to Llywelyn, the last native ruler of Wales. After her father's death, she was taken to Sempringham Priory, England, to be imprisoned for life.

Gwenn, Edmund (1875-1959): Glamorgan-born actor who went to Hollywood in 1940 to play roles such as benevolent shepherds and scientists or the occasional scoundrel; his Kris Kringle in *Miracle on 34th Street* won him Best Supporting Actor Award in 1947.

Gwent (Monmouthshire): a county made directly answerable to the courts of Westminster by the Second Act of Union, 1543 thus creating the impression that it had been annexed to England.

Gwerin: the country folk of Wales, upholders of the language and culture.

Gwerin (f. 1933): a group begun at Bangor University by Goronwy Roberts and others to join the principles of Socialism and Welsh Nationalism.

Gwir yn Erbyn y Byd, Y **(The Truth against the World):** the motto of the Gorsedd Beirdd Ynys Prydain (The Gorsedd of Bards of the Isle of Britain).

Gwlad y Gân ("the land of song"): 19th C. term for Wales which was becoming known for male voice choirs and its Cymanfaoedd Ganu (hymn singing).

Gwladgarwr, Y (the Patriot): two periodicals; a monthly published in Chester (1833-1841) with articles on all kinds of general topics; the other a weekly literary journal published in Aberdare (1858-1884).

Gwydyr Chapel, Llanrwst: (1633), perhaps designed by Inigo Jones, it houses the sarcophagus of Llywelyn the Great brought from Maenan Abbey.

Gwyddoniadur Cymreig, Y (the Welsh Encyclopedia): published in 10 volumes by Thomas Gee (1854-1879) that contains material on scientific, literary, Welsh and Celtic subjects including biographies.

Gwyl y Pasg: the festival of Easter.

Gwyliedydd, Y **(the Observer, 1877-1909):** Wesleyan newspaper that opposed the views of *Baner ac Amserau Cymru* to carry local and national news.

Gwylliaid Cochion Mawddwy (the red bandits of Mawddwy, 16th C.): a notorious band of thieves in Merioneth distinguished by their red hair, first mentioned by Thomas Pennant in *Tours of Wales* (1778). Somne of their descendants may still lve in the area.

Gwyn, Richard (Richard White, 1577-84): the first Catholic martyr in Wales (for refusing to accept Elizabeth as head of the Church of England). He was canonized in 1970.

Gwyn, Robert (1540-1592): Catholic priest, prolific Welsh writer; his *Y Drych Cristionogawl* (The Christian Mirror) was printed in a cave at Llandudno, 1586-7.

Gwynedd: the name of the northwestern kingdom that was the stronghold of the native-born Princes of Wales.

Gwyneddigion Society (f. London 1770): created to revive the Eisteddfod and seek recognition for Welsh culture; published manuscripts and periodicals, and helped send John Evans to search for the so-called Welsh Indians.

Gymdeithas Genedlaethol Gymreig, Y (f. 1922, National Welsh Society): a forerunner of Plaid Cymru: the Party of Wales.

Ng

The eleventh letter of the Welsh alphabet (pronounced as the *ng* in the English word *finger*). It appears at the beginning of many words as a mutation of the letter G

H

The twelfth letter of the Welsh alphabet (always heavily aspirated, never silent).

Hafod: a summer highland farm where the flocks and herds are sent to winter in the lower pastures.

Hailsingod (Hailsing, 17th C.): carols featured in S. West Wales; preserved in manuscript.

Hain, Peter (b. 1950): b. Neath. Labour M.P. who played a critical part in the winning of the referendum for the Welsh Assembly. He was appointed Secretary of State for Wales in 2002.

Haines Davies, Arfon: b. Caernarfon, he joined HTV in 1978 as an announcer to become one of its star presenters and a popular figure on Welsh television, presenting many programs inlcuding *Wales at Six* and children's events.

Haldane Commission, the (1916-18): set up to examine University education in Wales, it recommended that the University of Wales confer degrees and exercise general direction and control and was quickly followed by the founding of University College, Swansea and the Welsh National School of Medicine, Cardiff.

Hall, Augusta Waddington: (see Lady Llanover).

Hall, Benjamin (1802-1867): M.P. Monmouth Boroughs; a strong advocate of the use of Welsh in religious services. When Parliament refused to sanction its use in the Church of England in Wales, he built his own church, later donating it to the Methodists. He introduced the 1831 Truck Act to end the truck system, a major cause of discontent in Wales. "Big Ben," the bell of the famous clock at Westminster is named after him. He was married to Lady Llanover.

Hamer, Edward (1830-1901): from Llanidloes, historian of Powys and Montgomeryshire who wrote of the Chartist Outbreak at Llanidloes.

Hanbury, John (1664-1734): from Pontypool, a pioneer in the tinplate industry who produced rolled iron sheets known as "blackplate."

***Hanes Rhyw Gymro* (The Tale of a Certain Welshman, 1964):** a play by John G. Jones considered a milestone in the development of modern Welsh drama.

Hanmer: a village in Wrexham Maelor former part of flintshire), where Owain Glyndwr married Margaret, daughter of Sir David Hanmer.

Hannan, Patrick: (b. 1941): Aberdare writer and broadcaster for more than thirty years, industrial editor of *The Western Mail,* he spent thirteen years as BBC Wales' political correspondent, followed by six years producing television documentaries for BBC Two and BBC Wales and six years as presenter of *Good Evening Wales.* A newspaper columnist and a regular broadcaster on Radio Four for more than two decades, he is the editor of two books on broadcasting and the author of three books on contemporary Wales.

Hardie, James Keir (1856-1915): elected from Merthyr Tydfil in 1900, Scotsman Hardy was the very first Labour M.P. in Britain; he wore his cloth deer-stalker's hat in the House of Commons to signify his working class origin.

Harding, Lyn (David Llewellyn (1867-1952); b. St. Bride's, Newport; actor of stage, screen and radio. He performed Glendower with the BBC at age 80.

Harlech, Lord (William) David Ormsby-Gore, 5th Baron Harlech (1918-1985): from Brogyntyn, Shropshire: British Minister and politician educated at Eton College and Oxford During World War II, he served in the 'Phantom' reconnaissance unit, airborne, and other special units. Conservative MP for Oswestry 1950-61 Under Macmillan he was Minister of State for Foreign Affairs in 1957 but after the election of U.S. President John F. Kennedy in November 1960, as British Ambassador to the United States. He retired from the post in 1965, a year after his father died and took up his seat in the House of Lords as Lord Harlech, briefly also holding the position of Conservative party deputy chairman. He also had a successful career as a television executive, founding HTV, and served as president of the British Board of Film Classification. He died in North Wales in a car accident.

Harlech, Merioneth: After a three-year siege, its mighty castle fell to Owain Glyndwr; was retaken by the English and held out for eight years in the Civil Wars as a Lancastrian stronghold.

Harlech Television (HTV): began as Television Wales and the West in 1964, became Harlech TV in 1968. The bulk of its Welsh language programs were taken over by S4C in 1982; its presenters included Arfon Haines Davies.

Harp (Y Delyn): regarded as the national instrument of Wales, especially the triple harp with its three rows of strings that may have been introduced from Italy in the early 18th Century. Once played by professional musicians in the homes of the gentry, the native harp was forced to go underground during the excesses of the Methodists but was restored to popularity during the late Victorian period and has undergone something of a recent revival; many expert harpists are in much demand with orchestras and folk groups. Some Welsh harpists play gypsy style, with the harp resting on the left shoulder.

Harris, John (d. 1839): magician, from Cwrtycadno, Carmarthen, visited by those seeking a spell, a cure for sickness or a forecast of the future.

Harris, Joseph (Gomer, 1773-1825): from Llantydewi, Pembs; he published sermons in Welsh and English; also began and edited the first weekly newspaper in Welsh, *Seren Gomer,* in 1814 that became the official journal of the Welsh Baptists Union in 1880.

Harris, Hywel (1714-73): called the "father of the Methodist Revival in Wales," whose preaching activities led to thousands of converts.

Harry, Lyn: (b. 1930?): from Llanelli, educated at the Royal College of Music; Conductor Emeritus of the Canadian Orpheus Male Choir, which he founded in 1977. A former founder and conductor of the London Welsh Male Choir, then Music Director of the Morriston Orpheus, Swansea, before moving to Canada to teach at the Royal Hamilton College of Music.

Hartmann, Dr. Edward G. (1912-1995): Wilkes-Barre, Pa., son of Welsh-born mother, he taught at Suffolk University, New York. A pioneer in American ethnic history, his *Cymry yn y Cwm: The Welsh of Wilkes- Barre and the Wyoming Valley (1958)* and *Americans from Wales* (1979, rpt 2001), it is considered the definitive work on Welsh immigration to the U.S.

Hartson, John (b. 1975): b. Swansea, Welsh-international footballer with Glasgow Celtic (Britain's top scorer in 1987-8 season).

Heart of Wales Line (Central Wales Line): completed in 1868 from Shrewsbury to Swansea. In the 1960's, it survived when Secretary of State for Wales George Thomas reminded the Labour Government that it ran through six marginal constituencies. The line passes over 18-arch Cynghordy Viaduct down along the Tywi Valley to Swansea. If you have time to spare, this is the way to travel.

Hedd Wyn: (see Ellis, Humphrey Evans).

Heddiw **(Today):** a literary magazine (1936 and 1942) that also contained left-wing political editorials.

Heilyn, Rowland (1562-1631): London merchant of Welsh descent who used his wealth to publish Welsh books, including *Y Beibl Bach* of 1660.

Helena, St. (3-4th Century): the daughter of King Coel of Caer Collen (Colchester) and Stradwan (the daughter of Cadwan, King of North Wales). She married Constantius, Roman commander in Britain, later Emperor of the Western Empire. Their son Constantine became Emperor of Rome. Helena founded many Christian churches on the Continent and was responsible for choosing and thus commemorating Christian sites in the Holy Land.

Hemans, Felicia (1793-1835): poet raised at Gwrych Castle, Abergele. *Welsh Melodies of 1821* included her *Casablanca*, a favorite recitation piece ("The boy stood on the burning deck").

Hen Amddyffynfa, Y (the Old Fort): a collection of sun-dried mud huts built by Welsh pioneers at the mouth of the Camwy River in Patagonia in 1865.

Hen Benillion (Old Stanzas): traditional verses preserved orally and sung to the harp.

Hen Bersoniaid Llengar, Yr (Old Literary Clerics, 1818-58) a group of Anglican clergymen who fostered Welsh culture and acted as the guardians of the literary traditions of Wales before the arrival of the University, transforming the eisteddfod into an honoured and respected national festival.

Hendre: the traditional winter dwelling when the flocks are kept after they are brought down from the mountains.

Henry, Rhiannon (b. 1987): disabled Bridgend swimmer with 4 Gold medals at IBSA World Games (Quebec) and Welsh Young Athlete of the Year (2003).

Hen Wlad fy Nhadau **(Old Land of My Fathers)**: by Evan James and his son James, at Pontypridd in 1856. First sung in public at Tabor chapel, Maesteg in 1856, it

175

appeared in print two years later; the official national anthem of Wales.

***Herald Cymraeg, Yr* (The Welsh Herald, f. 1835):** weekly newspaper begun by John Rees in Caernarfon.

Herbert, Edward (1583-1648): the eldest Herbert brother; philosopher, writer; ambassador to France under James 1st. Known as "the father of deism." He became Lord Herbert of Cherbury for his services.

Herbert, George (1593-1633): b. Montgomery Castle, he was one of the Metaphysical School of poets led by John Donne. His poems, including the collection *The Temple*, were published after his death.

Herbert, William of Raglan: went to Parliament in 1461 as Baron Herbert, the first Welshman to become part of the English aristocracy, beginning a tradition that was to drain Wales of its many of its important potential leaders.

Herbert, Winifred (Lady Nithsdale 1665-1749): when her Jacobite husband was imprisoned at the Tower of London, Winifred, daughter of the Marquis of Powys, helped him escape disguised as her maid.

Hergest, 15th and 16th C.): Herefordshire home of a branch of the Vaughans that gave hospitality to many foremost Welsh poets of the period.

Heritage Lottery Fund Committee for Wales: appointed by the Secretary of State for Culture to give grants to protect Welsh heritage and the quality of life.

Heseltine, Michael Ray D. (b. 1932): b. Swansea; former M.P. for Tavistock,. Defense Secretary in 1983, he was Secretary of State for the government under John Major; with the Board of Trade under Thatcher, he presided over the closure of 31 mines. He resigned from the Cabinet in 1983 over the sale of Westland helicopters that caused an outrage in Parliament. His publishing business has made him one of Britain's richest millionaires.

Hewlett, Sylvia Ann (b. 1946): b. Bridgend, Glam; scholar at the School of International and Public Affairs at Columbia; taught at Barnard College, Columbia University and for six years was the Executive Director of the Economic Policy Council, New York. Sylvia founded the National Parenting Association in 1993 to develop family friendly policies in the workplace and the wider community. Her many books include *When the Bough Breaks*.

Hiraeth: a word expressing longing for home, one's childhood or one's native country; a motif for so much of Welsh literature that looks back to a former, more glorious (and thus imaginary) age.

Hirlas Horn, The: horn of plenty given to the Archdruid each year during the Gorsedd Ceremonies at the "National" by a young woman of the district.

***Historia Brittonum* (c.1100):** found in a number of manuscripts, of great importance for early Welsh literature with the history of early Britain, Roman Britain, the settlement of Armorica, the story of Vortigern, a reference to Arthur and so on.

***Historiae Britannicae Defensio* (The Defense of British History, 1573)**: a study of Welsh antiquity and history by John Price of Brecon to defend Geoffrey of Monmouth's history against the defamatory attacks of Polydore Vergil.

***Historia Regum Britanniae* (1136):** by Geoffrey of Monmouth; claims to be the history of the kings of Britain from Aeneas who founded Rome; through his grandson Brutus, down to Cadwaladr Fendigaid, who lost Britain to the Saxons.

Hoddinott, Alun (b. 1929): from Bargoed, Mid-Glamorgan; a distinguished composer. Former head of the music department at Cardiff University; founder of the Cardiff Music Festival and the National Youth Orchestra of Wales; he has won many awards for his musical compositions; became Doctor of Music in 1960; and awarded O.B.E. in 1991.

Hodge, Sir Julian (1905-2004): one of Britain's richest men, Sir Julian began as a railway clerk, began Hodge Bank in Cardiff, later helping to make the city an important financial centre. An important benefactor of Cardiff University, he established the Chair in Banking and Finance. Adamantly opposed to the creation of an Assembly for Wales, he spearheaded the "No" campaign.

Hollantide: festival held on the first day of November to celebrate the start of winter (see Samhain).

Holt Sweets: famous Swansea-made boiled sweets (candies) now available at Harrod's, London.

Holyhead (*Caergybi*, Anglesey): Celtic Christian settlement and Roman fortress, now a commercial and industrial town and port for ferries to Ireland.

Holywell (T*reffynnon*), Flintshire: (the Lourdes of Wales): site of St Winifride's Well, the finest surviving medieval well in Britain, a place of pilgrimage for many centuries attracting Richard lst, Henry V, James II and many others.

Homfray: a family of iron masters including Francis (1726-98), whose Penydarren factory bored cannon, Jeremiah (1759-1833), who began the iron works at Ebbw Vale, and Samuel, who helped finance the Glamorgan Canal in 1795 to carry iron to Cardiff.

Honorable Society of Cymmrodorion: begun in London by Richard Morris in the 1770's to give Wales a society equal to the English Royal Society.

Hooson, Isaac Daniel (1880-948): Rhosllanerchrugog, near Wrexham, whose works, found in *Cerddi a Baledi* (Songs and Ballads, 1936) are very popular with young folk as eisteddfod recitations.

Hopkin, Mary (1950): the Pontardawe girl with the lovely voice. Her *Those Were the Days* outsold all others in 1968, surpassing even *Hey Jude*.

Hopkins, Sir Anthony (b. 1937): b. Port Talbot, studied at the Welsh College of Music and Drama and RADA. He acted at the Old Vic under Laurence Olivier; in a long stage and film career won an Oscar for *Silence of the Lambs*. His films include *Howard's End, Armistad, The Elephant Man, The End of the Day, Nixon,* and *Meet Joe Black* and the *Hannibal Lecter* series. In 1996, he started directing stage plays with *August*, an adaption of Chekov's *Uncle Vanya*. Awarded the O.B.E. by the Queen in 1987, he became a U.S. citizen in 2000. Donated a million pounds to help preserve the footpaths of Snowdonia.

Hopkins, Gerard Manley (1844-89): English poet; after his theology studies at St. Asaph (*Llanelwy*) in Clwyd, his work was greatly influenced by his learning of the Welsh language and the form of cynghanedd. A major influence on Dylan Thomas, he also attributed the Welsh landscape to his maturing as a poet.

Horner, Arthur Lewis (1894-1968): b. Merthyr Tydfil; miners' leader and British Communist, whose tireless work with the S. Wales Miners' Federation and the National Union of Mineworkers endeared him to trade unionists and miners.

Houston, Donald (1923-1991): b. Rhondda, actor debuted with Jean Simmons in *Blue Lagoon* in 1949, starting a long career in film, television and theatre.

Howard, Michael (b. 1941): b. Llanelli, who led the Tory Party in 2003, following Ian Duncan Smith. Was President of the Cambridge Union in 1962; debuted as M.P. for Folkstone and Hythe in 1983; Home Secretary 1993-1997.

Howard-Jones, Ray (1903-1996): artist and writer from Penarth who was a star student at the Slade and one of the few female artists during World War ll, remembered chiefly for her landscapes of Pembrokeshire.

Howe, Geoffrey (Lord Howe, b. 1926): Aberavon-born, politician, the longest survivor of Maggie Thatcher's original 1979 cabinet; Tory M.P. for Bebbington, Cheshire in 1964; Solicitor General in 1970, then head of the Dept of Trade and Chancellor of the Exchequer and later Foreign Secretary. As Deputy

Prime Minister, he fought for Britain's entry into the European Union.

Howell, Gwynne (b. 1938): from Gorseinon, Swansea, one of the world's leading basses, with a long career at the Royal Opera; debuted at Covent Garden Opera, 1970; and starred at New York Metropolitan, 1985.

Howell, James (1593-1666): b. Abernant, Carms; Secretary to the Council for the North in 1626 and a year later M.P. for Bichmond, Yorkshire. He was appointed Historiographer Royal in 1661 with forty books to his name. His *Parly of Beasts* (1660) was a literary defence of Wales.

Howell, Dr. Kim (b. 1946): from Merthyr; art critic and culture minister; lectured and researched coalfield issues before being elected as Labour M.P. for Pontypridd in 1989. Has been Consumer and Corporate Affairs Minister, and Minister for Tourism, Film and Broadcasting, from which position he has let fly at all and sundry in the art world and the music and film industry.

Howells, Geraint (1925-2004): sheep farmer from Aberystwyth, Welsh Liberal Democrat leader, MP for Ceredigion and N. Pembroke, began as an Independent in 1952 with Cardiganshire County Council. He is a member of the Gorsedd of Bards.

Howley, Robert (b. 1970): from Bridgend, rugby scrum half and captain of Wales; debuted vs. Scotland in 1993.

Hudson-Williams, Thomas (1873-1961): b. Caernarfon, scholar and translator, lectured in Greek, Latin, French and Celtic at Bangor, published many translations from Russian into Welsh.

Hugh of Rhuddlan (Hue De Rotelande, 1180-90): author of romances in the Norman-French dialect, he is considered a pioneer in the literary genre.

Hughes, Annie Harriet (Gwyneth Vaughan, 1852-1910)): from Penrhyndeudraeth, Welsh writer of note, a fervent nationalist and supporter of Cymru Fydd.

Hughes, Beti (1926-81): from St. Clears, Carms. A teacher of Welsh: deputy head at Ysgol Bro Myrddin, Carmarthen: a prolific writer of popular novels.

Hughes, Brian: from Ponciau, well-known contemporary composer, conductor, accompanist and vocal consultant. Many years was Chorus Master and head of Opera music Staff at the Royal northern College of Music; accompanist to Joan Hammond, Joan Sutherland, and Sherill MIlnes. With son Daniel and daughter Miriam forms the musical group *A Family Affair*.

Hughes, Charles Evans (1862-1948): eminent Welsh-American (his father came from Tredegar), Governor of New York, influential Chief Justice of the Supreme Court, he narrowly lost the 1916 presidential election.

Hughes, Cledwyn (1920-78): Powys novelist and topographical writer; works include *The Civil Strangers* (1949) and *Portrait of Snowdonia* (1967*).*

Hughes, Cledwyn (Lord Cledwyn, 1916-2001): born in Holyhead, trained as a solicitor, served in the Royal Air Force. Elected Labour M.P. for Anglesey in 1951; Welsh Secretary in 1966, served as minister for Commonwealth relations, Agriculture Minister, and Chairman of the Parliamentary Labour Party (1974-79). He became a life peer in 1979, bravely supporting devolution amid much hostility, even from his own party.

Hughes, David Edward (1831-1900): from Corwen, Merionethshire; he went to the U.S. at age five; he was the first to transmit and receive radio waves (eight years before Heinrich Hertz). Professor of music at St. Joseph's College, Bardstown, Kentucky, he also patented a type printing telegraph and invented a forerunner of the carbon microphone.

Hughes, Edwin (Balaclava Ned, 1830-1927): Wrexham-born, the last survivor of the Charge of the Light Brigade. Injured in the attack and his horse killed, Edwin had a boot trapped under his horse and pulled one off a Russian corpse to get back to his lines.

Hughes, Ezekial (1766-1849) from Llanbrynmair, Montgomery who along with William Bebb, led a party of Welsh men and women to settle at Ft. Washington at the junction of the Big Miami and the Ohio in 1796 (now called Cincinnati).

Hughes, Gareth ("the Desert Padre" 1894-1965): from Llanelli, appeared in many Hollywood films in the early years, retiring from films to minister to the Paiute Indians in Nevada as *Brother David.*

Hughes, Hugh (1790-1863): b. Llandudno, artist and publisher whose famous map *Dame Venedotia, alias Modryb Gwen* (Auntie Gwen) of 1845 shows Wales as an old lady carrying a large bundle on her back. His *The Beauties of Cambria* (1823) helped establish North Wales as a tourist venue.

Hughes, John (1775-1854): Llanfihangel-yng-Ngwynfa, Mont.; Calvinist-Methodist minister, husband of maid Ruth Evans, who memorized the poetry and hymns of Ann Griffiths. He preserved Ann's hymns and letters and wrote biographies of fellow Methodists.

Hughes, John (1850-1932): b. Swansea; religious leader and writer; Moderator of the Methodist General Assembly, he wrote a number of theological works.

Hughes, John Ceiriog (Ceiriog, 1832-1887): from the Ceiriog valley in Clwyd, Hughes wrote of rural scenes and characters in poetry full of hiraeth (*longing*). A favorite of schoolchildren, he is much recited at youth eisteddfodau. He provided lyrics for the traditional folk tune *The Ash Grove*.

Hughes, John G.M. (Moelwyn, 1866-1944): from Tantygrisiau, Mer. prolific poet and hymn writer.

Hughes, Mark (b. 1963): (*the Ledge)* from Wrexham, international footballer with Manchester United with five cup winner's medals; awarded M.B.E. in 1998; became manager of Wales in 2001, leading his team to remarkable triumphs.

Hughes, Nathan (b. 1924): from Penygroes, Carms; former chief engineer at TWW and General Manager of Teledu Cymru in Cardiff, founder of the Dallas Welsh American Society, former board member of NWAF and member of the Gorsedd.

Hughes, Nerys (b. 1941): from Rhyl, Denbighshire; nationally known as a television actresss, appeared in countless TV dramas and comedies, including the all-'Welsh language "How Green Was My Valley." Nerys has worked with the Royal Shakespeare Company, as well as pantomime; she is a tireless worker for better health services in rural communities.

Hughes, Owain Arwel (b.1942): conductor of the world's finest orchestras and composers, including his 25 years with the Halle Orchestra. The driving force behind the Welsh Proms, he has conducted the Helsinki Philharmonic and the Prague Symphony, and has been a major music broadcaster with the BBC.

Hughes, Richard (1794-1871): publisher of religious works, the poetry of John Ceiriog Hughes, Sankey and Moody hymns, the novels of Daniel Owen; and the periodical *Y Llenor* (1922-1952).

Hughes, Richard Cyril (b. 1932): Anglesey-born writer of the life and times of Catrin of Berain.

Hughes, Richard Samuel (1855-88): Aberystwyth-born songwriter, famous for his accompaniment at National Eisteddfod; his songs include "Arafa Don" and "Suo Gan" (lullaby featured in the film *Empire of the Sun.*

Hughes, Roy (Lord Islwyn, 1922-2004): M.P. for Newport, for 31 years before going to the House of Lords. He fought hard for miners' rights.

Hughes, Stephen (1622-88): religious leader, "The Apostle of Carmarthenshire," who translated many works into Welsh, including the *New Testament* (1672), the *Bible* (1678), and *Pilgrim's Progress* (1688).

Hughes, Thomas Rowland (1903-49): b. Llanberis, produced feature programs for the BBC at Cardiff in the 1930's; wrote plays and poetry but is more well-known for his five novels, including *Chwalfa,* about the Penrhyn lockouts.

Hughes, William Morris ("the Little Digger," 1864-1952): Prime Minister of Australia from 1915-1923. From Llandudno, he emigrated in 1884, to become a mainstay of Australian politics for 50 years with the Labour Party and highly praised for his leadership and support of Britain during WW.I.

Hughes de Jones, Irma (1919-2003): born in Treorky, Chubut Province, Argentina, Irma won the Chair at the Patagonia Eisteddfod six times. Editor of *Y Drafod*, the Welsh language newspaper in Chubut for fifty years, Irma was initiated into the Gorsedd in 1969.

Hughes Jones, Gareth: accomplished contemporary musician, former conductor of Côr Meibion Caernarfon and producer for Sain Records.

Hughes Jones, Gwyn (b. 1969) from Llanbedrgoch, Gwynedd; an international star of opera, he won the Kathleen Ferrier Scholarship 1992, debuted with the Welsh National Opera in 1995. After switching from baritone to tenor, had starring roles at Paris, Lyon, Brussels, and Trondheim and finally a place at the New York Metropolitan Opera's *Nabucco* in 2005.

Hughesovska, (Yuzovk) Russia: named for John Hughes, Merthyr, who built iron and steel works in 1869 with Welsh workers; renamed Donetsk in 1961.

Humphries, Beverley: renowned opera star and the voice and brains behind BBC Wales' Showtime, Beverley has sung with the Welsh National Opera and at concerts worldwide. In 1992, she became the first singer in the history of Welsh rugby to lead the singing at the National Stadium, Cardiff.

Humphries, Edward Morgan (1882-1955): journalist at the *Liverpool Daily Post* and the *Manchester Guardian,* who saw the importance of producing interesting Welsh language reading material for young children.

Humphreys, Emyr (b. 1919): b. Prestatyn, Flintshire, raised in Welsh-speaking Trelawnydd. Widely read short-story writer with *A Man's Estate, Outside the House of Baal* and other works that put him in the front rank of Britain's literary men. His masterful patriotic works re-affirm the heritage of Wales.

Humphrey, Humphrey (1648-1712): from Penryndeudraeth, Mont; Bishop of Bangor (1689 and Hereford (1701), a supporter of S.P.C.K, he helped publish many books and encourage Welsh authors.

Humphries, Joshua (1751-1838): son of Daniel, of Merionethshire, and Hannah, daughter of Thomas

Wynne of Pennsylvania. He designed frigates for the American navy, including the *Constitution* ("Old Ironsides"). He helped prove the superiority of these ships against the navies of France and Britain. He can rightly be called "The Father of the U.S. Navy".

Humphries, Llewelyn Morris (Murray the Hump, 1899-1965) born to Welsh parents in Chicago; a trusted underling of Al Capone, organizing the crime syndicate's successful infiltration of legitimate businesses; said to have originated expressions "money laundering" and "being taken to the cleaners."

Humphries, Mary (b. 1865): the first Welsh child born in Patagonia.

Humphrys, John (b. 1943): from Splott, Cardiff; changed his name from Humphries, the name of a colleague at the *Western Mail*. Has spent over 40 years as a journalist; was the youngest foreign correspondent with BBC, which he joined in 1966. He is the long-serving presenter of Radio 4's *Today* program.

Hunting the Wren: a European Christmas folk-custom, practiced especially in Southwest Wales, where the wren, as king of birds, was paraded from house to house and shown in exchange for money or small gifts.

Hurn, David (b. 1934): born in England to a Welsh family and proud of his Cardiff roots, he is internationally known for his reportage photographs, including many of changing Bute Town, Cardiff.

Hwyl: spirit, or feeling of great emotion (as in a preacher or a conductor's hwyl), but it can be used to say goodbye or "go with spirit."

Hyder: a Cardiff-based company renamed from Welsh Water PLC that employs about 7,500 people in 30 countries providing water, energy, transport infrastructure and business services.

Hyddgen, battle of (1401): fought near Plynlimon; a victory for Owain Glyndwr over an English army that helped rally the people of Wales to his cause.

Hydref: tenth month of the year, called October in English. Also the Welsh name for autumn.

***Hyfforddwr, Yr* (the Instructor, 1807):** an influential book of the Welsh Methodist Revival.

Hywel ab Owain Gwynedd (d. 1170): prince and poet, who fought against his own brothers and sided with the Normans against the Lord Rhys. The earliest extant love poetry in Welsh, his praise of womanly beauty greatly influenced later poets.

Hywel ap Gruffudd (Hywel y Fwyall, d. 1381): a professional soldier who commanded a group of

Welshmen at Crecy (1346) and fought courageously at Poitiers (1356) with his battle axe.

Hywel Dda (Howell the Good: d. 950): Hwyel ap Cadell ruled a large part of Wales in the 10th century, bringing a period of peace and stability. His codification of Welsh law, *Cyfraith Hywel,* was one of the glories of Europe; some of its provisions were far ahead of anything produced in English law for a millenium, especially those dealing with the status of the victim and with the rights of women. Hywel was the only Welsh king to have coins bearing his name.

I

Thirteenth letter of the Welsh alphabet (pronounced as the Italian *pizza*, never as in the English *mite)*.

Ich Dien (I Serve): with the three feathers, the German motto of the Prince of Wales adopted from the plume of John, King of Bohemia slain at Crecy in 1346 by the Black Prince, son of Edward III.

**Iechyd da (*Good Health):* ** a toast for St. David's Day (March 1st) when leeks or daffodila are worn and quantities of good ale (*cwrw da)* are consumed after the singing of some great Welsh hymns.

Iestyn ap Gwrgant (ruled 1081-93): last independent King of Morgannwg; overthrown by the Norman invaders.

Ifans, Dafydd (b. 1949): from Aberystwyth, novelist Prose Medal winner, editor, and Keeper of Manuscripts at the National Library of Wales.

Ifans, Rhys (Rhys Evans, b. 1968): Wrexham-born actor, raised in Ruthin; former member of the rock group *Super Furry Animals*, began his acting career at Theatr Clwyd, Flintshire; the idiosyncratic star has appeared in Hollywood movies, including *The Sin Eater* and British films *Twin Town* and *Notting Hill.*

Ifor a Cadifor (Ifor Bach, 12th C.): Lord of Senghennydd who attacked Cardiff castle in 1158, capturing the Earl of Gloucester to have his lands restored.

Ifor ap Llywelyn (Ifor Hael, "The Generous" 1340-690): the friend snd chief patron of Dafydd ap Gwilym and ancestor of the Morgan family of Tredegar.

Illtyd, St. (late 5th century): founder of British Monasticism at Llanilltyd Fawr (Llantwit Major).

Institute of Welsh Affairs (f. Cardiff, 1987): independent think tank and research institute on Welsh public policy issues that publishes reports and policy papers and organizes seminars and conferences.

Interlude: see entry for Anterliwt.

Invasion of Britain, the Last (see entry under Fishguard).

Iolo Goch, (1320-1398): one of the poets of the gentry, his work includes praises of Owain Glyndwr and descriptions of the Welsh leader's fine mansion and gardens at Sycharth.

Iolo Morganwg **(1747-1826):** bardic title of Edward Williams, stonemason from Glamorgan, whose imagination began the colorful ceremonies of the Eisteddfod to create the Gorsedd, the society of bards.

Ionawr: first month of the year: January in English.

Islwyn: (see William Thomas).

Ivor the Engine: created in 1959 for B.B.C. television. Ivor was a railway engine of the Merioneth and Llantisilly Traction Company. The driver was *Jones the Steam. Dai the Station* was in charge. Ivor's great ambition was to sing in the choir like *Evan the Song.* The series ran for 30 years.

Ivorites: (see Philanthropic Order of).

Iwan Bala (b. 1956): one of Wales's most creative artists, who has won numerous awards for his work including the 1997 Gold Medal at the National Eisteddfod and the Owain Glyndwr Medal for his outstanding contributions to the arts in Wales.

Iwan, Dafydd (b. 1943): from the Amman Valley, one of Wales' most popular entertainers and song-writers whose support of the Welsh language made his name anathema to the authorities in the late 60's. Related to the Cilie family of poets, a member of the Gorsedd, he founded his own record company, Sain; he was imprisoned in 1970 (the same year he founded Cymdeithas Tai Gwynedd) for protesting English-only second homes taking over the Welsh countryside at the expense of locals. In 2004, he became president of Plaid Cymru.

Iwerddon: the Welsh name for Ireland (the Irish language is *Gwyddelig).*

J

There is no J in the Welsh alphabet (borrowings from English include *Jac, Jam, Jiwbili*; even the ubiquitous last name *Jones*).

Jac Glan y Gorse **(John Jones, 1766-1821)**: "the Welsh Thomas Paine" who helped organise the Cymmrodorion Society in 1751 in London to promote Welsh nationhood. A satirical poet and political writer and owner of the King's Head Inn at Ludgate, he coined the phrase *Dic Sion Dafydd* to describe one who forsakes his Welsh as his social status improves.

Jackson, Colin (b. 1967): from Cardiff; one of Britain's all-time great hurdlers, winning a Gold at the Stuttgart World Championships in 1953, setting a world record for the 110m hurdles in 1995, and winning two outdoor world titles.

Jackson, Kenneth Hurlstone (1909-1991): scholar at Edinburgh, Cambridge, and Harvard. His works deal with archaeology, history, languages and literatures of the Celtic world. *Celtic Miscellany* was published in 1951.

James, Carwyn Rees (1929-1983): from Cefneithin, Carms. regarded as "the prince of coaches," with Llanelli and the British Lions. A pioneer in modern rugby, he debuted with Llanelli, 1949 and was inducted into International Rugby Hall of Fame in 1999.

James, Daniel (*Gwyrosydd*, 1847-1920): poet whose words "Nid wy'n gofyn bywyd moethus" are sung by Welsh men and women all over the world to the tune of *Calon Lan.*

James, David Emrys (Dewi Emrys, 1881-1952*): b.* New Quay, Cards, Eisteddfod Crown winner and four-time Chair winner, greatly influenced other poets.

James, Evan (Ieuan ap Iago, 1809-78): author of *Hen Wlad Fy Nhadau,* (The land of my Fathers) the Welsh national anthem, with the music composed by his son James (1833-1902).

James, Dr. Haydn: from Llanfyllon with a Ph.D. in physics, has earned an outstanding reputation as a musical director, arranger and adjudicator of choral music. Director of the London Welsh Male Voice Choir, and Cor Meibion De Cymru; conducted the British Lions Choir in Australia; guest conductor at many U.S. singing festivals.

James, Sian (b. 1932): from Llandysul, author of more than six novels (in English) with Welsh settings.

James, Thomas (1593-1635): Abergavenny-born navigator whose voyage in search of the Northwest passage on the *Henrietta Maria* in 1631 may have inspired Coleridge's "The Rime of the Ancient Mariner." With Admiral Thomas Button, he mapped parts of the coast of Hudson Bay, named it New South Wales and the River Severn.

Jarman, Alfred Owen J (1911-1998): from Bangor; Professor of Welsh, University College of Wales, Cardiff, expert on Myrddin (Merlin), Geoffrey of Monmouth and Arthuriana, co-editor of *A Guide to Welsh Literature* (1976, 1979) and co-author with his wife Eldra of *Y Sipsiwn Cymreig (*The Welsh Gypsies, 1979).

Jarman, Eldra: (d. 2002): one of Wales's great triple harpists, a direct descendant of the Welsh gypsy patriarch Abram Wood whose family helped preserve much of their adopted country's folk music. Eldra was the great-granddaughter of John Roberts of Newtown, known as *Telynor Cymru* (the harpist of Wales). Married to A.O. Jarman, she was the acknowledged authority on the history of the Romany in Wales. With her husband, she authored *Children of Abram Wood.* Her life story is told in the award-winning film *Eldra* produced by S4C in 2002 shortly after her death.

Jarman, Geraint (b. 1950): poet and singer from Denbigh; a well-known Cardiff-based exponent of the reggae style in Welsh with many recordings.

Jazz Bands: 1918-1940): playing gazookas, many groups in fancy dress marched in the South Wales Valleys between the Wars.

Jarrett, Keith: during the 1967-8 season, in his first international rugby match, Jarrett scored 19 points for Wales against England, equaling a record set by J. Bancroft against France 57 years before.

Jeffreys, Judge George (1648-1689): b. Wrexham, educated at Cambridge. Appointed Solicitor General to the Duke of York, Lord Chief Justice and a privy counselor at age 33, and Lord Chancellor in 1680. Known as "Hanging Judge" Jeffreys: for his severe treatment of those who had joined the Duke of Monmouth, he died in the Tower of London after James II had fled.

Jenkins, Clive (1926-1999): from Port Talbot, a respected Union Leader and National Officer of Assoc. of Scientific Workers in 1946 (it became M.S.F.U. in 1988). He was also President of TUC, working for professional workers.

Jenkins, Dafydd (1911): critic and historian, London-born, at Carmarthen as a lawyer he organized the Welsh Language Petition calling for legal recognition of Welsh. Lectured as Aberystwyth, where he retired in 1978 as Chair of Legal History and Welsh Law. He wrote many books on Medieval Welsh Law.

Jenkins, David (1843-1915): b. Trecastle, Brecon, an influential conductor and composer, studied under Joseph Parry at Aberystwyth, where he became Professor of Music in 1910, raising the standards of music and choral singing. He edited *Y Cerddor,* a magazine devoted to Welsh music.

Jenkins, Geraint Huw (b. 1946): from Aberystwyth; a senior lecturer in Welsh history with a number of books on historical subjects (and one on football).

Jenkins, Gwilym Meirion (1932-1982): from Gowerton, noted statistician who innovated systems engineering with the Royal Aircraft Establishment at Farnborough, then taught at Imperial College, London and Lancaster University before starting his own consulting company looking at and solving some of the world's major problems.

Jenkins, John (Ifor Ceri, 1770-1829): musicologist and antiquary who helped begin the practice of collecting and publishing Welsh manuscripts and was a member of the first Gorsedd at Carmarthen in 1819.

Jenkins, John (Gwili, 1872-1936): Hendy, Carms; theologian and poet, Professor of New Testament Greeek in the Baptist College and lecturer at Bangor. Contributed to the history of theology in Wales, won the Crown as a member of the Bardd Newydd school of poetry and was Archdruid 1932-1936.

Jenkins, John Geraint (b. 1929): b. Penbryn, Cards: Keeper of Material Culture in 1969 at the Welsh Folk Museum; Curator of the Welsh Industrial and Maritime Museum in 1979; has written many books on traditional folk life in Wales.

Jenkins, Joseph (1886-1962): from Pontrhydygroes, Cards. Won the O.M. Edwards Memorial Prize in 1947 for his contribution to Welsh literature as an author of children's books.

Jenkins, Joseph (19th century): farmer who claimed to have left his native Cardiganshire "because of a nagging wife. His exploits as "the Jolly Swagman" of song "Waltzing Matilda" earned him a prominent place among Australia's most loveable folk heroes.

Jenkins, Karl (b. 1944): the best-selling living composer; creator of the "Jenkins Sound." Formerly principal oboe with the National Youth Orchestra of Wales, he founded jazz group Nucleus; wrote the children's opera *Eloise; the Adiemus- Songs of Sanctuary; the Fanfare for Four Trumpets,* and *Dewi Sant* (for the Millenium celebrations).

Jenkins, Katherine (b. 1980): from Neath. Following her scholaship to the Royal College of Music, London, and a few years spent teaching singing in to schoolchildren, she is the fastest selling female opera singer in the world since Maria Callas with an exciting future awaiting.

Jenkins, Leoline (1625-85): from Llantristant, Glam; a Principal of Jesus College; elected M.P. for Hythe in 1671; a generous benefactor to Jesus College, where he endowed the library and scholarships for Cowbridge School.

Jenkins, Neil (b. 1971) "the Ginger Monster," the highest points scorer in the history of international rugby union reaching 925 points. Jenkins matched Ieuan Evans by getting his 92nd Welsh cap. On March 18, 2001, he reached 1000 international points, helping Wales defeat France at Stade de France.

Jenkins, Nigel (b. 1949): poet from Gower, former journalist, shared Welsh Arts Council's first Young Poets' Prize; helped create the Welsh Union of Writers, of which he was the first Secretary.

Jenkins, Rachel: pioneer Welsh woman whose suggestion to build an irrigation canal from the Camwy to the Chubut Valley helped saved the Welsh colony in Patagonia in its early days.

Jenkins, Rae (in the 1940's and 50's, regarded as the best conductor of light music in Britain, he became household name on the radio show ITMA with Tommy Handley's catch phrase "Play, Rae."

Jenkins, Robert Thomas (1881-1969): Liverpool born, brought up at Bala, taught at Llandysul, Brecon and Cardiff, Professor of Welsh History at University

College, Bangor and regular contributor to *Y Llenor*; published short stories for the general reader in Welsh and an historical novel. Helped edit and write the *Dictionary of Welsh Biography* (1953).

Jenkings, Roy (1920-2003): from the mining valleys of Gwent, rose to become Home Secretary in the Wilson Government, Lord Chancellor, and president of the European Commission in 1976. As Home Secretary, he legalized abortion and homosexuality, made divorce easier, and abolished the long-standing theatre censorship. Lord Jenkings of Millhead was one of the "Gang of Four" who broke with Labour to form the Social Democrats (SDP) in 1981, thus making it possible for Tory Party leader Maggie Thatcher to become Prime Minister. During W.W.II, as captain in the Royal Artillery and a codebreaker, Jenkins helped crack the secrets of the Nazi Enigma machine. In 1975, he led the successful referendum campaign to keep Britain in Europe. He also wrote highly acclaimed biographies of Winston Churchill and Gladstone.

Jesus College, Oxford (f. 1571): originally for sons of the Welsh gentry, it has educated many generations of prominent Welshmen.

John ap John (1625-97): from Trevor, near Ruabon, Denbs, he was the first Quaker evangelist in Wales.

John, Augustus (1878-1961): b. Tenby; painter, and print-maker, famous for his portraits (including those of

James Joyce, G.B. Shaw and Dylan Thomas); served in W.W.I as an official war artist with the Canadian Army. John traveled over the British countryside learning Gypsy customs and language.

John, Barry (*King John*, b. 1945): an all-time great of Welsh rugby. With the British Lions in New Zealand in 1971, he scored 30 points but retired from rugby at age 27 to the disappointment of thousands of his fans.

John, Edward Thomas (11857-1931): from Pontypridd; M.P. for East Denbighshire (1910-1918): a keen advocate of Home Rule, he was President of the Union of Welsh Societies and of the Peace Society from 1924-1927.

John, Gwen (1876-1939): b. Haverfordwest, sister of Augustus John; she was a great painter who refused to exhibit but who won fame after her death. She was the model for Rodin's *The Muse*.

Johnes, Arthur James (1809-71): from Garthmyl, Mont., a lawyer very active on behalf of Welsh culture, promoted the *Cambrian Quarterly Magazine* (1830-33), translated Dafydd ap Gwilym. Awarded Royal Medal by London Cambrian Institution in 1831 for his essay on the dissent in the Church in Wales.

Johnes, Thomas (1748-1816): agriculturalist whose spacious mansion and grounds at Hafod, Cards, a mecca for artists, writers and agriculturalists, are described in *Peacocks in Paradise*, 1950. (Hafod was demolished in 1962).

Johns, Glynis (b. 1923): husky-voiced star of stage and screen; debuted in London at age of twelve; she received a Tony for *A Little Night Music* on Broadway in 1975. Starred in many Hollywood movies.

Johns, Mervyn (1899-1992): Pembroke-born star of British films beginning in 1934, father of Glynis.

John, William Goscombe: (1860-1952): Cardiff-born sculptor who studied under William Burgess, then Rodin; noted for his equestrian statues of prominent British statesmen and military leaders.

Johnny Onions (Sioni Nionod, or Sioni Wynwns): Breton onion sellers in the South Wales Valleys until the 1950's. Their dialect was similar to Welsh.

Jones, Aled (b. 1971): singer began with the Bangor Cathedral choir, going on to make 14 recordings, several of which won Silver, Gold and Platinum. Aled trained at the Royal Academy of Music and has performed worldwide. In 1985 he sang with the Los Angeles Philharmonic in front of Queen Elizabeth with Joan Sutherland and Leonard Bernstein. He has retained his popularity with *Songs of Praise* on B.B.C. television.

Jones, Allan (1907-1992): born in Scranton, Pa., of Welsh parents; one of U.S.A.'s top singers in musicals and movies 1930-50's's after a short career following his Cwmbach born father into the mines. He sang his famous "Donkey Serenade" in the movie *Firefly*.

Jones, Dr. Alun Denny Wynn (b. 1937): b. Amman Valley, a Senior Research Fellow with Lockheed Missiles and Space Co. in California (1964-6): joined MacMillen & Co., publishers (1999); he was an adviser to British Steel, British Library Council, the National Library of Wales, and governor of U.C.W., Aberystwyth.

Jones, the Rev. Alwyn Rice (b. 1934): b. Capel Curig, Vicar of Porthmadog, Dean at Brecon Cathedral, and finally Archbishop of Wales, 1991-99.

Jones, Aneurin (*Aneurin Fardd*, 1822-1904): from Bedwas, Gwent, came to the US in 1864 to become superintendent of the New York and Brooklyn Public Parks. He was well-known as an eisteddfod adjudicator and master of the Welsh classical poetry metres. Aneurin Bevan was named after this gifted poet.

Jones, Arthur Llywellyn (Arthur Machen, 1863-1947): b. Caerleon, prose writer and translator of French; wrote many tales of the supernatural; began a new career as an actor in 1901. In his book, *The Bowmen*, he created the enduring legend of the ghostly medieval archers led by "the angel of Mons" to fight alongside British soldiers in the trenches of W.W.I.

Jones (Stephen), Barry (b. 1937): Labour M.P. for Delyn and Deeside, Flintshire (1983-2002); Chief Opposition Spokesman on Wales, 1983-87; 1988-92. Labour Shadow Cabinet 1983-87, 1988-92: member Court of Governors, University of Wales and the National Library of Wales.

Jones, Bedwyr, Lewis (1933-1992): b. Wrexham, educated Bangor and Oxford, distinguished, influential professor of Welsh at Bangor, editor of *Yr Arloeswr* (the Pioneer, 1957-60): essayist in *Writers of Wales* series (1972).

Jones, Bobi (Robert Maynard (b. 1929): Cardiff-born ex- professor of Welsh at Aberystwyth, and prolific writer and critic. He taught himself Welsh; won Welsh Arts Council's Book of the Year Award for *Ysbryd y Cwlwm* (1999). Committed to the Welsh language, he has written many books for learners and children.

Jones, Rev Calvert Richard (1802-1877) a Swansea pioneer in early photography who created the first known photograph in Wales (of Margam Castle, taken 9 March, 1851).

Jones, Captain Dan (d. 1861): the father of Welsh Mormonism who converted many at Merthyr Tydfil in 1843, leading them to the Promised Land in Utah.

Jones, Carol (b. 1968): from Maesteg, she emigrated to Australia in 1955 to star in television to win Most Popular Actress awards, later becoming a successful internationally known pop singer.

Jones, Catherine Zeta (b. 1969): b. Treboaeth, Swansea, started singing at an early age, starring in musicals before moving to television to star in *The Darling Buds of May.* She became a Hollywood star in *Mask of Zorro* and other movies including *Chicago.* She is married to actor Michael Douglas. Her name Zeta comes from a grandmother who was named after a ship that used to come into Swansea harbor.

Jones, Cliff (b. 1935): from Swansea, where he partnered Ivor Allchurch, he went to Tottenham Hotspur to help win the Double in 1961. One of the all-time great wingers in professional soccer, he played 50 times for Wales.

Jones, Clive William (b.1949): from Newbridge, chief executive at Carlton T.V. since 1996: former TV Controller: News, Current Affairs and Sport.

Jones, Dafydd (1711-77): from Caeo, Carmarthen: hymn writer and translator of many hymns and psalms of Isaac Watts into Welsh.

Jones, David (1895-1974): born in England to a Holywell family; served with the Royal Welsh Fusiliers; established a reputation as a painter and engraver and a scholar-poet deeply concerned with modern man's loss of spiritual identity.

Jones, David Bevan (1807-1863): from Llandysul, converted to Mormonism helping the movement grow rapidly in Wales. In 1862 he took 900 converts with him to Zion (Utah) sailing from Liverpool on the *William Tapscott*.

Jones, David James (Gwenallt, 1899-1968): from Alltwen, Swansea Valley; poet, critic and scholar, deeply influenced by the nationalistic traditions of Wales' heartland and the countryside in contrast to the industrial landscape; won the Chair in 1926; published five volumes of poetry beginning in 1939.

Jones, David Lewis (b.1945): from Aberaeron, has served as Librarian at the House of Lords since 1991: former librarian at U.C.W. Aberystwyth; member of the Gorsedd; his works concern the Soviet Union, Paraguay, the House of Lords, and *The Glorious Revolution.*

Jones, Delme Bryn (1935-2001): Brynamman baritone with many leading opera companies. Regarded as too cherubic looking for villainous parts, he had an illustrious career, finding the money to pay for his music lessons by working on a coal tip. His career coincided with those of Tito Gobbi and Geraint Evans, but he was their match in lyrical expertise.

Jones, Derek William (b.1952): director, Economic Affairs at the Welsh Assembly, former Head of Japan Desk and Overseas Trade Policy 1987-89 and held various positions with the Welsh Office.

Jones, Dillwyn Owen (1923-84): from Neath, called "Jones the Jazz," he was regarded as one of world's great jazz pianists, playing mainly in the U.S.

Jones, Edward (*Bardd y Brenin,* 1752-1824): harpist to the Prince of Wales, he helped revive the ancient eisteddfod to counteract the decline of minstrelsy and harpists in Wales, with the first meeting held at Corwen in 1788. His major work was *The Musical and Poetical Relicks* of *the Welsh Bards (1784).*

Jones, Edward Morus (b. 1944): from Llandegfgan, Sir Fôn, where he was headmaster for 18 years; former pop singer with Dafydd Iwan; peace campaigner active with Christian Aid Society; recently retired Chairman of Undeb Cymru a'r Byd (Wales and the World) and tireless worker for Urdd Gobaith Cymru.

Jones, Elias H. (1883-1942): b. Aberystwyth, lawyer who worked in Burma before serving with the Indian Army in W.W.I; wrote *The Road to En-dor* (1920) about his escape from a Turkish prison camp. He edited *The Welsh Outlook* from 1927-1933.

Jones, Elin (b. 1966): agricultural economist; singer with *Cwlwm*; member of Plaid Cymru; has served the

Development Board for Rural Wales and the Welsh Development Agency; in 1997 became the youngest-ever Mayor of Aberystwyth.

Jones, Elinor: a native of the Swansea Valley. A veteran of broadcasting in the Welsh language, she appeared in *Heno, Hawlio*, and other popular programs.

Jones, Elizabeth Mary (Moelona, 1878-1953): from Rhydlewis, Cards. A teacher and author of more than thirty books for children and adults: a champion of women's rights in her later novels.

Jones, Ellis J. (b. 1924): N.W.A.F. Heritage Award winner from Minnesota, Dr. Jones retired as Executive Director of W.N.G.G.A. in 2003 and more than 40 years of service to Welsh Americans.

Jones, Elwyn (1923-82): from Cwmaman, Glam. Joined BBC Television in 1957, working on documentaries and plays, creating the character of Inspector Barlow, and publishing a number of books.

Jones, Emma (b. 1975): from Mold, former editor of "Smash Hits" magazine, worked on *The Mail on Sunday* and *The Sun*, for whom she was the youngest columnist. Twice nominated for the UK press Gazetteer Young Journalist of the Year award.

Jones, Emyr (b. 1914): from Waunfawr, quarryman and teacher who wrote of John Evans' search for the Welsh Indians in his prize-winning novel of 1969.

Jones, Ernest Alfred (1897-1958): b. Llwchwr, near Swansea; an all-time "great" in the field of psychoanalysis, he helped Carl Jung set up the world's first psychoanalytic congress in 1908. In 1911 he established the American Psychoanalytic Association, winning general acceptance for psychoanalysis. In 1913 he founded the British Psychoanalytical Society and launched the prestigious International Journal of Psychoanalysis in 1920. A member of Plaid Cymru, he is the author of the 3-volume *Life of Freud* (1953-57).

Jones, Eurfron Gwynn (b.1934); from Aberdare Girls' Grammar to Director of Education, BBC (1992-94); distinguished as a writer and broadcaster.

Jones, Evan (Ieuan Gwynedd, 1820-1852): born near Dolgellau; a minister and outstanding champion of the Welsh language against the government reports on the state of the Welsh language: *Brad y Llyfrau Gleision* (Treachery of the Blue Books). In addition to editing many quarterly magazines, he also edited *Y Gymraes,* the first Welsh language paper for women.

Jones, Evan David (1903-1993): b. Llangeitho, Cards. Scholar, Head of Department of Manuscripts in 1938 and Librarian at National Library of Wales, an authority on poet Lewys Glyn Cothi and editor of the *Journal* of the Merionethshire Historical Society.

Jones, Sir Ewart (1911-2002): from Wrexham, professor at Oxford, Manchester, Illinois and Wisconsin, won awards from Royal Institute of Chemistry and American Chemical Society.

Jones, Gareth Vaughan (1905-1935): b. Barry; prolific correspondent in Welsh and English, a journalist with the *Western Mail* who detailed the starvation of the Russian peasants by Stalin in the 1930's but unjustly denounced by Walter Duranty of the *New York Times* and Eugene Lyons of the *United Press*. Jones was right; a former aide to Lloyd George. He had audiences with Adolf Hitler, Herbert Hoover, William Randolph Hearst and Frank Lloyd Wright. On a world tour, he may have been murdered in Inner Mongolia by bandits.

Jones, Gareth (b.1936): b. Cardiff, Professor of Anesthesia at Cambridge (1990-99): leading author of books on anesthesia and pulmonary mechanisms.

Jones, Gareth "Gaz Top," (b. 1961): from St. Asaph, television presenter and actor, former punk rocker and mainstay of BBC afternoon science television.

Jones, Geraint (b. 1977): born in Papua to Welsh parents. Learned cricket in Austalia, plays for England as wicket keeper.

Jones, Geraint Stanley (b.1936): b. Pontypridd, Head of Programs, BBC Wales (1974-81), Director of Public Affairs (1986-87).

Jones, Glyn (1905-1995): b. Merthyr; short-story writer and poet, pioneer of a generation of Anglo-Welsh writers; his *The Dragon has Two Tongues* (1968), is a critical appreciation of other Anglo-Welsh writers.

Jones, Glynne (1927-2000): b. Merthyr Tydfil, Fellow of the Welsh College of Music and Drama, conductor of Pendyrus Choir, music advisor to County of Gwent (1965-1990), adjudicator, lecturer, radio and popular Welsh television broadcaster.

Jones, Griffith (1683-1761): Curate at Laugharne, where he helped found S.P.C.K. School, moved to Llanddowror, preaching and converting. In 1731 he began the circulating schools movement to help make Wales one of the most literate countries in Europe.

Jones, Gwenfyl (d. 2004): from Llanelli, former president of the Vancouver Welsh Society and supporter of Welsh activities in North America, a former president of the W.N.G.G.A., a member of the Gorsedd.

Jones, Gwilym Richard (1903-1993): b. Talysarn, Caerns; poet and journalist, worked on a number of North Wales newspapers, then editor of *Baner ac*

Amserau Cymru (1939-1977); an accomplished poet, Crown and Prose winner, novelist and short story writer.

Jones, Gwyn (1907-1974): Blackwood, Monmouthshire, internationally known critic, short-story writer and novelist, translator of Icelandic sagas and author of short stories about the Valleys, historical novels and essays. In 1939, he founded *The Welsh Review*, and co-edited a new translation of the *Mabinogion*.

Jones, Gwyn Erfel (b. 1924): born in Llanerfel, Montgomeryshire; poet and editor, winner of many international prizes for his TV documentaries.

Jones, Gwyn Owain (1917-1992): from Port Talbot, with a career in physics, including U.K. Atomic Energy Project 1942-46; Professor at Queen Mary College 1953-56: member of Academi Gymreig; the Gorsedd; and a Director of National Museum of Wales, 1968-77.

Jones, Dame Gwyneth (b. 1937): from Pontnewydd, internationally known operatic soprano, starred at Covent Garden for many years, praised for her *Turandot* and *Trovatore*, also for Brunnhilde at Bayreuth.

Jones, Sir Henry (1852-1922): influential author and philosopher, whose autobiography *Old Memories*

(1923) describes his work on educational reform that brought about the Intermediate Education Act of 1889.

Jones, Hugh Robert (1894-1930): quarry worker at Deiniolen who founded Byddin Ymreolaeth Cymru, the nucleus of Plaid Cymru, serving as its first secretary until his early death from tuberculosis.

Jones, Humphrey (Bryfdir, 1867-1947): from Cwm Croesor, Merioneth; winner of sixty-four chairs and eight crowns at eisteddfodau.

Jones, Humphrey Owen (1872-1912): from Ebbw Vale, pioneering research chemist who discovered carbon monosulphide, worked in the analysis of nickel and metal carbonyls, and did early reseach in crystals. He and his wfe were killed climbing in the Alps.

Jones, Humphrey R. (1832-1895): "the Revivalist," from Llangynfelyn, Cardiganshire; moved to Tre'r Ddol, near Aberystwyth; returned to Wales from Wisconsin to start the great Welsh Revival of 1858-1860.

Jones, Huw (b.1948): went from Cardiff High to Jesus College, Oxford; Chief Executive of S4C; co-director of Sain Records with Dafydd Iwan.

Jones, Idwal (1895-1937): from Lampeter, playwright and humorist, author of light verse, poems and stories and a member of the musical group *Adar Tregaron* and a script writer for radio.

Jones, Ieuan Gwynedd (b. 1920): emeritus professor at University of Wales; influential author of many books on social conditions and religion in Wales, especially during the Victorian era. A pioneer in Welsh social and political history, named "The most important historian of modern Wales" *(Planet).*

Jones, Inigo (1573-1652): the great architect of the early Stuarts; born in England to a Welsh family. According to Thomas Pennant, he designed Gwydir Chapel and the graceful bridge over the Conwy at Llanrwst.

Jones, J.E. (1905-1970): from Corwen, the first secretary of the Bangor College branch of *Plaid*, later secretary of the London branch, then of Plaid itself, building a party from scratch. He organized campaigns, and established the Welsh Listeners' Society to protest English-only television broadcasting.

Jones, Jack (1884-1970): Anglo-Welsh writer born in Merthyr, son of a coal miner, he was wounded in WWl after which he joined the Communist Party, then joined Labour, the Liberals, and Oswald Mosley's New Party. His *Rhondda Roundabout* (1934), about life in a Welsh industrial valley, was followed by the biography of Dr. Joseph Parry: *Off to Philadelphia in the Morning*

(1947) and many others, mainly about working-class life in the South Wales industrial valleys.

Jones, Jenkin (b. 1623): Puritan preacher from Llanddeti, Brecons. Leading his own troop, he fought for Parliament, was imprisoned at the Restoration.

Jones, Joey (b. 1955): from Bangor, Welsh international footballer with careers at Liverpool where he helped win two European Cups, two League Championships and Wales defeat England. As a youth he played for the Llandudno Swifts along with Neville Southall.

Jones, John (*Shoni Sgubor Fawr*, Johnny Big Barn, 1811-1858): of immense strength, he helped demolish the tollgates at Pontyberem in the Rebecca Riots, but sadly betrayed many of his companions. For shooting a man in a tavern he was transported to Van Diemen's Land in 18143 but later pardoned.

Jones, John (or Griffith, 1559-98): born Clynnog, Caerns. A Franciscan friar executed in London and canonized in 1970 as one of the "Forty Martyrs."

Jones, John (1597-1660): from Ardudwy, Mer. Fought for Parliament: M.P. for Merionethshire; Commissioner for the Propagation of the Gospel in Wales (1650): Commissioner for Ireland (1650) and North Wales (1655): a signer of the death warrant for Charles lst, he was executed as a regicide at the Restoration.

Jones, John (Ioan Tegid, 1792-1852): from Bala, a poet and orthographer, chaplain at Jesus College, Oxford, he helped translate the notorious Report of the Commission on Education in Wales of 1847.

Jones, John (Jones Y Seerdydwr) (1918-1898): from Bangor, Jones "the astronomer" constructed his own telescope to examine Mars. He taught himself Greek and Hebrew.

Jones, John Ackerman (b. 1934): from Maesteg, a poet and critic whose study of Dylan Thomas (1964) did much to establish the poet's standing.

Jones, John Gwilym (1904-1988) from Groeslon, Caernarfon, he was recognized as one of the greatest Welsh dramatists of the 20th century and a distinguished literary critic. He produced radio plays with the BBC in Bangor from 1949-53. His masterpiece is *Ac Eto Nid Myfi* (1976).

Jones, John Morgan (1818-1912): from Glandulais Isaf, near Llanidloes, came to U.S. in 1832, became a successful broker in New York City and began publishing *Y Drych* in 1851 as owner-editor.

Jones, Sir John Morris (1884-1929): his many books include *An Elementary Welsh Grammar,* 1921 and *Welsh Grammar Historical and Comparative*, 1913.

Jones, John Puleston (1862-1925): born in Dyffryn Clwyd: blinded at 18 months, educated at Universities of Glasgow and Oxford, essayist and developer of a Braille system for Welsh.

Jones, John Richard (1765-1822): from Llanuwchllyn, he left the Baptists in 1798 to form a new connexion known as the Scotch Baptists, permanently impairing the cause of the Baptist Church in North Wales.

Jones, John Robert (1911-70): b. Pwllheli, philosopher who greatly influenced Plaid Cymru: the Party of Wales; and Cymdeithas Yr Iaith Cymraeg.

Jones, John Tudor (John Eilian, 1904-85): poet and journalist from Anglesey, editor of *Y Cymro,* won both Chair and Crown at the National Eisteddfod.

Jones, Jonathan (b. 1948): advocate for Wales: became Chief Executive of the Wales Tourist Board in 1999 after directing the British Tourist Authority Office in the Netherlands, Regional Liaison Manager in London, and Senior Marketing Director in Wales.

Jones, Dr. Keith Howard (b.1937): Cardiff born, Chief Executive at Dept of Health; formerly adjunct Prof. of Medicine at Thomas Jefferson Medical School, Philadelphia, and Prof. of Pharmacology, University of London.

Jones, Lewis (1836-1904): from Caernarfon, he encouraged emigration to Patagoni; Trelew is named after him. As Governor of Wladfa, upholding Welsh interests, he was imprisoned by the Argentine government. He founded two newspapers and wrote the history of the settlement, *Y Wladfa Gymreig* (1898).

Jones, Lewis (1897-1939): b. Rhondda; Marxist political activist involved in hunger marches, strikes, and demonstrations of the 1930's, author of *Cwmardy* (1937) and *We Live* (1939); died speaking in favor of Spanish Republicans.

Jones, Mai (Gladys Mary, 1899-1960): musician, broadcaster, and writer of the radio program *Welsh Rarebit* during WW II up to the early 1950's. She wrote the music for "We'll Keep a Welcome," almost a second Welsh National Anthem.

Jones, Mary (1784-1872): as a 16-year old, walked barefoot from Llanfihangel to Bala to buy a Welsh Bible from Thomas Charles. Her 25-mile walk inspired Charles and others to found the British and Foreign Bible Society (1814).

Jones, Mervyn Thomas (b. 1942): from Swansea, Governor of Turks and Caicos Islands following a distinguished career with H.M. Diplomatic Service.

Jones, Michael Daniel (1822-98): tireless patriot for Wales, he founded the Brython Association in

Cincinnati in 1847 to help Welsh immigrants. Principal of the Independent College, Bangor, he formulated plans to establish Wladfa, Patagonia. He is regarded as one of the founders of the modern Welsh nation.

Jones, Owen (1809-1874): influential interior designer and architect, the son of a prosperous Welsh furrier, Owen's painting tour of the Middle East led to the publication of *Plans, Elevations, Sections and Details of the Alhambra* in 1842. He was appointed Superintendent of works for the Great Exhibition of 1851; published (with Matthew Wyatt, the monumental *Grammar of Ornament* in 1856; won gold medals for his interior designs at International Exhibitions of Paris, 1867 and Vienna, 1873.

Jones Owen (Owain Myfyr), 1741-1814): from Llangfihangel, Denbs. Earned a fortune in London, where he founded and supported the Gwyneddigion Society in 1770 and paid for the works of Dafydd ap Gwilym and parts of the *Mabinogion* to be published.

Jones, Owen Glynne (1867-99): he popularized rock climbing in his *Rock-Climbing in the English Lake District* (1897) and provided written materials for Adams' *Rock-Climbing in North Wales* (1906).

Jones, Owen Thomas (1878-1977): from Newcastle Emlyn, member of Geological Survey of Britain in 1903: twice President of the Geological Society, he played a major role in mapping the western part of south Wales coal field and Plynlimon. Writing in Welsh and English, he was first Chair of Geology at Aberystwyth in 1910; then Chair at Manchester.

Jones, Patrick (b. 1966): b. Blackwood, Gwent; poet, writer, and dramatists bringing new audiences to Welsh theatre where his works reflect economic, social and political changes.

Jones, Paul Carey (b. 1974): b. Cardiff; after studying at the Welsh School of Music and Drama, taught at Ysgol Glantaff before becoming a full-time singer; won the W. Towyn Roberts Scholarship at the National Eisteddfod, and has worked with some of the world's leading conductors in concerts and opera.

Jones, Peter (Pedr Fardd, 1775-1845): from Garn Dolbenmaen, Caerns, he was one of the last great hymn-writers of the Methodist revival.

Jones, Philip (1618-74): b. near Swansea; Puritan soldier and administrator, friend of Cromwell; Governor of Swansea in 1645 and virtually the whole of South Wales.

Jones, Rhiannon Davies (b. 1921): b. Llanbedr, Mer.; major historical novelist, whose work includes *Llys Aberffraw* (the Court at Aberffraw), *Dyddiadur Mari Gwyn* (Diary of Mary Gwyn), and *Fy Hen Lyfr Cownt* (My Old Account Book) about Ann Griffiths, for which she won the prose Medal.

Jones, Rhydderch (b. 1935): from Aberllefenni, Mer., former teacher who joined BBC Wales in 1965 and became a producer of Light Entertainment in 1973 with many Welsh plays and comedy series. His program *Cofiant Ryan* (1979) remembers comedian and actor Ryan Davies.

Jones, Richard (b. 1926): from Rhydyfelin, Carms, former journalist with the *South Wales Echo;* appointed to a lectureship at University of Virginia in 1973: has published four novels.

Jones, Richard Lewis (Dic Jones, b. 1934): from Tre'r-ddol, Cards, a distinguished poet and master of the *awdl*; five time Chair winner and publisher of volumes of his poetry.

Jones, Richard Robert (see Dic Aberdaron).

Jones, Robert (1560-1615): from Chirk, a member of the Society of Jesus who was unsuccessful in bringing the Counter-Reformation to Wales.

Jones, Robert Ambrose (Emrys ap Iwan 1851-1906): influential writer on religion and politics. Concerned with English immigration and loss of the Welsh language, he preached uncompromising nationalism and Home-rule in a federal system, coining the word *ymreolaeth* for self-government.

Jones, Dr. Robert Brinley (b.1929): President, National Library of Wales, Director, Univ. of Wales Press, 1969-76; Member of Welsh Arts Council, British Council; prolific writer of biographies of influential Welshmen including those of William Williams and William Salesbury.

Jones, Robert Gerallt (b. 1934): holder of many important posts in education in and out of Wales, prolific writer of radio and television programs; literary critic; author of five novels and poetry in both English and Welsh.

Jones, Robert Isaac (Alltud Eifion, 1815-1903): poet and editor who published the literary and antiquarian journal, *Y Brython* from 1858 to 1863.

Jones, Robert Maynard (Bobi Jones b. 1929): professor of Language and Literature at Univ. of Wales 1960-89: prolific author, taught at Trinity College, Carmarthen; and Professor of Welsh at Aberystwyth: a member of Yr Academi Gymreig. Has written many books for children and for Welsh learners.

Jones, Robert Trent, Sr. (1906-2000): born in England to Welsh parents; came to the U.S. at age six. A designer of over 400 courses 29 countries, the first architect inducted into the World Golf Hall of Fame.

Jones, Robert Tudor (b. 1921): prolific writer on religion and politics and fervent patriot.

Jones, Rowland (1722-74): philologist; his *The Origin of Languages and Nations* purported to show that words were derived from monosyllabic roots and that the primeval language was Celtic.

Jones, Rowland (Rolant o Fon. *1909-1962*): b. Anglesey an accomplished poet, a master of cynghanedd and two-time Chair winner.

Jones, Sally Roberts (b. 1935): librarian, poet and publisher, co-founded Alun Books in 1977 and owner of Barn Owl Press.

Jones, Simon (b. 1978): b. Morriston, Swansea, bowler with cricket teams Glamorgan and England. Simon debuted against India in 2002.

Jones, Stephen: (b. 1944): b. Wirral of Welsh parents, Professor at University College, London; internationally known expert on genes and genetics.

Jones, Steve (b. 1955): winner of the London Marathon in record time in 1985; he was the first Briton to win the New York Marathon (1988).

Jones, Professor Steven (b. 1944) from Aberystwyth, author and scientist of international renown. Pofessor of Genetics at University College, London, he has written several books including *The Language of the Genes* that won the Rhône-Poulenc prize for the best science book of 1994, and *In the Blood*, which was shortlisted for the 1997 Rhône-Poulenc prize. In his 1999 book, *Almost Like a Whale* Steve Jones has taken Charles Darwin's *On the Origin of Species* and updated it for the 21st Century. In 1996, the Royal Society presented Steve Jones with the Michael Faraday Award, given annually to the scientist who has done the most to further the public understanding of science. As a professor of genetics, author, presenter of the Reith Lectures (1991), television presenter and newspaper columnist, Professor Jones deals with some of the most important issues in genetics today.

Jones, Terry (b. 1942): from Colwyn Bay, film and TV producer and former wacky member of the Monty Python group, he co-wrote and directed *The Life of Brian* and has written many children's books.

Jones, Thomas (1648-1713): bookseller and writer of Welsh almanacs in London, and in Shrewsbury, where he was known as *Thomas Jones the Stargazer*.

Jones, Thomas (Pencerrig, 1742-1803): from Trefonnen, nr. Llandrindod, he studied under Richard Wilson to become internationally known for his landscapes. He popularized the myth of the Wild Welsh Bard in many of his paintings, including the famous illustration to Thomas Gray's "The Bard."

Jones, Thomas (1756-1820): b. Caerwys; Calvinistic Methodist preacher, author, friend of Thomas Charles. His press at Rhuthin was later sold to Thomas Gee.

Jones, Thomas (1870-1955): b. Rhymney, he was Secretary, National Health Insurance Commissioners 1912. As Deputy-Secretary of David Lloyd George's Cabinet in 1916, he helped negotiate the Anglo-Irish Treaty of 1921, but was staunchly anti-Nationalist in Wales. He helped found and was President of Coleg Harlech and the Arts Council of Great Britain.

Jones, Thomas (1910-72): professor at Aberystwyth, translator of Geraldus Cambrensis and early Irish and Breton. With Gwyn Jones, he published the authoritative version of the *Mabinogion* in 1948.

Jones, Thomas Artemus (1871-1943): b. Denbigh, a journalist and judge who won an important libel case in 1908, following which publishers could not in future use living persons and characters in novels. His tireless work to have the Welsh language used in courts of law led to the Welsh Courts Act of 1942.

Jones, Thomas Gwynn (1871-1949): poet, scholar, dramatist and journalist, known for his poetry on Celtic themes and legends, including *Ymadawiad Arthur* (the departure of Arthur), and *Tir n-Og* (land of Youth), a lyrical play. He also translated Goethe's *Faust* into Welsh as well as a selection of Greek poems and Latin epigrams.

Jones, Thomas Henry (1921-65): contributed to many literary journals, moved to Australia where his writing evoked his hiraeth for Wales. After his accidental death by drowning, a collection of his work is *Collected Poems* (1977).

Jones, Thomas Llewelyn (b. 1915): Associated with the Cilie Poetic Circle; he wrote over 50 books in Welsh, including detective stories and children's literature.

Jones, Tom (*Tom the Voice*, b. 1940): stage name for Thomas Woodward popular Pontypridd singer who went from working men's clubs in Wales to Las Vegas theatres and television performances, often returning to Wales in concert. In 1965, "It's not Unusual" made him a star. His hits include "Delilah" and "The Green, Green Grass of Home." He is a director of the World Foundation that raises money for women and children in Vancouver, Canada.

Jones, Tommy George (1918-2004): B. Connah's Quay, Flints, an international footballer with Everton and Wales. Known as "the prince of half backs."

Jones, Tom Parri (1905-80): Chair and Crown-winner, poet and short-story writer of Anglesey life.

Jones, Tristan (b. 1924): born at sea to Welsh-speaking parents; torpedoed three times with the Royal Navy in World War II, sailed single-handed in his tiny yacht across the Atlantic, on Lake Titicaca, down Europe's rivers, and in the Arctic, all of which are related in more than 15 books.

Jones, Tudor Bowden (b. 1934): from Ystradgynlais, distinguished contemporary physicist, Professor of Ionospheric Physics (1980-98) at the University of Leicester, a guest research scientist at many leading U.S. government establishments, including the National Oceanics and the Atmospheric Administration Laboratory, Boulder, Colorado.

Jones, William (1675-1749): b. Anglesey, he is credited with being first to use the 16th letter of the Greek alphabet Pi to represent the ratio of the circumference to the diameter of a circle.

Jones, William (1726-95): from Llandgadan, Tannat Valley; self -educated, poet, musician, astronomer and healer who did nore than any one else to focus Welsh minds on the idea af a *Gwladfa*, a National Home for the Welsh in the New World.

Jones, William John (b. 1928): from Ystradmeurig, Cards, lecturer, Welsh Dept. Head at Cardiff College of Education; a prolific writer of children's books.

Jones, William, Sir (1746-94): London Welsh scholar whose service with the East India Company led him to discover that Welsh had similar roots to Sanskrit, thus leading to theories about an Indo-European language group. He gave status to the Welsh language. He helped publicize the legend that the Mandans were descended from explorers led by Prince Madog.

231

Jones, William Samuel (b. 1920): b. Llanystumdwy, Caerns; short-story writer and playwright, with many scripts for radio and television and publishing many plays in Welsh, mostly humorous.

Jones-Davies, Henry (b. 1949): from Caerfyrddin, the editor and publisher of *Cambria*, the National Magazine for Wales, which he founded in 1997and a leading member of the "yes" campaign for the Welsh Assembly. A journalist and writer who appears regularly on Welsh and UK TV and radio and Chairman of the Welsh Heritage Campaign; co-founder of World Wide Welsh Award.

Jones-Evans, Dylan: b. Pwllheli, Director of Enterpreneurship at the Northeast Wales Institute of Higher Education in Wrexham, helping develop world-class small firms and linkages between academia and industry; author of *Enterprise and Small Business* (Financial Times).

Jones-Griffiths, Philip (b. 1936): from Rhuddlan, Flintshire, a teacher at State University New York, and internationally known award winning sculptor.

Jones-Parry, Dr. Emyr (b. 1947): from Gwendraeth Grammar to Univ. College, Cardiff, then to H.M. Diplomatic Service; holding many important overseas posts before becoming Political Director of Foreign and Commonwealth Office in 1996 and NATO permanent representative of the U.K since 2003.

Josephson, Brian David (b. 1940): from Cardiff, Physics professor with dozens of medals and prizes from prestigious institutions, including the Nobel Prize for Physics, 1973. Has taught at Cambridge, Illinois, and Cornell Universities. He discovered "the Josephson Effect," dealing with the flow of electrical currents.

Juvencus Manuscript: (9th Century): a Latin manuscript containing the earliest surviving poetry in Welsh.

K

There is no K in the Welsh alphabet. Borrowings from English include Kerry (*Ceri*) and Kidwelly and many names listed below.

Karrie, Peter (b.1946): b. Bridgend; star of musicals, regarded as the best of all in *Phantom of the Opera*; also starred as Valjean in *Les Miserables* and Judas in *Jesus Christ Superstar.* Played rugby with Newport, then played the piano in nightclubs; he got his big break in London in *Che Guevera.*

Keating, Joseph (1871-1934): from Mountain Ash, novelist. Supporter of the Irish Nationalist Movement, he was a pioneer in the Anglo-Welsh novel.

Keenor, Fred (1894-1972): captain of Cardiff City when it beat Arsenal to win the F.A. Cup at Wembley, the only time the cup has left England.

Kelsey, Jack (1929-92): from Llansamlet, Swansea. A legendary goalkeeper with Arsenal (1950-62); he played for Wales 41 times.

Kemble, Charles (1775-1854): Breconshire-born Shakespearean actor, brother to Sarah Siddons. A theatre manager, he was the first to use detailed historical sets and costumes. He successfully toured the U.S.

Kempster, David: b. Chirk, contemporary baritone who left a career as a building surveyor to turn professional with the English National Opera after winning the Young Welsh Singer of the Year Contest in 1998.

Kilvert, Francis (1840-79): English diarist included here for his writings that detailed every-day life as curate at Clyro, Radnorshire.

Kinmel Camp Riots (1919): after W.W.I had ended, Canadian soldiers at Kinmel Camp, Flintshire, were unhappy at the slow pace of their discharge. In a riot, five soldiers were shot and were buried at the Marble Church. British War Records lists the cause of death as disease (see Bodelwyddan).

Kinnock, Neil (b. 1942): Labour, M.P. Bedwellty (1980-83), later Islwyn, Mid-Glam; led Labour from 1983-1992, defeated in the General Election. Known as "the nearly man of British politics," since 1995 served in the European Commission, becoming Vice-President in 1999. In the 1997 Referendum, he was noted for his negative views towards the Welsh language and the Assembly.

Kinnock, Glenys (b. 1944): b. Anglesey, politician, a Fellow of the Royal Society of Arts, President of Coleg

Harlech, first elected to the European Parliament in 1994, Vice-President of the United Nations Association, and wife of Neil.

Knight, Bernard (b. 1931): from Cardiff, barrister and doctor, prominent forensic pathologist (professor of forensic Medicine at Cardiff and Home Office Pathologist, he has international reputation for his work, his medical textbooks, and his involvement with high-profile forensic cases.

Kynniver Llith a Ban **(Many Lessons and Excerpts, 1551):** translation by William Salesbury of some Epistles and Gospels with an enormous influence on the Welsh Bible and Prayer Book.

L

Fourteenth letter of the Welsh alphabet
(it often appears as a mutation of Ll after prepositions).

Ladies of Gregynog (See David Davies, Llandinam).

Lady Llanover (see Hall, Augusta Waddington).

Lake Vyrnwy (*Llyn Llanwddyn*): mid-Wales, a
reservoir built to supply water for Liverpool
Corporation in the 1880's that completely drowned the
vibrant village of Llanwddyn, a center of Welsh culture
and language.

Lampeter (*Llanbedr Pont Steffan*): home of St.
David's College, the oldest degree-granting institution
in Wales, now part of the University of Wales.

***Land of My Fathers*:** (see Hen Wlad fy Nhadau).

Largest leatherback turtle: (2119 lb or 961 kg)
drowned on the beach off Porthmadog on 22 Sep 1988,
caught on a fishing line, the preserved creature is
exhibited at the National Museum of Wales.

Last Invasion of Mainland Britain: (see Nicholas,
Jemima).

Last Suspect:: a horse trained by Welshman Hywel Davies that won the Grand National in 1985 at 50-1.

Laugharne (Talacharn), Carmarthenshire: named after a Civil War general, but famous for its association with Dylan Thomas and Caitlin who lived and fought here and where he wrote many memorable poems.

Laverbread (*Bara Law*): a dish of boiled seaweed, mixed with oatmeal and fried in bacon fat. Known as *Welsh caviar*, a gourmet dish in the Swansea area.

Lawn Tennis: begun at the home of Major Wingfield, Cerrig y Drudion in N. Wales. In 1874 he took out a patent after publishing rules for "Sphairistike, or Lawn Tennis" (Marylebone Cricket Club, London also has a claim).

Lawrence, T.E. (Lawrence of Arabia (1888-1935): b. Tremadoc; explorer and military leader, led Arab forces against the Turks and agitated for Arab independence. His story is told in his *Seven Pillars of Wisdom* and in the movie *Lawrence of Arabia*.

Laws of Hywel Dda, The: (see Hywel Dda).

Lee, Lisa Scott (b. 1976): from St. Asaph, a star in the British pop industry, former member of *Steps*, enormously successful on TV, in magazines etc.

Lee, Rowland (d. 1543): Anglican Bishop, President, King's Council in the Welsh Marches in 1534, noted for his cruel measures against the Welsh.

Leek (Cenhinen): praised by the Physicians of Myddfai for its healing properties, adopted in Wales as a national emblem, Its colors of green and white were worn by the victorious Welsh archers at the Battle of Crecy.

Leland, John (1506-52): author of *The Itinerary of John Leland*, consisting of notes from tours through England and Wales during 1534-1543. It greatly influenced later antiquarians and topographers.

Leonowens, Anna (1831-1915): Caernarfon-born governess to King Mongkut of Siam and instructress to his children. Her story is told in *Anna and the King of Siam* and *The King and I*. She later became involved in education and women's rights in Canada.

Levi, Thomas (1825-1916): from Ystradgynlais; composer of hymns including *Oleuni Mwyn* (lead, Kindly Light), and religious and historical books, editor of the children's magazine *Trysorfa Plant* (Treasures for Children, 1862-1911).

Lewis, Alun (1915-44): Cwmaman poet and short-story writer, many of whose poems were written as a soldier in World War Two in which he died of wounds. His first collection of poetry, *Raiders' Dawn* (1942), was followed by short stories written in India, and the collection of poems titled *Ha, Ha, Among the Trumpets.*

Lewis, Ceri Williams (b. 1926): b. Treorchy, former coal miner, professor of Welsh at University College Cardiff in 1979; has published many books on Welsh history and language.

Lewis, David (*Tad y Tlodion.* 1617-79), called the "father of the poor," Catholic martyr executed at Usk, canonized in 1970.

Lewis, Eluned (1900-1979): b. Newtown, Mont; asst. editor of *The Sunday Times,* winner of the Gold Medal of the Book Guild in 1934.

Lewis, Edward Arthur (1880-1942): historian who pioneered in Welsh social and economic history.

Lewis, Francis (1713-1803): b. Llandaff, Welsh-born signer of the American Declaration of Independence; orphaned at five, went to the US in 1735. As a prosperous merchant, he supplied British troops in the French-Indian Wars, supposedly had his life spared at Ft. Oswego by conversing in Welsh to an Indian chief; his house destroyed by British soldiers, he died in poverty.

Lewis, Geoff (b. Talgarth): the first Welsh jockey to win the English Derby (on *Mill Reef* in 1971.

Lewis Glyn Cothi (Lewys Glyn Cothi, 1420-89): 15th century Welsh poet who composed verses that described his life as an outlaw and many elegies and eulogies for wealthy patrons that are found in a collection compiled by John Davies of Mallwyd in 1617.

Lewis, Henry (1889-1968): first Professor of Welsh at Swansea University College where he popularized Celtic studies, publishing many medieval texts.

Lewis, Howell Elvet (Elfed, 1860-1953): preacher at King's Cross Welsh Chapel, London; winner of the Crown and the Chair as National Eisteddfodau; his collection, *Caniadau* (Songs) made him important in Welsh poetry. In 1890 he published *Sweet Singers of Wales*, a study of hymns and their authors. One of his hymns, "Cofio'n Gwlad" (Remembering the Land) is often called the second national anthem of Wales (in addition to "We'll Keep a Welcome").

Lewis, Hugh (1562-1634): cleric whose translation of Coverdale's *A Spiritual and most Precious Pearl* (1595) was the first Welsh book to be printed at Oxford, creating great interest in all things Celtic.

Lewis, John (1548-1616): historian whose sole work, *The History of Great Britain until the Death of Cadwaladr* (1729) was written to counteract Polydor Vergil's denigration of Geoffrey of Monmouth.

Lewis, John David (1859-1914): publisher whose Gomerian Press at Llandyssul, Ceredigion, published many of Wales's prominent 20th century authors.

Lewis, John Llewelyn (1880-1969): American-born son of Welsh immigrants, worked in mines till aged 15. Became president of A.F.L. and later the C.I.O, which he led to organize within the major U.S. industries. Hated by the establishment, he achieved much for his workers, including travel time and a welfare fund.

Lewis, Lewis (Lewsyn yr Heliwr): b. Penderyn, Rhondda, sentenced to life imprisonment in Australia following his leadership of the Merthyr Riots of 1831, On the prison ship *John*, he taught English to fellow Welsh and Irish convicts.

Lewis, Lewis William (Llew Llwyfo, 1831-1901): b. Pensarn, Anglesey; poet, novelist, and journalist, former copper mine worker, founded or edited a number of newspapers in Wales, Liverpool and the USA; a prolific writer of heroic verse and a popular figure at eisteddfodau.

Lewis, Michael: Aberystwyth-born contemporary composer; won the Ivor Novello Award for a film score in *The Madwoman of Chaillot*, his first of many, including the movie *Titanic*. In 1998, he formed the Welsh Choir of Southern California. Their debut CD is *Hearts Afire* (Calonnau ar Dân).

Lewis, Richard: (see Dic Penderyn).

Lewis, Robyn (b. 1929): b. Llangollen, Denbs; distinguished lawyer, former Deputy Judge and Assistant Recorder at the Crown Court, London; elected by the Gorsedd of Bards to be Archdruid of Wales in 2001—the first to be elected rather than appointed to the office. The first National Prose Medalist to be so honoured, he is the author of 19 books, his latest the most substantional and ambitious—the *New Legal Dictionary: Eiriadur Newydd y Cyfraith.*

Lewis, Saunders (1893-1985): poet and dramatist, co-founder and early president of Plaid Cymru. Twice nominated for the Nobel Prize in literature, he wrote 19 plays from 1921 through 1980 as well as religious poetry. In 1962, his radio speech *Tynged Yr Iaith* (fate of the language) was a signal for Welsh youth, leading directly to the founding of Cymdeithas Yr Iaith Gymraeg.

Lewis, Sir Thomas (1881-1945): born Taff's Well, he pioneered the development of the electrocardiograph, often using his own body to experiment. At Univ. College Hospital, London, his life's work was studying the operation of the heart and the blood flow.

Life of St. David **(1090 A.D.):** earliest of the lives of the Welsh saints; by Rhygyfarch (Ricemarch).

Lilly, Gweneth (1920-2004): b. Liverpool, former teacher at St. Mary's College, Bangor, a prize-winning prolific writer of novels for children.

***Lilting House*, the (1969):** 20th C. Anglo-Welsh poetry anthology, ed. Meic Stephens and John Williams.

***Liverpool Daily Post*:** the main daily newspaper for North Wales' readers, keeping them informed of local happenings, and the Liverpool and Everton football teams. Has excellent coverage of the National and International Eisteddfodau.

Liverpool Welsh, The: a sizeable community settled on Merseyside who kept up their culture and language through many publishing companies and through *Y Angor* Presently led by Rev. Ben Rees, still active in Welsh affairs.

Livesey, Roger (1906-1976): from Barry, popular theatre and movie actor with unmistakable husky voice starred *The Life and Death of Colonel Blimp* (1945).

Lob Scows: a dish popular in N. Wales made from lamb and vegetables. It may have originated in Liverpool as a dish (scouse) made for sailors.

Lockley, Ronald Mathias (1903-2000): b. Cardiff naturalist, founder of bird observatories in Britain and New Zealand; author of sixty books on nature that inspired Richard Adams' *Watership Down*.

***Lolfa, Y* (f. 1966)** (tr: "the lounge" or "place of nonsense"): outliving an early irreverent reputation, now a respected and influential Welsh book publisher appealing to a Welsh language readership.

London Welsh, The: largest and most active of all the communities of Welsh men and women outside Wales. The Cymmrodorion Society provided impetus for the establishment of many leading institutions including the National Library, Museum, and the University of Wales. Active are the London Welsh Association, a Welsh primary school, and the London Welsh Rugby Club.

London Welshman, The: periodical founded in 1894 as *The Kelt*, changing to *Y Ddolen* and *Y Ddinas* before becoming *The London Welshman* in 1959 with news of the London Welsh societies.

Longbow: feared medieval weapon of Welsh origin, (1337-1453). Its archers could shoot six times a minute to 200 yards with great effect, helping to demolish the French army at the battles of Crecy, Poitiers, and Agincourt.

Loomis, Roger Sherman (1887-1966): American scholar; co-founded the International Arthurian Society in 1930; he contributed enormously to the study of *Arthuriana* and Celtic literary traditions.

Lord Rhys (12th century): set up by Henry II as a deputy in Wales, Rhys ap Gruffudd took back much of Ceredigion from Norman control. In 1176, he hosted an eisteddfod at Cardigan in which contests were set between harpists and crowthers and pipers, and with chairs to be awarded as prizes.

Love Spoon (*Llwy Caru*): a carved wooden spoon with intricate, symbolic shapes and patterns to be given to a sweetheart. Superb examples are on display at the National Folk Museum, St Fagan's.

Lowe, Harold (1982-1944): born Deganwy, Gwynedd, he was the real hero of the *Titanic*, being the only officer who returned to the sinking ship to search for survivors. As Fifth Officer, he helped load the lifeboats before taking charge of boat Nr. 14 and rowing away, but after dispersing his occupants he returned to rescue many from the freezing waters.

Ll

Fifteenth letter of the Welsh alphabet: pronounced as an aspirated "L." It mutates to a single L after prepositions (ex: *i Landudno "to Llandudno"*).

***Llafur* (labour f.1970)**: published by the Society for the Study of Welsh Labour History, a major contributor to the industrial history of Wales.

Llais Llafur (The Voice of Labour, 1898-1971): a weekly Socialist newspaper published at Ystalyfera, Glam. that became *Labour Voice* in 1915 and *South Wales Voice* in 1927.

Llan: appearing in Welsh literature in the early 8th century, it signifies a church settlement, originally a small enclosure. The circular walls of the Llan, usually bordered with the sacred yew, had no corners in which the Devil could hide.

Llancarfan, Vale of Glamorgan: site of an ancient monastery founded by Cadog in the 6th century. The church has an ancient carved stone. Iolo Morgannwg, stonemason, poet and inventor of tradition, was born and buried here (See Edward Williams).

Llandaff, Cardiff: founded to honor Saints Dyfrig, Teilo and Euddogwy in the 6th century, the cathedral has suffered storm damage, an attack by Owain Glyndwr, bomb damage in WWll, and centuries of neglect, but now fully restored.

Llandovery (*Llanymddyfri*), Carmarthenshire: small town where The Bank of the Black Ox (now Lloyds Bank) was founded in 1799 for cattle drovers on their way to English markets.

Llandovery College: begun in 1848 as the Welsh Collegiate Institution to provide public school education entirely in Welsh.

Llanddewi Brefi, Teifi Valley: a village connected with St. David, who preached here against the Pelagian Heresy in 519 A.D.

Llanddowror, Carmarthenshire: the village where Griffith Jones began the Methodist Revival in the late 18th century and where, helped by Sir John Phillips of Picton, he began the traveling schools to teach people how to read their Welsh Bibles.

Llanelian yn Rhos, Denbighshire: the Church of St. Elian is the burial place of Ednyfed Fechan, chief minister of Llewelyn the Great (*Llywelyn Fawr*). Ednyfed's descendants became great landowners in Wales and the ancestral family of the Tudors of Penmynydd.

Llanelli, Carmarthenshire: In June, 2003, Corus opened the new Trostre Tinplate Works, the largest in Europe and the third largest in the world to make light gauge steels. A fine new park alongside the river has transformed the old industrial area and brought a renewal of hope to what was once called "Tinopolis" where tinplate was first made in 1846 at the Dafen Works. Stradey Park is the home of "the Scarlets," internationally known rugby union team.

Llanelwdd, Powys: near Builth, the home of the annual Royal Welsh Agricultural Show, the largest and finest in Britain (see separate entry).

Llanerch or Gwysaney Manuscripts, The: a collection with many valuable early manuscripts, including *The Book of Llandaf* and the *Brut Chronicle*, and a version of Nennius's *Historia Brittonum.*

Llanfaches, Gwent: part of Chepstow, and home of the first Independent Congregation in Wales.

Llanfair P.G., Anglesey: a shortened form of the name that has brought countless tourists to photograph the sign: Llanfairpwllgwyngyllgogerychwrn-drobwyllllan-tisiliogogogoch (count the letters but remember that ll and ch count as one letter each). Llanfair means Church of St. Mary.

Llanfyllyn and Dolwar Fach, Montgomeryshire: an annual summer festival brings a world-class chamber orchestra to perform in the Parish church. Ann Griffiths' memorial is at nearby Llanfihangel yng Ngwynfa.

Llangollen, Denbighshire: Little town on the Dee; the International Eisteddfod attracts competitors from all over the world and thousands of spectators who thrill to music, dancing and to concerts by international guest stars.

Llangorse Lake (*Llyn Syfadden*), Brecon: the largest natural body of water in S. Wales, where many legends and folk tales may be based on historical fact. The lake sheltered an Iron Age crannog mentioned in the *Anglo Saxon Chronicle* of 916 as destroyed by the English under Aethelflaed (female ruler of Mercia, daughter of Alfred the Great).

Llanidloes, Montgomeryshire: Its chief claim to fame comes from the Chartist Riot of April 1839 in which the Trewythen Arms was broken into, prisoners rescued, and a pike run through the hat of the resident magistrate. The John Wesley Stone commemorates his preaching here. The town is also home to the W.H. Smith Shop and Museum as well as the Textile Museum.

Llanilltud Fawr (Llantwit Major, Glamorgan): site of the monastery founded by Illtud (6th Century).

Llanover, Lady (Augusta Waddington Hall, *Gwenynen Gwent* (*Bee of Gwent*), 1802-96): Abergavenny patron of folk culture who collected important manuscripts, helped revive interest in Welsh music, folk dancing and traditional costumes as well as such important traditions as Plygain, Mari Lwyd, and others. She encouraged Welsh language and Welsh dress at her house and hired a triple harpist.

Llanrheadr ym Mochnant, Montgomeryshire: Bishop Morgan was vicar here when he began the task of translating the Bible into Welsh.

Llansanfraid, Conwy Valley: home of Total Network Solutions F.C., champions of the Welsh League in 2000 and 2005.

Llanstephan Manuscripts, The: a collection containing valuable medieval and Renaissance Welsh literature, including *The Red Book of Talgarth.*

Llantrisant, Mid-Glamorgan: since 1967 the home of the Royal Mint, one of the world's largest.

Llantwit Major (*Llanilltud Fawr*): near Cardiff, an important church in early Welsh Christianity on the site of the monastery of St. Illtud, a famous seat of learning and scholarship in 7th century Europe.

Llanwchllyn, Merionethshire: home of Sir Owen M. Edwards and his son Sir Ifan ab Owen Edwards, pivotal figures in the long struggle to preserve the Welsh language and culture, commemorated by statues in the village.

Llanybydder, Cardiganshire: market town where dealers and buyers look over ponies, cobs, hunters and foals on the last Thursday of each month in one of the largest horse sales in Europe.

Llanystumdwy, Caernarfonshire: a small museum commemorates local boy Lloyd George, who became Prime Minister of Britain. His modest grave is by the side of the River Dwyfor.

Llatai (a love-messenger): a poetic convention much used by medieval Welsh poets by which a message is sent to a loved one by means of a bird or animal.

Llay Main, Wrexham: the largest Welsh colliery closed in 1966 after 44 years; it had a work force of 2,500.

Llechwedd Slate Caverns, Blaenau Ffestiniog: a former massive quarry with two underground tours, one an inclined railway, the steepest in Britain.

Llen Cymru **(Welsh Literature)**: an annual magazine begun in 1950 by the Board of Celtic Studies to publish works of Welsh literary history.

***Llenor, Y* (The Writer, 1922-55)**: a magazine that published literary criticism and scholarship.

Lleufer (Light, 1944-1979): a magazine for the Workers' Education Association.

Llewelyn Gwyn (b. 1942): Anglesey broadcaster, worked for *The North Wales Chronicle* and the *Western Mail* before joining BBC Wales in 1979 as an introducer and news reporter.

Llewellyn, Carl: jockey who won the 1992 Grand National Steeplechase on *Party Politics*, standing in for the injured Andy Adams, and the 1998 race, standing in for Tom Jenks on *Earth Summit.*

Llewellyn, Desmond (1914-1999): son of a mining engineer, his role as Q in the James Bond films from 1963-1999 made him famous. Captured at Dunkirk with the Royal Welch Fusiliers, he was interred until the end of the War. Known to have hated gadgets of any kind, he was killed in a car crash.

Llewellyn, Gareth (b. 1969): Cardiff-born, forward; in March, 2004, with 87 games for Wales International Rugby, he passed the record of Neil Jenkins.

Llewellyn, Grant (b. 1960): b. Tenby; conductor with the BBC Symphony, Boston Symphony, Houston Symphony, the St. Paul Chamber Orchestra, the BBC National Orchestra of Wales and other prestigious orchestras; chosen in 2004 to lead the North Carolina Symphony.

Llewellyn, Sir Harry (1911-1990): from Abergavenny, Britain's leading horseman of the post-war years. Won the Gold at Helsinki on *Foxhunter* in 1952. Horse and rider won the George VI Gold Cup three times at the Royal International Horse Show. His ashes are buried near *Foxhunter's* on Blorenge Mountain.

Llewellyn, Martin (1565-1634): the first British cartographer; a survivor of a Dutch trading expedition; his charts covering the Far East and the Cape of Good Hope were only discovered in 1975.

Llewellyn, Richard ((Richard Ll. Lloyd, 1906-1983): from St. David's, Pembs, he spent a few months at Gilfach Goch Colliery to gather material for his masterpiece *How Green Was My Valley* (1939) his first published novel, made into an Oscar-winning Hollywood movie (1941).

Llewellyn-Jones, Frank (1907-1997): Mountain Ash; an authority on the physics of electrified gases and electrical contact phenomena. At the R.A.F. Establishment, Farnborough, he solved the problems caused by spark plug ignition and erosion in switches in aircraft engines.

Lloegr: the Welsh name for England (land of the Angles, called *Loegres* in medieval English poetry).

Lloyd family: Montgomeryshire iron-masters and bankers persecuted for its Quaker beliefs in the 17th century. Thomas became Deputy-Governor of Pennsylvania under William Penn; Charles (1748-1828) developed the Taylor and Lloyd Bank in Birmingham (to become Lloyd's Bank).

Lloyd, David (1912-69): b. Trelogan, Flintshire: one of Wales' best-known tenors, famed in Europe for his singing of Verdi and Mozart; in Wales for concerts.

Lloyd, David Myrddin (1909-81): distinguished staff member at the National Library of Scotland; author of essays, short stories, and translations from Irish.

Lloyd, David Tecwyn (1914-1992): pseudonym of E.H. Francis Thomas, essayist, short story writer and literary critic; editor of *Taliesin* magazine.

Lloyd, Elis (1897-1939): b. Newport, Mon., journalist and novelist with the *Glamorgan Gazette*, the *South Wales News and Echo* before studying law and entering politics as M.P. for Llandaff and Barry in 1929.

Lloyd, Henry (1720-1783): b. Llanbedr, Mer., Jacobite writer and soldier whose books on military strategy may have been read by Napoleon.

Lloyd, Herbert (1720-69): from Lampeter, a notoriously corrupt and lawless squire who became M.P. for Cardigan Boroughs in 1761.

Lloyd, John (1630-79): from Brecon, executed during the *Popish Plot* of 1678, he was canonized in 1970.

Lloyd, John Ambrose (1815-74): b. Mold, a composer of two important collections of hymn tunes and anthems.

Lloyd, John Edward (1861-1947): historian of early and medieval Wales; called "The old Magician of Bangor" by Saunders Lewis, author of *A History of Wales to the Edwardian Conquest* (1911) and *Owen Glendower* (1931).

Lloyd, John Selwyn (b. 1931): from Tal y Sarn, Caerns, teacher and prize-winning novelist.

Lloyd, Owen Morgan (1910-79): b. Blaenau Ffestiniog, an Independent minister and poet prominent at Eisteddfodau and on Radio Wales.

Lloyd, Robert (Llwyd o'r Bryn, 1888-1961): b. Llandderfel, Mer., a public speaker, author and adjudicator who coined the phrase *Y Pethe* to describe the values of traditional Welsh culture.

Lloyd, Thomas (1640-94): from Dolobran, Meifod, Montgomershire, persecuted as a Quaker, came to Pennsylvania to become one of the most importantfigures in the colony's civil life as President of the Presidential Council and Deputy Governor under William Penn.

 **Lloyd-George, David (1863-1945): b.** Manchester but raised in Llanystumdwy, Caernarfonshire, elected for Caernarfon Borough in 1890, rising rapidly through the ranks to become President of the Board of Trade, Chancellor of the Exchequer and Prime Minister (the latter during World War One). As Chancellor he introduced social security (Old Age Pensions), National Insurance against sickness and unemployment, a lessening of the miners' work hours, and the establishment of labor exchanges. Totally committed to the war against Germany, Lloyd-George was a leading figure in the peace negotiations of 1919 at Versailles. In 1921, opposed to Woodrwow Wilson. His employment of the infamous Black and Tans and his ultimatum to Irish leader Michael Collins led to the establishment of the Irish Free State and civil war.

Lloyd-George, Gwilym (1894-1967): served in France during W.W.I; elected Liberal M.P. for Pembrokeshire in 1919, was defeated in 1924; became managing director of United Newspapers in 1925: returned to Parliament in 1925; rose to become parliamentary secretary of Board of Trade under Churchill; become Viscount Tenby in 1957.

Lloyd-George, Megan (1902-1966): b. Criccieth, elected in 1929 as Liberal M.P. for Anglesey; he was president of Parliament for Wales Campaign in 1951; switched to Labour in 1955 defeating the Liberals at Carmarthen in 1957. A superb speaker in English and Welsh; died two weeks after being re-elected.

Lloyd Jones, Rev. Gareth (b. 1938): from Tremadog, Chair of the Dept of Theology and Religious Studies at Univ. of Wales, Bangor; Anglican priest and a Canon of Bangor Cathedral; author of several books in Welsh and English; a Fulbright Scholar at Yale University; has preached in several Welsh American churches; Dr. Jones is one of the eight scholars chosen to translate the Old Testament from Hebrew into modern Welsh (to celebrate the 400th anniversary of the first Welsh translation by Bishop Morgan).

Lloyd-Jones, John (1885-1965): b. Dolwyddelan, Caerns; Professor at University College, Dublin; master of the *awdl*, and Chair winner.

Lloyd-Price, Richard J. (1843-1923): from Rhiwlas, Mer., whose former whisky distillery became Camp Frongoch for Irish Republican prisoners from the Easter Rising of 1916.

Llwyd, Alan (b. 1948): from Dolgellau, Mer.; poet, and critic, editorial officer for the Welsh Joint Education Committee; has won both Crown and Chair on two occasions, and has edited several major anthologies of Welsh poets; editor of *Barddas* since 1976 and organizer of *Cymdeithas Cerdd Dafod.*

Llwyd, Angharad (1780-1866): antiquarian, essayist; wrote *The History of the Gwydir Family* (1827) and *The History of the Island of Mona* (1832).

Llwyd (Lhuyd), Edward (1660-1709): from Llanforda, Oswestry, linguist, Keeper of the Ashmolean Museum, Oxford. Known as "the father of British palaentology," he pioneered studies on Celtic languages and natural history.

Llwyd, Humphrey (1527-1568): antiquary and mapmaker from Denbigh who produced the first maps of Wales as a distinct unit from England.

Llwyd, Morgan (1619-59): from Ardudwy, Gwynedd; agent of the Commonwealth in Wales charged with dispossessing regular clergy. A prolific author, his *Llyfr y Tri Aderyn* (Book of the Three Birds) urged the Welsh people to prepare for Christ's return.

Llwyd, Richard (1752-1835): known as the Bard of Snowdon, poet and antiquary, with works on Welsh geneology and heraldry.

Llwyn Onn: *The Ash Grove;* popular melody published as a harp tune in 1802.

Llwyau Serch:(see Welsh Love Spoons).

Llyfr Tonnau Cynulleidfaol (Congregational Tune Book): edited by John Roberts (*Ieuan Gwyllt*) in 1859; the basic hymnbook for the Cymanfa Ganu (hymn-singing meeting) as an integral part of Welsh culture.

***Llyfrau Deunaw* (Eighteen Pence Books, 1948 to 1957)** a series published by University of Wales Press featuring contemporary Welsh writing.

***Llyfrau Pawb* (Everyone's Books, 1843-48):** a variety of cheap volumes of Welsh poetry and short stories.

Llyfrau'r Dryw (Wren's Books, 1940-52): a very popular series of books published by Aneurin Talfan Davies and his brother Alun on various subjects.

Llyfrau'r Ford Gron (Books of the Round Table 1931-2): twenty books with selections from Welsh classics published by Hughes a'i Fab.

Llygad Gwr (13th century): court poet whose praise of Llywelyn ap Gruffudd views Wales as a national entity, not an insignificant appendage of England.

Llyn Eigiau Dam (Dolgarrog, Gwynedd): in 1925, site of the last British dam to burst, killing sixteen local inhabitants.

Llyr: a character in the *Mabinogion*, written as *Leir* by Geoffrey of Monmouth and eventually as *Lear* by William Shakespeare.

Llysfasi (Denbighshire): home to the annual International Sheep Shearing Competition at Coleg Llysfasi, which specializes in agriculture and farm management. In the first Wool Handling competition (1997), Wales won Gold, Silver and Bronze.

Llywarch ap Llywelyn (1173-1220): a poet known as *Prydydd y Moch*, Poet of the Pigs) closely connected with praise of Llywelyn Fawr and the need for national unity under a strong leader.

Llywelyn ap Gruffudd (1225-1282): *Y Llyw Olaf* (The Last Ruler), grandson of Llywelyn Fawr, he united much of his country to assert his claim to be called "Prince of Wales" (officially recognized by Henry III in 1267 at the Treaty of Montgomery). At the accession to the English throne of Edward I in 1272, lacking significant support, Llywelyn was forced to accept humiliating terms and to give up most of his recently acquired lands. He then led his younger brother Dafydd's revolt against oppressive English rule. Separated from his army at Cilmeri, he was killed by an English knight unaware of the Welsh prince's identity. A poignant ballad by modern Welsh songwriter and nationalist Dafydd Iwan expresses the intense grief of the Welsh people: "Collir Llywelyn, colli'r cyfan" (losing Llewelyn is losing all).

Llywelyn ab Iorwerth, (1173-1240): the grandson of Owain Gwynedd, Llywelyn became ruler of the kingdom of Gwynedd in 1200; under his strong leadership, Wales was united as a single political unit. In 1204 he was recognised by King John of England, who gave him his daughter Joan in marriage. Known to posterity as Llywelyn Fawr (*Llywelyn the Great*), he was pre-eminent in Wales.

Llywelyn ap Rhisiart (Lewis Morgannwg: 1520-65): one of Glamorgan's great poets, the recognized head of the bardic order in mid 16th century Wales.

Llywelyn Bren: lord of Senghenydd who rebeled against Edward II in 1316 after the king had refused justice for the people of Wales. Llywelyn yielded rather than sacrifice his own men and was executed at Cardiff.

Llywelyn, Sion (1540-1615): poet and copyist whose transcriptions of early literature helped enormously in preserving priceless Welsh manuscripts.

Llywelyn-Williams, Alun (1913-1988): essayist, poet and critic, radio-producer and college professor.

Llwyd, Elfyn (b. 1951): from Betws y Coed, Gwynedd: M.P. since 1992 for Plaid Cymru, working with Home Affairs, Transport and Agriculture: he is the leader of Plaid Cymru's Parliamentary Group.

M

Sixteenth letter of the Welsh alphabet.

Mabinogion, the **(Pedair Cainc y Mabinogi, 11th century):** Wales's great contribution to medieval European literature, twelve anonymous tales named by Lady Charlotte Guest between 1838 and 1849. The original texts, dealing with the four "Cainc" (branches) of Pwyll, Pryderi, Branwen, and Manawydan are found in The *White Book of Rhyderch* and *The Red Book of Hergest.*

Mabon (Gwyl Canol Hydref): the Autumn Equinox; the festival of Mid-Autumn, during which the Green Man (the God of the Forest) is honoured.

Mabon: a Glamorgan based band that has toured the Continent, the USA, and Australia with their brand of Celtic music.

Mabon (1969-1976): a North Wales Arts Association magazine: an unsuccessful attempt to stimulate an interest in creative writing among young people.

Mabsant: a festival in honor of the patron saint of the local parish church that became secular by the early 19th century. It is also the name of a popular Welsh folk music group of the 1970's and 80's.

MacDonald, Julien (b. 1972): from Merthyr, trained as a dancer, but studied fashion design at Cardiff Art College to become a leading designer of knitwear at Chanel. His shows have become internationally famous for their creativity.

MacDonald, Tom (1900-80): novelist from Llandre, Cards; a journalist in China, Australia and S. Africa who wrote in Welsh and English.

Machen, Arthur (1863-1947): Caerleon-born actor, and journalist, author of *The Angel of Mons*, *The Great God Pan*, and other works.

Machynlleth, Merionethshire: the town where Owain Glyndwr created his first parliament in 1404, with parts of the original building remaining in the Old Court House. A major attraction is *Celtica*, an exhibition that tells the story of the Celtic inheritance of modern Wales. The Centre for Alternative Technology, is a microcosm of a modern world, using renewable energy sources of wind, water, solar energy and bio-fuels.

Mackworth, Humphrey (1637-1727): member of an influential family with mining and copper smelting at Neath, he was a founder member of S.P.C.K. in 1699.

Madog, Philip (b: 1934): from Merthyr, actor of stage, screen and television, known for his roles in *Last of the Mohicans* and *Dad's Army* on T.V.

Madocks, William Alexander (1773-11828): industrialist from Denbighshire who gave up a career in Parliament to develop the towns of Tremadoc and Porthmadog and to build the road from London to Holyhead, including the Cob embankment across the River Glaslyn. He died broke in Paris.

Madog ap Owain Gwynedd (or Madoc, 12th century): a legendary prince who sought lands away from the troubles of his native Wales. His eight ships led by the *Gwennan Gorn* reached what is now Mobile Bay, Alabama in 1169. He then returned for additional settlers. Sailing from Lundy Island in 1171, they were never heard from again. Tradition has it that the adventurers settled in the Mississippi Valley, being discovered at the time of the Revolutionary War as the Mandans of N. Dakota but decimated by smallpox in 1838 (see John Evans).

Madog ap Gruffuddd (d. 1236): the ruler of a region of northern Powys who founded the Cistercian Abbey at Valle Crucis, Llangollen.

Madog ap Maredudd (d. 1160): the last King of Powys who extended his boundaries during the reign of weak King Stephen of England, but allied himself to Henry II against Owain Gwynedd.

Maelgwn Gwynedd (Magloconus, 490-549 A.D.): the son of the king of Gwynedd (Cadwallon Lawhir) who was educated at Llanilltud Fawr before taking over the throne of Gwynedd to extend its influence through much of Britain. He was known as *Insularis Draco* (Dragon or High King of the Island).

Maelor: divided into Maelor Saesneg and Maelor Gymraeg; became detched parts of Flintshire in 1284 but now parts of Wrexham-Maelor in Clwyd.

Maen Achwyfan (Stone of Lamentation), Flintshire: a 10th or 11th century cross, named for St. Chwyfan, that stands in isolated splendor three miles from Holywell. The 12ft high cross is inscribed with crude Christian and pagan carvings. Locals say it commemorates a British victory over invading Saxons. In a nearby field, Queen Boadicea, fearing capture, committed suicide. Local legend has a treasure buried beneath the Cross protected by bolts of lightning.

Maen Ceti (*Arthur's Stone):* a cromlech in mid-Gower; the site of many legends concerning future husbands of the girls who must spend a night there.

Maen Llog, Y (the Logan Stone): from which the archdruid conducts the ceremony of the Gorsedd.

Maes Garmon (*Germanus Field*): near Mold, Flintshire: the site of the *Alleluia Victory* of 430 AD, when the native Britons, under Bishop Germanus, defeated the invading army of Saxon Pagans.

Magnus Maximus (335-388 A.D.): Romano-British political and military leader who may have built the foundations of the Welsh nation before leaving for the Continent after he had been proclaimed Emperor by his troops. Known to the Welsh people as Macsen Wledig, he has a place in legend in *The Dream of Macsen Wledig* second only to Arthur.

Magor, Gwent: a Norman church sits on an original site founded in the 7th century by Cadwaladr, the last Welsh prince to be King of Britain.

Mai: fifth month of the year (called May in English).

Maid of Iowa: the little ship captained by Dan Jones that carried many Welsh converts to Mormonism up the Mississippi River in the early 1840's.

Mainwaring, Evelyn (1916-2004): from Aberafan, she was known as the most famous fan in Welsh rugby, following Aberfan for 75 years; her son Billy played for Wales six times. She received an ovation during a game against Neath.

Malcolm, Christian (b. 1977): internationally known athlete, Chris became World Junior 100m and 200m Champion in 1998. In 1997 he had beaten Carl Lewis in a race at Zurich. On 26 Feb 2000, he won his first senior title.

Mamau: (see Tylwyth Teg or Welsh Fairies).

Manic Street Preachers: a rock band from Blackwood, Glam, their major label debut was 1992's *Generation Terrorists*. Guitarist and lyricist Richey Edwards disappeared in 1995. The trio then had a huge success with their 1996 *Everything Must Go* winning three major British awards. In 1999 they signed with *Virgin* in the U.S., and were the first major rock band to play in Cuba.

Manorbier, Pembrokeshire: birthplace of Geraldus Cambrensis.

Mansell, Admiral Sir Robert (1573-1656): b. Margam; explorer and adventurer, Treasurer of the Royal Navy, Vice-Admiral of the Realm and M.P. for various constituencies including Glamorgan.

Mantell Gwynedd (the Mantle of Gwynedd): an independent charity that supports and promotes voluntary and community groups and develops voluntary action in Gwynedd.

Marchia Wallia **(the Welsh Marches)**: a chain of lordships from Denbigh to Pembroke set up by William 1st to control the Welsh borders.

Maredudd ab Owain (935-999 A.D.): grandson of Hywel Dda, he ruled most of Wales during the time of the Danish invasions, helping preseve its unity to earn the title "Most praiseworthy king of the Britons."

Mari Lwyd (**or Lhwyd**): a horse head skull sheathed in white robes paraded in a survival of the cult of the horse goddess. Since the language revival of the 1960's, the custom, almost extinct, has been resurrected in many villages. The Mari Lwyd was originally known as Aderyn bec y Llwyd "Bird with the grey beak."

Marley, Bob (1945-81): highly influential Jamaican rock musician, Rastafarian and pioneer of Reggae, son of a Welsh army officer and plantation manager.

Math: a Celtic deity, "the Guardian of the Center," representing the power of pure consciousness.

Mathew, David (1902-76): prolific historian and novelist, Bishop Auxiliary at Westminster and Catholic Archbishop of Apamea in Ethiopia.

Mathews, Abraham (1832-99): from Llanidloes, a minister at Aberdare; he went with the first settlers to Patagonia where he wrote its early history.

Mathias, Roland (b. 1915): b. Talybont-on-Usk: poet, editor and critic, headmaster at Pembroke Dock for ten years; a member of the Welsh Arts Councils' Literature Committeee and *Yr Academi Gymreig*; editor of *Dock Leaves* from 1961-1976; an extensive contributor to Anglo-Welsh literature.

Mathias, Tom (1866-192?): born near Cilgerran, a self-taught photographer, in a 40-year career documenting the lives and people of his time.

Mathias, William (1934-1992): from Whitland, Carmarthenshire, a noted composer and pianist. Educated at Bangor and R.A. M, was a lecturer at Bangor University College, later Head of Music Dept; curtailed by illness, he composed in virtually all the musical genres. In 1972 he founded and directed the North Wales Music Festival at St. Asaph.

Mathrafal: important church and principal court of the rulers of Powys, near Meifod (the site of the 2003 National Eisteddfod of Wales).

Matter of Britain, The: one of the three main categories of medieval French literature based on Celtic or Welsh traditions of the Arthurian period.

Matthews, Sir Terry (b. 1943): from Newbridge, Gwent; contemporary businessman who began a career with British Telecom; chairman and chief executive of March Networks Corporation, the world's leading supplier of ATM technology; co-founder of Mital Networks Corporation; Fellow of the Institute of Electrical Engineers, University of Wales. He created the huge hotel and golf complex at Celtic Manor, Newport; knighted in 2001.

Mawrth: third month of the year known in English as March; also the third day of the week (Tuesday).

McBride, Robin (b. 1970): b. Bangor, he is one of the few North Walians to play first class rugby, moving from Mold, to Swansea and Llanelli, which he captained in 1998 and 1999 to win championships.

McKinley Tariff (1891): passed by the U.S. Government to boost American industries, ending its dependence on Welsh tinplate, creating depression in areas of Wales that produced it.

McCready, William: playhouse manager who satisfied the local taste for spectacle and melodrama at the Swansea Theatre from 1819 to 1829.

Medi: ninth month of the year known in English as September; it is also the Welsh for *harvest*.

Meddwl Modern, The (*Modern Thought*, f. 1980): a series of monographs on great thinkers and writers of the modern world published by Gwasg Gee.

Medrod (Mordred or Medraut): the betrayer of Arthur who fell with him at the Battle of Camlan.

Mehefin: sixth month of the year (June in English).

Meibion Glyndwr (Sons of Glyndwr): a Nationalist group that carried out arson attacks against English-owned holiday cottages in Wales in the 1980's (always when the house was empty).

Meifod, Vale of (Powys): seat of the Princes of Powys for centuries. William Penn worshipped at Dolobran, a small Quaker Meeting House.

Meilir Brydydd (1100-37): one of the early poets and chief poet to Gruffudd ap Cynan who began a bardic revival in Gwynedd.

Meirionydd (Merioneth): N. Wales county created along with Anglesey and Caernarfon by the Statute of Rhuddlan in 1284; part of Gwynedd 1974 to 1996.

Meistri'r Canrifoedd (Masters of the Centuries, 1973): a volume of 37 essays by Saunders Lewis on the history of Welsh literature.

Melangell (6th C.): patron saint of all small creatures, a princess in Welsh folk tales who sheltered a hare.

Menai Bridge, Gwynedd: Telford's magnificent suspension bridge (1826) to connect the island of Anglesey with the mainland (to allow Irish M.P.'s to reach London). Ship owners insisted on a height of 100 feet at high tide.

Merchant, Moelwyn (b. 1913): b. Port Talbot: a poet and critic, lecturer at Cardiff, Professor at University of Exeter; vicar of Llanddewibrefi; author of critical studies and essays, and libretti for Alun Hoddinott's operas.

Merched y Gerddi (The Girls of the Garden, 18th-19th C.): girls from Mid-Wales who walked to London to find work in the public gardens.

Merched y Wawr (Daughter of the Dawn, f. 1967): founded after the National Federation of Women's Institutes had refused to allow the official use of Welsh at Parc, Near Bala. It publishes *Y Wawr* and has many branches.

Meredith, Billy "Old Skinny" (b. 1884): "the Welsh Wizard". From Chirk, Billy went to City from Wrexham, working in the mines and playing the next day. He won 48 caps for Wales, including the day they beat England for the first time when he was 48 years old.

Merfyn Frych (790-844 A.D.): King of Gwynedd who resisted the English of Mercia and who began a cultural revival in Wales that brought about the flowering of poetry, history, and religious works.

Merlin (Myrddyn): the magician or seer of Welsh legend that had him fleeing to Celyddon Wood after a battle to live as a wild man and receive the gift of prophecy. The tale is retold in *Vitae Merlini* and *Historia Regum Britanniae* by Geoffrey of Monmouth and in ancient poetry where he is a chief character in the *Arthuriana*. He is also found in "Armes Prydain" in *The Book of Taliesin*.

Merthyr Tydful: By 1831, the former pastoral oasis, was the center of the Welsh iron industry, its population the largest of any town in Wales, its furnaces, forges and factories blackening the hillsides. John Guest began at Dowlais in 1759, quickly followed by Crawshay at Cyfarthfa, and Homfray at Penydarren. Composer Joseph Parry is honored here as well as Robert and Lucy Thomas, pioneers in the export of South Wales steam coal. The Ynysfach Iron Heritage Center tells the story of the town's industrial history.

Merthyr Rising, the (1831): revolt led by Thomas Llewelyn, a Cyfarthfa miner protesting low wages, poor working conditions, and seeking parliamentary reform, The marchers raised the red flag of rebellion, on its staff a loaf of bread, but were shattered by a volley of rifle fire from soldiers waiting at the Castle Inn (see Dic Penderyn).

Methodist Revival (18th century): a cultural phenomenon that helped change the face of Wales sparked by the religious vision of Hywel Harris in 1735 and other religious leaders including Daniel Rowlands and William Williams.

Metoka, the: the little ship that took the first Welsh Mormons from Liverpool to the U.S. in September, 1843.

Meyrick, Robert K. (b. 1958): from Ogmore Vale, Glamorgan, senior lecturer and Keeper of Art at the University of Wales, Aberystwyth with a career as educator, researcher, writer, artist and innovator.

Miles, Gareth (b. 1938): b. Caernarfon, short story writer; Organizer of the Teacher's Union who helped write the manifesto of the Welsh Republican Movement, *Socialism for the Welsh People* (1980).

Miles, John (1621-83): set up the first Baptist church in Wales in 1649 at Ilston, Gower. He founded Swanzey, Massachusetts in 1663.

Milland, Raymond (Reginald Truscott Jones, 1907-1986): b. Neath; actor and film-director took his stage name from the flat Mill land around Neath. After service with the British army, his first English film was *The Flying Scotsman* (1929). One of Hollywood's most versatile actors, he won an Oscar for *The Lost Weekend* (1945): his baldness came from hot curling irons used on his hair in *Reap the Wild Wind* (1946).

Millenium Falcon: a full-scale model of the spaceship from the original *Star Wars* trilogy that was built in a hanger at the Royal Dockyard, Milford Haven, Pembs, in 1979 under the code name "Magic Roundabout."

Millenium Stadium, Cardiff: one of the most spectacular sports stadiums in the world, with its retractable roof. Seating 75,000, it was completed just in time to host the Rugby World Cup in 1999 and after Wembley's demolition, for various English cup finals and Welsh soccer and rugby internationals.

Mills, Dr. Donald (d. 2003): b. Llanelli, Don moved to Canada in 1961 to work for the National Research Council in Ottawa to join Terry Matthews at Mitel. A major contributor to Welsh life in Canada, Don was president of the WNGGGA from 190-92, President of the Ontario Gymanfa Ganu Asociation 1978-1980, and President of the Ottawa Welsh Society and the Ottawa Welsh Choral Society.

Mills, John (Ieuan Glan Alarch, 1812-73): from Llandidloes, a musician whose numerous books greatly improved the common people's knowledge of music and singing. He also wrote books on Britain's Jews.

Mills, Robert Scourfield (Arthur Owen Vaughan), 1863-1909): Anglo-Welsh writer brought up at Tremeirchion, Flints, cavalry commander in the Boer War, wrote stories for boys and novels; *Flamebearers of Welsh History* (1905).

Mimosa, the: ship that took 200 Welsh people from Liverpool in May, 1865 to begin life in Patagonia.

Miners' Federation of Great Britain (1889): founded in Newport, Gwent; it argued for the creation of a Board of Arbitration to replace the Sliding Scale and to restrict the working day to eight hours. Its activities were to dominate life in the five great industrial Valleys of South Wales.

Minogue, Kylie (b. 1968): sensational pop star from Australia, her mother was from Maesteg, and her grandmother came from Blaenau Ffestiniog.

Mistar Urdd: the green, red, and white mascot of the Urdd Gobaith Cymru.

Mitchinson, Maureen Guy: b. Penclawdd, Swansea, has achieved worldwide renown as a mezzo soprano, including principal roles with the the Royal Opera, Covent Garden, the Frankfort Opera; and many of the world's concert halls.

Mochyn Du, Y (The Black Pig, 1854): a well known ballad written by a farm servant, John Owen but sung mockingly about Crawshay Bailey's engine.

Modern Welsh Poetry (1944): an anthology of Anglo-Welsh poets edited by Keidrych Rhys.

Mold (*Y Wyddgrug*), Flintshire: the county town and administrative and marketing center for Clwyd. Theatre Clwyd presents Welsh and English language films and plays. Nearby Maes Garmon saw an important victory for the native Welsh against an army of invading Pagans in 430 A.D.

Monmouth (*Sir Fynwy*): strategically situated at the confluence of the Monow and Wye Rivers, the town was the birthplace of Henry V. The town possesses a rare 13th Century fortified bridge over the River Monnow. The County, known in Welsh as Gwent, was created out of the old marcher lordships in 1536, but was made driectedly answerable to the Courts of Westminster and not part of the Great Sessions of Wales. It has very few Welsh speakers though 62 percent of its population is Welsh born.

Monmouthshire and Brecon Canal: two canals, one from Newport to Pontnewydd opened in 1796; the other from from Brecon to Newport (the Brecknock and Abergavenny Canal) opened in 1812; in use up to 1938.

Monmouthshire and S. Wales Coal Owner's Association: companies owning over 200 mines who formed a united front against the unions in 1877; it set up the 'sliding scale" tying wage levels to the selling price of coal.

***Montgomery, the Treaty of,* 1267:** after Llywelyn ap Gruffudd's alliance with Simon de Montfort, he was recognized as Prince of Wales by King Henry lll.

Montgomery (*Drefaldwyn*): mid-Wales county created out of the Marcher lordships in 1536. From 1974 to 1996, it was part of the new county of Powys.

Morgan, Barry Cennydd ((b. 1946): from the Neath area, Bishop of Llandaf and former Bishop of Bangor, who became the Archbishop of Wales in 2003 succeeding Rowan Williams who moved to Canterbury.

Morgan, Captain Henry (1635-1688): born at Llanrhymny, famous buccaneer of the Golden Age of Piracy. After thwarting Spanish attempts to capture Jamaica, he was knighted by Charles II, who made him Deputy Governor of the island.

Morgan, Cliff (b. 1930): from Trebanog, played in 29 rugby internationals,. Editor of *Rugby: the Greats*. In 1958, joined BBC as Sports Organizer for Wales; edited *Sportsview,* later becoming Head of Outside Broadcasting for BBC TV. In 1997, inducted into the International Rugby Hall of Fame.

Morgan, Daniel (1756-1802): son of a Welsh iron master in New Jersey, Brigadier General Daniel defeated a British force at Cowpens, N.C. in January, 1781. He later helped suppress the Whiskey Rebellion and served as U.S. Congressman.

Morgan, Derec Llwyd (b. 1943): b. Carmarthenshire; an accomplished author and eisteddfodwr and critic, senior lecturer at Aberystwyth and Bangor; has written on Welsh authors, the history of Methodism and collections of poems; a frequent broadcaster, Chairman of the Council of the National Eisteddfod (1979-82), currently Senior Vice-Chancellor of the University of Wales.

Morgan, Dyfnallt (b. 1917): b. Dowlais, Merthyr, a writer, critic and translator and BBC producer who taught at Bangor University; has written verse, literary criticism, and translated plays into Welsh.

Morgan, Elaine (b. 1920): b. Pontypridd, known for her controversial theories of evolution as expressed in such books as *Descent of Woman* (1972), *The Aquatic Ape* (1982) and others.

Morgan, Eluned (1870-1938): born on a voyage to Patagonia, Elunded became a leading figure in the cultural and religious life of Wladfa (the Colony).

Morgan, Enoch (1676-1740): minister at Welsh Tract Church, Delaware, he published the second Welsh language book in the USA (*Cyd-gordiad Egwyddorawl o'r Scrythrau)* in 1730 (written by his brother Abel).

Morgan, George Osborne (1820-97): born in Sweden, educated at Bangor; lawyer and Liberal M.P. in 1868 for East Denbigh who ended the Wynn hegemony after 160 years. He became Judge Advocate-General and Parliamentary Under-Secretary for the Colonies. In 1880, he secured the Burials Act, allowing Nonconformist to perform burials with their own form of service; he strongly supported the Welsh Sunday Closing Act of 1881 (which recognized Wales as a separate entity), and he helped Hugh Owen promoted the idea of a National University for Wales.

Morgan, Gerald (b. 1935): b. Sussex of Welsh parents, learned Welsh at Jesus College, Oxford; tutor-librarion at Aberystwyth University then head of Llangefni School, then Ysgol Penweddig, Aberystwyth; has many books to his credit.

Morgan, Griffith (see Guto Nyth Bran).

Morgan, Helen (b. 1952): from Barry, as Miss Wales she won Miss World title in 1974 but was stripped of her title after four days when it was disclosed she had an 18 month old son. Helen kept her Miss Wales title, returning from Spain in 2004 to judge the Miss Wales contest.

Morgan, John Rhys (1760-1804): from the Rhymney Valley, a Baptist minister who, inspired by the French Revolution, campaigned vigorously throughout Wales for political and religious freedom. Moving to the United States, he founded a company to establish a Welsh colony Cambria in Ohio.

Morgan, Kenneth Owen (Baron Morgan of Aberdovey, b. 1934): Professor and later Principal, University of Wales, Aberystwyth 1989-95: senior vice chancellor, 1985-89; has a distinguished career in education and college administrator in Wales and abroad with over 50 works on British and Welsh history and society. He was elected a Fellow of the British Academy in 1983.

Morgan, Morgan: founder of the first permanent European settlement in West Virginia, at Mill Creek in 1731. Coal was discovered there in 1742.

Morgan, Sir Morien Bedford (1912-1978): from Bridgend, Fellow of the Royal Society, played a pioneering role in in the world of aerodynamics. After serving an apprenticeship at Vickers Aviation, he saw through countless engineering projects, including the development of the Concorde.

Morgan, Prys (b. 1937): b. Cardiff, a prolific writer, broadcaster and editor with many published works.

Morgan, Rhodri (b.1939): Cardiff-born Rhodri is back in the capital city as First Minister for the National Assembly of Wales after serving in Westminster as Labour M.P. for Cardiff West (1979-2000). Educated at Oxford and Harvard, Welsh-speaking Rhodri served as Economic Development Secretary for the Assembly (1999-2000).

Morgan, Richard (d. 1918): the last British service man to die in W.W.I (serving on *HMS Garland*). On Armistice Day, November 11th, 1918, Seaman Morgan joined 40,000 Welshman who died in the war.

Morgan, Richard William (1815-1887): Llangynfelyn, Cardiganshire, clergyman and leading figure in eisteddfodau and the Gorsedd; wrote many books on Wales and the Church.

Morgan, Robert Erwyn (Erwyn, 1929-1999): born in U.S. raised in Usk, after a distinguished career at the University of Alabama. In 1970, he was admitted to the *Gorsedd* for his tireless work on behalf of Wales and Welsh Americans. He served as vice-president of the Honorable Society of the Cymmrodorion; received the Hopkins Medal from the St. David's Society of New York; and helped found the annual Welsh Academic Conference that began at Rio Grande. Dr. Morgan also helped establish a medical school at Benin, Nigeria. He was particularly proud of his work with the fledgling W.D.A. on programs to benefit the future of Wales.

Morgan, Thomas (1542-95): b. Pencarn, Mon., known as *The Warrior*, he fought in the Netherlands, served as Governor of Flushing and Bergen-op-Zoom; instructed British soldiers in the use of the musket.

Morgan, Thomas, (1604-79)): b. Llangattock, Mon., known as *The Dwarf,* a soldier on the Continent and in the service of Parliament against the Crown before becoming Governor of Jersey (Channel Islands).

Morgan, Thomas John (b. 1907): from Glais, Cardiff; Registrar at University of Wales in 1951; then Professor of Welsh Language and Literature at Swansea with important works of scholarship and authoritative studies of Welsh.

Morgan, William (1545-1604): vicar of Llanrhaeadr-ym-Mochnant, later Bishop of Llandaff and St. Asaph whose unmatched scholarship chose him to complete the work begun by William Salesbury to bring the whole scriptures to the Welsh people in their own language. His Bible of 1588 and later editions were of enormous influence on the future of Welsh literature and language (see entry for Welsh Bible).

Morgan le Fay: a fairy enchantress who ruled Avalon where she helped heal King Arthur's wounds. Her feats exemplified in Continental literature, she is remembered in Sicily in the Fata Morgana mirage.

Morgans, John O. (1915-2003): b. Cilrhedyn, Carmarthen; began as newspaper career with *Cardigan and Towy-Side Advertiser*, then with Gregynog Press before serving in W.W.II. Jones then moved to Toronto, later Boston and New York to become a leading figure in Welsh-American activities for 50 years.

Morgannwg: the medieval name for Glamorgan.

Moris, Carey (1882-1968): from Llandeilo, painter and survivor of gassing in the trenches of World War I whose most famous work is "Welsh Weavers" showing the Edwards family of Rhosmaen.

Mormon Tabernacle Choir: after their arrival at Salt Lake City in 1847, Welsh pioneers began a choir under conductor John Parry. The first performance took place on August 22, 1847. Other choirs at Provo, under James Daniels, and the Deseret Philharmonic Society, under John M. Jones, soon augmented the Tabernacle Choir that became an American national institution by 1890 under the leadership of Evan Stephens, from Pencader.

Morris, Andrew (b. 1962): from Abergavenny, Professor at the University of Houston, Texas, who is working on a vaccine to cure viral diarrhoea, a disease that kills millions of children each year in undeveloped countries of the world.

Morris, Billy (1918-2003): soccer star with Burnley and Wales; served with Royal Welch Fusiliers in World War Two; played in F.A. Cup Final against Charleton in 1947; then managed Wrexham.

Morris, Jan (b. 1926): born Somerset, resident of Wales, and a committed Welsh nationalist; before a sex change was a military intelligence officer who became a newspaper journalist (first to report on the British ascent of Everest in 1953), and critically-acclaimed author of *Pax Britannica, Our First Leader*, and *The Matter of Wales* among countless others. Jan is a member of the Gorsedd.

Morris, Lewis (1701-65): Anglesey-born cartographer and mapmaker whose *Tlysau yr hen Oesoedd* (Treasure of the Ancient Ages), published in 1717, was the first Welsh periodical most influential in the study of the history of Wales.

Morris, Margaret (1776-1885): from Tanrallt, Taliesin; still in charge of her faculties at aged 108, she was considered something of an oracle and authority on local history.

Morris, Roy (b. 1938): deserving of mention is this gentleman from Monmouth who caught a record-breaking 33lb salmon in the Wye (March, 2004).

Morris-Jones, John (1864-1929): born Trefor, Anglesey, a founder member of Gymdeithas Dafydd ap Gwilym in 1886; Professor of Welsh at Bangor in 1895: published many books to help set studies of the Welsh language and literature on a firm academic foundation and had a great influence on the development of Welsh poetry in the early part of the 20th Century.

Morys, Huw (Eos Ceiriog, 1622-1709): "the Ceiriog Nightingale," a most prolific and gifted Welsh poet who founded a new school of poets.

Morys, Twm (b. 1961): Welsh language poet and essayist, using the sounds and rhythm of cynghanedd.

Mostyn, Flints: the Hall is home to the family who dominated the political and social scene of Flintshire for many centuries. It keeps a place at the table for the return of Prince Henry (later Henry VII) who jumped through a window to escape capture by Richard lll's forces. The Mostyn Manuscripts are an important source for scholars of Welsh history. The Point of Ayr Colliery, known as *Parlwr Du* (the Black Parlour) closed in the early 1990's.

Mudiad Ysgol Meithrin (Nursery School Movement (f. 1971): a movement that grew out of the nursery school begun in 1943 at Aberystwyth when Sir Ifan ab Owen Edwards opened a nursery class to educate the younger children of Wales through the medium of the Welsh language. One year later, parents at Cardiff followed suit at Ty'r Cymry. Enlisting the aid of English-only families, the first Yssgol Meithrin opened at Barry in 1951.

 **Mumbles and Oystermouth Railway (f.1804):** brought to an untimely end in 1960 by Swansea Council (who had sold it to a bus company) the world's first passenger railway, accepting passengers in its horse-drawn carriages as early as 1807 (it had begun three years earlier, carrying mineral ores to Swanse Docks. Part of the last tram is in the Swansea Transport Museum located at the restored dock area.

Murray the Hump: popular Welsh rock band founded 1997 in Aberystwyth, named after Llewelyn Morris Humphreys, of Welsh parents, a close confidant of Al Capone (see separate entry).

Murphy, Paul (b. 1948): Usk-born, M.P. for Torfaen since 1987, holding many influential posts in Parliament. Secretary of State for Wales 1999-2002; then Secretary of State for Ireland.

Myddfai, The Physicians of (see Physicians of Myddfai)

Myddleton family, The: owners of Chirk Castle, Denbs., influential in North Wales politics for centuries. The family vacated the castle in 2004 due to lack of privacy from the many tourists.

Myddleton, Sir Hugh (1559-1643): b. Denbigh; son of Sir Richard, governor of Denbigh Castle, he became a successful London goldsmith and is ceredited with contruction of the New River scheme to supply the city with fresh water.

Mynydd Newydd Colliery, Swansea: services were held here hundreds of feet underground in chapels hewn out of solid coal from 1843 to 1929.

Mytton, John (1796-1834): as M.P. for Shrewsbury (attended Parliament for 30 minutes) he inherited a huge estate at Dinas Mawddwy, where he paid local children to roll down the mountain.

N

Seventeenth letter of the Welsh alphabet.

Nadolig (*Christmas*): celebration of Christ's birth celebrated on December 25th. In Wales, an old custom was to worship by candlelight through the night or early dawn on Christmas Eve (see Plygain).

Nanmor, Dafydd (1450-80): a master of the poetic form *cywydd* whose praise of the Anglesey Tudors helped make the family popular in most of Wales.

Nant Eos (*Stream of the Nightingale*), Aberystwyth: a mansion where Wagner may have stayed to work on his opera *Parsival* inspired by the local legend that an ancient wooden cup is a Holy Grail, a replica of the cup used at the Last Supper once kept at Strata Florida (now kept in a secret location).

Nant Gwrtheyrn, Gwynedd: a quarrying village near Llythfaen, abandoned in the 1950's but restored in the 1970's as the National Welsh Language Centre.

Nash, Richard (Beau) 1674-1761): b. Swansea, educated at Carmarthen and Oxford; moved to Bath in 1705 to set up the Assembly Rooms, and greatly influencing society manners, helping Bath to become a center of fashion and a fashionable resort.

Nash, Malcolm: the unfortunate bowler for Glamorgan Cricket off whom Gary Sobers scored six consecutive sixes in a single over on August 31, 1968.

Nash-Williams, Victor Erle (1897-1955): b. Mon.; became Keeper of Archaeology at the National Museum of Wales in 1926; made many contributions to learned journals and two major works on early Wales.

National Assembly for Wales (Cynulliad Cenedlaethol Cymru): a quasi-parliament that came into being as a result of the referendum of September 20, 1997. The Government of Wales Act established the National Assembly for Wales, enabling the transfer of the devolved powers and responsibilities from the Secretary of State for Wales to the Assembly to take place on 1 July, 1999. A directly elected body responsible for government policies and public services in Wales, it has secondary powers, linked to Westminster through the Secretary of State for Wales. Of its 60 members, 40 are directly elected, and 20 by proportional representation. The five electoral regions return four Members each. Housed in Cardiff, it depends on Westminster for funding, but is allowed to decide on its priorities and allocation of funds.

National Botanic Garden of Wales (Llanarthne, near Carmarthen): one of the world's great botanical gardens, created in a former 18th century regency park of Middleton Hall, with a blend of scientific education and artistic beauty. Its great Glasshouse is 100 metres long, 60 metres wide.

National Council for Education and Training for Wales (b. 2001): the largest National Assembly-sponsored public body in Wales designed to secure, fund, promote, and widen access to post sixteen education and training in Wales.

National Library of Wales (Llyfrgell Genedlaethol Cymru, Aberystwyth, f. 1907): based mainly on the collection of Sir John Williams, created through public donations and government funds (It certainly helped that the Chancellor of the Exchequer was David Lloyd George at the time). Its collections include all material relating to Wales and other Celtic countries.

National Museum of Wales (f. 1922): Cardiff; one of the largest and finest museums in Britain, it has six departments: archeology and numismatics, art, botany, geology, industry, and zoology.

National Welsh American Foundation (N.W.A.F.): a non-profit membership organization (f. 1980) with officers in the U.S. and Wales to promote knowledge of Wales, to provide scholarships and financial assistance to Welsh American or Welsh individuals, and to groups and organizations, including the National Eisteddfod of Wales, and to co-ordinate activities of Welsh Americans. Its annual award is given to an outstanding Welsh American.

National Welsh Centre for Children's Literature, (f. 1979): an important collection of Welsh books (in Welsh and English), manuscripts, magazines and audio-visual material at Aberystwyth.

Nationalist, The **(1907-1912):** a literary magazine written in defence of Wales.

Neath (S. Wales West Electoral Region): parliamentary constituency in West Glamorgan including Neath and the Upper Swansea Valley.

Neath Port Talbot (*Sirol Castell-Nedd Poet Talbot*): blackened Neath Abbey shows centuries of heavy industry. Cefn Coed Colliery was the world's deepest anthracite mine.

Needs, Chris (b. 1954): from Cwmafon, Port Talbot; one of Wales's best loved radio presenters, actor in *Pobol y Cwm* (the Welsh soap opera); the host of the late night show on Radio Wales and a Garden Club.

Nennius (9th Century): monk who compiled *Historia Brittonum*, the source of most the nation's early history, including *Arthuriana*.

Nest (1080-1145): daughter of the Lord Rhys, seduced by Prince Henry to produce Henry, Duke of Gloucester, she married the Norman Earl of Pembroke. Widowed, she married Stephen of Cardigan, to sire Robert Fitzstephen, one of the conquerors of Ireland. After his exile, she married the Sheriff of Pembroke. Many of her illustrious offspring became known as "the race of Nest." She was grandmother to Geraldus Cambrensis.

Nevern (Nanhyfer) **Pembrokeshire**: at St. Brynach's Church the first cuckoo of spring is reputed to sing from the top of the 13ft high Celtic cross. In the church, named for a 5th century Irish saint, ancient memorial stones include one inscribed in Latin and Ogham.

Newcastle Emlyn (*Castell Newydd Emlyn, Ceredigion***):** a little town where the very first book printed in the Welsh language appeared in 1719. The Museum of the Welsh Woollen Industry is at nearby Drefach Felindre.

Newport (*Sirol Casnewydd***):** the third largest city in Wales, home to St. Woolos Cathedral, Westgate Square, and a unique transporter bridge.

Newport Rising, the **(Nov 4,1839)**: about 5,000 men and women marched to Westgate Square, where soldiers inside the hotel opened fire, leaving over a score dead and many more wounded. The Chartist leaders, including John Frost, were sentenced to death, but their sentences were commuted to life in Tasmania. A group of statuary commemorates the affair.

Newtown, Montgomershire: former center of a huge woolen and flannel industry; home of Price Jones

Warehouse, the world's first mail order store; the birthplace of Robert Owen, socialist reformer and founder of the co-operative movement; a textile museum; and Owain Glyndwr's Parliament House, brought from Dolgellau.

New Wales: the name proposed by William Penn for his colony that later became Pennsylvania.

New South Wales: the first British colony in Australia named by Capt. James Cook in 1770 (his ship's surgeon was Welshman David Samwell).

Nichol, William (d. 1558): from Haverfordest, one of the three Protestant martyrs burned in Wales during the reign of Mary Tudor.

Nicholls, Gwyn (1874-1939): captained Cardiff and Wales in rugby, including the victory over New Zealand in 1905, the only Welsh player in the British team to tour Australia in 1899.

Nicholas, James (b. 1928): poet from St. David's, Pembs; teacher and headmaster, published volumes of verse; Archdruid, 1981-84.

Nicholas, Jemima (1750-1832): a Fishguard lady who captured 14 French soldiers with her trusty pitchfork during the last invasion of mainland Britain.

Nicholas, Thomas Evan (Niclas y Glais, 1878-1971): b. Llanfyrnach, Pembs; prolific poet, ordained minister, and eloquent spokesman for the Labour Party in the Welsh language; editor of *The Merthyr Pioneer*, lectured on the Soviet Union as a political journalist.

Nicholas, William Rhys (1914-1996): poet and hymn-writer whose most famous hymn is *Pantyfedwen,* composed in 1967 for an eisteddfod at Lampeter.

Nine Three **(1972):** the title of a poem by Max Boyce to celebrate Llanelli rugby's win over New Zealand.

Ninnau: (founded in New Jersey in 1975 by Arturo Roberts), a North American Welsh newspaper that combined with *Y Drych* in 2003. It includes news of events in Wales as well as the U.S.

Noble, Roy (b. 1942): b. Brynamman; entertainer; joined BBC Radio Wales presenting *Letters from Aberdare.* The daily *Roy Noble Sho*w earned him a Sony Award in 1999; well known for presenting programs in English and Welsh, he co-presented *Heno* from 1994-2001; awarded O.B.E. in 2001.

Nod Cyfrin, Y (The Mystic Mark): symbol devised by Iolo Morganwg to represent Love, Justice and Truth. Also known as *Nodyn Pelydr Goleun,* "the mark of the shaft of light," it is used in the ceremonies and the regalia of the Gorsedd.

Non: the mother of St. David, buried in Brittany, but whose Chapel and Well at St. David's, in Pembrokeshire still attract pilgrims. The well is found in a meadow near the cathedral.

Norris, Leslie (b. 1921): b. Merthyr Tydfil, a former teacher, headmaster and college lecturer, has published nine volumes of poetry beginning in 1941. He made a second home in Carmarthenshire, of which he writes with passion as well as melancholy for his native Merthyr. He has been a professor at many universities in the United Sates, including University of Washington in Seattle and Brigham Young in Utah.

North American Association for the Study of Welsh Culture and History (NAASWCH, f. 1995) founded to advance scholarship on Welsh studies, support the study of Welsh culture and foster bonds between scholars, teachers, and the Welsh-American community. It holds a bi-annual conference and publishes the *North American Journal of Welsh Studies*.

***North Wales Gazette, The (1808-25)*:** a Bangor weekly with articles on Welsh history and Welsh affairs, succeeded by *The North Wales Chronicle*.

North Wales Newpapers Ltd: owned by the Thomas family for generations, its flagship paper is the *Evening Leader* (Wrexham, Chester, Deeside, and Rhyl). Supported by the *Chronicle* (Ynys Mon, Bangor,

Gwynedd and Colwyn Bay). The company also owns Radio Ceredigion.

Norton's Coin: Carmarthenshire-trained horse that caused one of the biggest upsets in racing history on March 15, 1990, by winning the Cheltenham Gold Cup at 100-1, entered by his owner who had forgotten to put him in a race the day before.

Nos Galan Gaeaf (*All Hallow's Eve*): the ancient Celtic New Year's Eve when spirits walk abroad. On gates or entrances to footpaths, ghosts appear at midnight.

Noson Lawen (*Merry Evening*): held to celebrate the hay harvest, always a big event. Festivities included penillion (reciting of verses) to the sound of the harp, dancing, and recitation. It gives a chance to show one's talents in village halls throughout Wales and keeps pace with the local Eisteddfod as a living reminder of an old cultural tradition.

Novello, Ivor (David Ivor Davies, 1893-1951): popular actor in many early movies, but best remembered as a song writer and creator of musicals (he wrote eight between 1935 and 1951), including *The Dancing Years* (1939), and *King's Rhapsody* (1949). His most famous songs are "We'll Gather Lilacs," and "Keep the Home Fires Burning."

O

Eighteenth letter of the Welsh alphabet

Offa's Dyke: a mid-8th century earthen barrier constructed by Mercian king Offa to divide the Welsh to the west from the Saxons to the east. It extended the earlier *Wat's Dyke*, built on the old Roman boundary known as *Gaual*. The newer Dyke ran 150 miles, from Prestatyn on the Irish Sea to Sedbury on the Bristol Channel; much of it is now a hiking trail.

Old Man of Pencader, Prophecy of (1163): recorded by Giraldus Cambrensis, supposed to have been spoken to Henry ll, a king who was determined to "tame the wild Welsh. It reads: "This nation, O King, may now, as in former times, be harassed, and in a great measure weakened and destroyed by your and other powers, and it will also prevail by its laudable exertions, but it can never be totally subdued through the wrath of man unless the wrath of God shall concur. Nor do I think that any other nation than this of Wales, or any other language whatever may hereafter come to pass, shall on the day of severe examination before the Supreme Judge answer for this corner of the earth."

O'Neill, Dennis (b. 1948): operatic tenor born at Pontarddulais, Swansea Valley, early eisteddfod winner, has sung in the greatest opera houses, specializing in Italian roles; has been named one of the world's six best tenors.

Ormond, John (b. 1923): b. Dunvant, Swansea; post-war poet writing in the English language; joined *Picture Post* in 1945, returning to Wales to begina distinguished career with BBC Wales ad director and producer of documentaries. His first major volume of poetry was *Requiem and Celebration* (1969) followed by *Definition of a Waterfall,* (1973).

Osborne Family: from Ogden, Utah (the state with the highest percentage of citizens of Welsh descent): a musical group that became an American institution in the 1970's; they are directed descendents of John Davies and Elizbeth Landark of Llantwit Major and make much of their Welsh heritage.

O'Shea, Tessie (*Two-Ton Tessie*, 1918-1995): Cardiff-born, with an infectious laugh: much loved star of stage and screen in the U.K. and the U.S. with her trademark ukelele.

Oswestry, (*Croeswallt*) Shropshire: east of Offa's Dyke, yet very Welsh in character, for many years the home of *Y Cymro*, the Welsh-language weekly.

Ottowa Welsh Society (f. 1988): one of the most active in Canada with an annual St. David's Day Dinner, Cymanfa Ganu, Noson Lawen, that supports Welsh cultural events and language classes.

Overton Yew Trees, Wrexham Maelor: located at St. Maryís Church, Overton, some of the 21 yews are said to date to the 12th century, when the first stone church was built. They are included in the so-called *Seven Wonders of Wales*, perhaps because the yew tree furnished bows for the Welsh archers who helped win the battles at Agincourt and Crecy.

Owain Gwynedd (1100-1170): ascended to the throne of Gwynedd in 1137 to rule for 33 years; he defeated the armies of Henry ll. His stature is indicated by his title, *Princeps Wallensium.*

Owain Gwynedd (1545-1601): one of the last of the Poets of the Gentry; he graduated as master-poet at the Caerwys Eisteddfod of 1567.

Owain Lawgoch (*Owain of the Red Hand*): a brave, skilled soldier who fought for France against the English; hailed by the Welsh poets as a deliverer. Betrayed and killed in 1378, his legends inspired Owain Glyndwr.

Owen, Alun (1925-1994): actor and screen play writer (including the script of the Beatles' hit *A Hard Day's Night*) who acted in many BBC television programs.

Owen, Daniel (1836-95): from Mold, Flintshire, Welsh-language novelist. Though perhaps poorly constructed, his novels show skill in the observation of society and character.

An Alphabetical Guide to Wales and the Welsh

Owen, Goronwy (1723-69): a poet who revived the study of ancient Welsh traditions, he came to William and Mary College, Virginia in 1757.

Owen, Sir Hugh (1804-81): a pioneer of education whose open letter to the Welsh people in 1843 urged the acceptance of the schools of the British and Foreign Bible Society; his efforts to secure a university for Wales led to a commission to promote the idea in 1854.

Owen, John Dyfnallt (Dyfnallt, 1873-1956): b Llangiwg, Glam, poet and prose writer, Crown winner, and nfluential editor of *Y Tyst* (The Witness 1927-56).

Owen, Morfydd Llwyn (1891-1918): from Treforest, near Swansea; beautiful, talented musician, composer, and songwriter who died from appendicitis only one year after marrying psychoanalyst Ernest Jones, thus having an illustrious career cut short.

Owen, Nicholas (Little John d. 1606): born to a prominent Welsh Catholic family at Oxford, a member of the Society of Jesus, he was executed following the Gunpowder Plot.

Owen, Robert (1771-1858): factory owner, socialist visionary from Newtown, Montgomeryshire, forerunner of the co-operative movement and inspirer of trade unions, whose socialist philosophy was put into practice at the New Lanark Mills in Scotland and at New Harmony, Indiana.

Owen, Robert (Bob Owen Croesor, 1885-1962): b. Llanfrothen, Mer.; antiquqary and book collector in great demand for his genealogical expertise (see Cymdeithas Bob Owen).

Owen Pughe, William (1759-1835): b. Llanfihangel y Pennant, Mer; an active member of the Gwyneddigion and the London Welsh Society, he edited numerous books on Welsh History, Language and Grammer including *Geiriadur Cymraeg a Saesneg* (A Welsh and English Dictionary, 1803).

Oxford Book of Welsh Verse, The (1962): an anthology of poets from the early period to the middle of the 20th Century.

P

Nineteenth letter of the Welsh alphabet
Sometimes mutated to ph at the beginning of words

Pais (**Petticoat, f. 1978**): a monthly magazine for women, with book reviews, poetry and short stories.

Panic Attack: a fighting robot from Torfaen, 1999 winner of the BBC Technical Knockout Tournament.

Panton, Paul (1727-97): b. Bagillt, Flintshire; historian, collector of ancient manuscripts.

Pantyfedwen: a favorite hymn tune on both sides of the Atlantic, composed in 1968 by M. Eddy Evans to win the first prize at the National Eisteddfod at Lampeter (Llanbedr Pont Steffan).

Papur Bro (Local newspaper): any number of Welsh-language newpapers, beginning with *Y Dinesydd* (The Citizen) in Cardiff, 1973.

Papur Pawb (Everyone's Paper, f. 1893-1917, 1922-55): a weekly newpaper from Caernarfon, merged with *Y Werin a'r Eco* in 1937.

Parker, John (1922-82): from Cardiff; journalist and novelist; feature editor at the *Western Mail* and news-editor with *The South Wales Echo*; later worked with the Welsh Office, at the U.N. in New York City, and as the Deputy Director of Information at the Home Office in London.

Parliament for Wales Campaign (b. 1951): an all-party effort under the chairmanship of Lady Megan Lloyd George, presented in 1957 by Goronwy Roberts, Labour M.P. for Caernarfon. Supported by only 6 of the 36 constituencies in Wales, it failed.

Parlwr Du (the Black Parlour): local name for the colliery at Point of Ayr, Flintshire, that once employed 900 men but was forced to close in 1993.

Parri, Dafydd (b. 1926): from Dyffryn Conwy, Carns; a prolific, and successful children's writer in Welsh, famed for his *Cyfres Y Llewod* (1975-80), and his stories about a sheep-dog named *Cailo*.

Parry, Lord Gordon, Baron of Neyland (1925-2004): teacher, librarian; writer, broadcaster and TV panel chairman; Chairman of the Wales Tourist Board, and president of man companies and institutions. A director of NWAF, his autobiography is *Trinity 1943-4, a Legacy for Life (1996)*.

Parry, Gwenlyn (b. 1932): b. Deiniolen, Caerns; playwright, BBC producer.

Parry, John (1750-82): b. Nefyn, Caerns; blind harpist of the Williams Wynn family whose tune collections are a major part of the Welsh cultural tradition.

Parry, John (1775-1846): for a century his catechism for children, *Rhodd Mam* (1811), was a primary source of religious instruction.

Parry, Joseph (1841-1903): b. Merthyr, he went to Danville, Pa. at age 13 to work in steel mills. Won several prizes at National Eisteddfod and was sent to study at Royal Academy of Music on subscriptions from Welsh chapels in U.S. He became the first Professor of Music at University of Wales, Aberystwyth. He composed operas, oratorios; hymn tunes, including "Aberystwyth."

Parry, Richard (1560-1633): from Flintshire, Dean of Bangor, he succeeded William Morgan as Bishop of St. Asaph in 1604 and worked on the revised editons of the *Welsh Bible* (1620) and the *Book of Common Prayer* (1621).

Parry, Robert Williams (1884-1956): from Dyffryn Nantlle, Caerns; author of one of the most well known of all modern Welsh poems, "Yr Haf," giving him the title of *Bardd y Haf* (Poet of Summer).

Parry, Thomas (1904-85): teacher and librarian, Principal, Univ. College of Wales, Aberystwyth. His literary contributions include a survey of Welsh literature entitled *Hanes Llenyddiaeth Gymraeg* (The History of Welsh Literature, 1945); an anthology of Welsh poetry titled *Llyfryddiaeth i Lenyddiaeth Gymraeg* 1976; and an edition of Dafydd ap Gwilym that established the poet's authenticity and genius.

Parry, William John (1842-1927): from Bethesda, Caerns; workers' leader who helped create the North Wales Quarrymen's Union in 1874 serving as Secretary and President. Author of several works in Welsh and English, he helped found the newspaper *Y Werin* in 1885.

Parry-Jones, Daniel (1891-1981): b. Llangeler, Carms; clergyman who wrote four volumes of autobiography in which customs and farming methods of his time are detailed.

Parry Jones, Richard (b. 1952): b. Bangor; motor rally driver. Began as an apprentice in 1952 to become vice-president for product development and quality and helped develop the Ford Focus for international markets, including the U.S., where it almost overnight became the best-selling car—voted the Car of the Year for 2000, an honor duplicated in Canada and Europe.

Parry Thomas, John Godfrey: (d. 1926): from Wrexham, chief engineer at Leyland Motors in the early 1920's, broke many speed records; killed in his car *Babs* at Pendine Sands, Carmarthenshire, trying to break his own world record. *Babs* lay buried in the sand for many years before being dug up and placed in exhibition.

Parry-Williams, Thomas Herbert (1876-1975): b. Rhydd-ddu, Caerns; literary giant; scholar, poet and essayist, twice winner of the Chair and the Crown at Nationals; Chairman of the Dept of Welsh at University College of Wales, Aberystwyth. His last collection of poems and essays appears in *Bro* (Neighborhood) and *Casgliad o Ysgrifau* (Collection of Writings 1984). From 1920-32 he was Chair of Welsh at Aberystwyth.

Patrick, St. (4th century): Patricius (or *Padrig*) may have been born around 385 A.D. in Strathclyde or in southwest Wales. He vowed to serve God at Glyn Rhosyn (now St. David's). In his *Life of St. David*, Latin author Rhygyfarch tells of Patrick's being shown Ireland in the distance and vowing to evangelize the distant land.

Patti, Adelina (1843-1919): popular American opera singer (who retired to a mock castle *Craig y Nos* (Rock of the Night) in the Swansea Valley, there to entertain many famous people and to give concerts to distinguished guests.

Paviland, Gower: The site of the "Red Lady of Paviland," the skeleton of a youth ritually buried in a cave about 24,000 B.C.

Paxton's Tower, Tywy Valley: a huge folly built by William Paxton to honor Lord Nelson; locals say it was built with money that failed to get him into Parliament.

Payne, Ffransis George (b. 1900): folk historian whose important studies in Welsh agriculture, folk customs and country life were completed at the National Folk Museum, San Ffagan.

Peate, Iorwerth Cyfeiliog (1901-82): the first curator of the National Welsh Folk Museum; San Ffagan, he was an important author, specializing in the culture of rural Wales. His essays and poems show his deep commitment to the preservation of the Welsh language and his lament for the loss of much that was good and honorable in Welsh life.

Pedair Cainc y Mabinogi (the four branches of the Mabinogi) see *Mabinogion.*

Peers, Donald (1908-1973): "The Cavalier of Song," Ammanford-born Donald debuted at New Theatre, Lowestoft in 1927, rising through the ranks of show business to become a great success in the 1940's and 50's and making many hit records. His theme song was "By a Babbling Brook." He was severely disabled in a freak accident on the stage in Australia in 1971.

Pelagius (350-418): theologian who taught the unspeakable heresy that man can live without sin and was thus condemned by Rome and combated by Germanus and St David.

Pembroke (Sir Penfro): "Land's End" county created out of the kingdom of Deheubarth in 1080 by Norman King William. It is divided into the Welsh speaking areas to the north and the English-speaking areas to the south by the invisible boundary "Landsker."

Pembroke: walled town dominated by a massive Norman keep, birthplace of Henry Tudor, 13th Century St. Mary's and St. Michael's Churches, and the National Museum of Gypsy Caravans.

Pembroke Dock: formerly Britain's chief naval dockyard, where the very first steam-driven man of war, the first iron-class warship, and the first royal yacht were built.

Pembrokeshire National Park: the only coastal nation park in Britain, encompassing 225 square miles around the rugged coast, it spreads inland some 10 miles to include the Preseli Hills and the Gwaun Valley.

Penal Laws (1401-02): a series of restrictions placed upon Wales, especially its poets, after the initial successes of the Glyndwr Revolt.

Pencarreg Three, the: in November, 1979, the Pencarreg television transmitter was switched off by Pennar Davies, Meredydd Evans, and Ned Thomas to contest the lack of Welsh broadcasts. Their act, punished by heavy fines, contributed greatly to the eventual success of the Welsh language channel.

Pencerdd: the chief bard of the Royal Courts of Wales before the Edwardian Conquest.

Penderyn: (b. March lst, 2004): a brand of Welsh whiskey from Gwalia Distillerry, Brecon Beacons.

Pendine, Carmarthenshire: an expanse of flat, smooth sands, site of attempts to break the world's land speed records during the early 20th century. In 1927 Sir Malcolm Campbell reached 174.88 mph in *Bluebird,* the same year that Welsh driver J.G. Parry Thomas was killed in *Babs*, which remained buried in the dunes until 1969.

Penhow Castle, Gwent: claims to be the oldest inhabited castle in Wales;

Peniarth Manuscripts, The: more than 500 manuscripts formed by Robert Vaughan of Hengwrt, Mer., covering almost every aspect of Medieval and Renaissance Welsh literataure (housed in the National Library of Wales.

Penillion: a style of singing in which the vocalists provide the accompaniment and the instrument (usually a harp) plays the melody. Singers sometimes have to fit set pieces to music or they improvise in this difficult art.

Penllyn: a district around Bala, Merioneth., a center of rich literary and cultural traditions, birthplce of leading poets and prominent figures in Welsh life.

Penllyn Manuscript, the (see Robert ap Huw).

***Pennal Letter, the* (1406):** also named the *Pennal Policy,* part of an official document sent to the French King by Owain Glyndwr seeking recognition from the Avignon Pope for Welsh control over Welsh dioceses, the establishment of Welsh universities, and the training of officials for an independent state (housed in Archives Nationales, Paris).

Pennant Melangell, Powys: site of a little church in the Tanat Valley dedicated to St. Melangell who sheltered the hares. Her feast day is 27 May.

Pennant, Thomas: from Downing Hall, near Holywell, antiquarian and naturalist (who helped name New South Wales), whose *Tours of Wales* (1778, 1781) encouraged English interest in Wales.

Penrhyn Castle, Bangor: a massive pseudo-Norman edifice, now owned by the National Trust, built with the profits from the nearby Bethesda slate quarries. The second Baron Penrhyn, refusing to give his workers a decent salary, caused the Great Strike of 1900-1903, "the Penrhyn Lockouts" the longest in Britain's industrial history, causing deep divisions in an area noted for its close family ties and fellowship and creating scars that never healed.

Penry, John (1563-93): religious leader and pamphleteer who satirized the Church of England in the *Martin Marprelate Tracts* (1588-89); often imprisoned for his attacks on episcopacy, he petitioned Queen and Parliament for the translation of the Bible into Welsh, but executed for his extreme views.

Pentre Ifan: Pembrokeshire: on the edge of the Preseli Hills, the largest and most impressive of megalithic chambered tombs in Wales.

Pen y Darren, Merthyr: site where the first steam locomotive to run on rails, Cornishman Richard Trevithick's *Catch-me-Who-Can*, made its journey to Abercynon in 1804. It hauled a five-wagon load of 10 tons of iron and 70 persons for nine miles at 5 mph. The world changed forever from that day on.

Perllan (the Orchard): part of the Wassailing ceremony of New Year's Day in which a small tray decorated with an apple, leaves and a bird was carried around the houses.

Peter, John (Ioan Pedr, 1833-77): b. Bala, Mer; self-taught master of many languages, college tutor and pastor and pioneer in the field of comparative philology.

Peters, Mike (b. 1959): from Prestatyn, Flintshire; lead singer with the 80's rock band *The Alarm* now a successful solo artist, he now presents Raidio Wales' Bedrock programme. *The Alarm* and resurrected itself in 2003. Mike appeared in the movie *Dead Man Walking*.

Philanthropic Order of the True Ivorites: a Friendly Society founded in Wrexham in 1836 to give members financial support during sickness and to promote the Welsh language and culture.

Philips, Katherine (1632-1664): b. London, raised in Picton Castle, married to James Philips M.P. and Mayor of Haverfordwest), her poetry and membership of the Society of Friendship made her the first woman writer in Britain to receive professional and public recognition. Her collected works was published in 1993.

Phillips, Edgar (Trefin, 1889-1962); Penbrokeshire, soldier in WWl, then Welsh teacher; Chair winner and prominent member of the Gorsedd; Archdruid from 1960-62; and writer of poetry for children.

Phillips, Eluned (b. 1915): from Cenarth, poet and biographer, the only woman to have won the Crown twice at the National Eisteddfod (1967 and 1983).

Phillips, Sian (b. 1934): internationally-known actress from Bettws, Carms, perhaps best remembered for her television role as Livia in *I, Claudius*, she began in BBC Radio alongside Dylan Thomas and Richard Burton when she was only eleven years old. Once married to Peter O' Toole, the bilingual actress's long, distinguished film and stage career has included *Marlene*, a tribute to Marlene Dietrich; a starring role in the musical version of *Sunset Boulevard*, and many other stage and television triumphs.

Phillips, Thomas (1801-67): b. Llanelli; Mayor of Newport during the Chartists March; a successful London barrister and author of a masterly refutation of the negativity of the Blue Book Commissioners.

Physicians of Myddfai: a family of Carmarthenshire doctors whose skills in herbal medicine were famous throughout Europe to the end of the 18th Century.

Pibgorn: a musical hornpipe very popular in Wales up until the end of the 18th century, recently revived by such groups as *Cras Dant,*.

Picton, Sir Thomas (1758-1815): a Pembrokeshire soldier appointed governor of Trinidad for services against the Spanish, distinguished himself in the Peninsular Campaign of Wellington, and died leading *The Thin Red Line* at Quatre Bras, Waterloo.

Pierce, Thomas Jones (1903-64): b. Liverpool; on the staff of the History Dept at Bangor, he pioneered research into the structure of medieval Welsh society, wrote papers on the Laws of Hywel Dda and human settlements in Gwynedd: Chair of Medieval Welsh History; also President of the Cambrian Archeological Association in 1964.

Pilkington Report, The (1962): by which the government charged BBC Wales with the responsibility of preparing 12 hours of TV programs per week, half of which were to be in Welsh.

Pilnos: a tradition when neighbors gathered to peel rushes for candle making during the winter nights, and singing.

Pilleth, Battle of (1402): a humiliating defeat of an English army by Edmund Mortimer and Owain Glyndwr at Bryn Glas, Radnorshire.

Plaid Cymru The Party of Wales: formed in 1925 at Pwllheli by Saunders Lewis and friends to further the aims of self-government and to try to stop the decline in language and culture. In 1966, Gwynfor Evans was elected at Carmarthen to become the party's first M.P. It paid a crucial part in the 1997 referendum that gave Wales its first Assembly and by 1999 had become the second largest Welsh political party, making inroads into previously impenetrable Labour strongholds. Dayfdd Iwan became Chairman in 2004.

Planet (f. 1970): a nationalist magazine containing book reviews, essays, and translations of verse and prose. After ceasing publication in 1977, it was revived in 1985.

Plas Newydd, **Llangollen:** former home of Sarah Ponsonby and Eleanor Butler, *the Ladies of Llangollen.* Visitors included Wellington (who claimed to have learned Spanish from a book he found there) Shelley, Byron, and Scott.

Plas Newydd, Anglesey: former home of the Marquis of Anglesey who lost a leg as commander of cavalry at Waterloo. Owned by the National Trust, the mansion has the largest mural painted by Rex Whistler.

Plas Penmynydd, **Anglesey:** seat of the Tudors, so influential in British history, birthplace of Owen Tudor who married Catherine of Valois, widow of Henry V, and grandmother of Henry Vll.

Plygain: a candle-lit carol service held in the early hours of Christmas morning in Parish churches.

Pobol y Cwm (**People of the Valley**): a popular Welsh-language television "soap" shown on S4C. Set in fictional Cwmderi, it is one of the longest-running programs in the U.K., having begun in 1973.

Poco Bara (a little bread): an expression learned by the Tehuelche Indians in Patagonia, who exchanged meat for bread with the Welsh pioneers.

Poets of the Gentry (13th and 14th centuries): after the death of Llywelyn ap Gruffudd, landowning classes encouraged a new class of professional poet who praised the hospitality of the patron. They included such masters as Dafydd ap Gwilym, Sion Cent, Lewys Glyn Cothi, and Tudur Aled.

Poetry Wales **(b. 1965):** published by the Poetry Wales Press after some years by the Triskel Press, it has consistently encouraged Anglo-Welsh poets.

Pontcysyllte (*Connecting Bridge*) Wrexham and Maelor: a wonder of Wales, the aqueduct, built by Thomas Telford to take the Shropshire Union canal across the Dee valley is the longest and highest in Britain. Completed in 1805, its watertight cast iron trough is supported by 18 piers at a height of 121 feet.

Pontnewydd Cave, Clwyd: in the Elwy Valley, the site where a human tooth was found dating 25,000 years, the oldest object ever found in Britain.

Pontypridd, Rhondda: former center of the coal and iron industry where the anchor chains for Lord Nelson's fleet were manufactured as well as those for the *Queen Mary* and *Queen Elizabeth*. Its unique bridge was built of stone by self taught William Edwards in 1755.

Poole, Edwin (1851-95): b. Oswestry, a journalist, printer and county hisotiran of Breconshire and founder of the *Brecon and Radnor Express* in 1889.

Pope, Mal (b. 1960): from Brynhyfryd, Swansea; musician, songwriter, and performer of international fame who began singing at chapel and at the Gospel Hall, Manselton. His career guided by Elton John, he has made numerous television appearances in Britain, the US and Europe, including the highly popular "The Mal Pope Show."

Portmeirion, Gwynedd: on the coast of Llyn near Porthmadog, the village was built from 1925 to 1975 to fulfill a dream of Sir Clough Williams Ellis. He took interesting buildings scheduled for demolition to create his Italianate masterpiece, the setting for the cult B.B.C. series of the 1960's, *The Prisoner*.

Porthmadog, Gwynedd: former ship building center, in the 19th century its schooners took roofing slate from the quarries to many parts of the world. Porthmadog pottery is internationally known for its quality and design.

Potato Jones (birthdate and birthplace unknown): Ih his 50's, David John Jones was one of three Welsh sea captains (along with corn Cob Jones and Ham n' Chips Jones) who ran guns to Spain to fight Franco. On the *Marie Llewellyn,* sailing from Swansea, he had guns under sacks of potatoes.

Povey, Michael (b. 1950): actor, and writer for television, has helped create many programs in the Welsh language.

Powel, David (1552-98): historian and scholar whose *Historie of Cambria, now called Wales* (1584) was the standard work on Welsh history for 200 years and of immense importance to later historians.

Powell, Anthony (1905-2000): novelist famed for his 12-volume novel *A Dance to the Music of Time*. The son of an officer in the Welsh Regiment, he served in W.W.II with the same regiment.

Powell, Philip (1594-1646): from Breconshire, educated as a Catholic priest at Louvain, arrested in the Civil War and executed in London.

Powell, Rees (1638-65): a Parliamentarian, Governor of Tenby, commanded Cromwell's' forces in West Wales before negotiating with the King over a pay dispute. Sentenced to death, he was reprieved by Cromwell.

Powell, Vavasor (1617-70): Puritan evangelist whose enthusiastic preaching swept throughout Wales in the latter half of the 17th century.

Powell, William (Gwilym Eryri, 1841-1910): b. Beddgelert, steward of Bryn y Felin Copper Mine, came to Wisconsin in 1865 to become leading figure in

Welsh-American circles, taking settlers to the Dakotas, helped organize the Eisteddfod at Chicago World's Fair in 1893.

Powys: county created in 1974 from Radnorshire, Montgomershire, and Breconshire. It is also the name of an ancient mid-Wales kingdom.

Powys Castle: inhabited for over 500 years, a huge red pile surrounded by magnificent terraces, gardens, woodlands and parkland, defended by Royalists in the Civil War; home of the Herbert family for many centuries. In 1667, its owner, a supporter of James ll, was once smuggled out of the Tower of London by his wife, Lady Nithsdale.

Poyer, John (d. 1649): merchant and military commander who committed Pembroke to Parliament against the King, but whose acceptance of Prince Charles's commissin in 1647 began the Second Civl War. Later opposing Parliament, he was executed.

***Prayer Book, the* (Kinniver Llyth a Ban, 1567):** by William Salesbury, the first complete Welsh translation of the Prayer Book, and thus of incalculable influence on the survival of the language. It was revised by Bishop Morgan in 1599, and by John Davies in 1620.

Preece, Sir William Henry (1834-1913): from Caernarfon, a major figure in the development of wireless telegraphy and the telephone in Britain.

Studied under Michael Faraday, became an engineer with the Post Office, and worked with and encouraged Marconi. He introduced the Bell telephone to Britain.

Preseli, Pembrokeshire (Mid and West Wales Electoral Region): parliamentary constituency created in 1997 out of parts of Ceredigion and Pembroke, much of it lies in the Pembrokeshire Coast National Park.

Price, Henry (1899): b. Neath; philosopher who won acclaim for his pioneering work on perception and logic. In 1935, he was appointed Mykeham Professor of logic and New College, Oxford.

Price, Hugh (1495-1574): the founder and principal benefactor of Jesus College, Oxford, for centuries closely associated with Wales.

Price, John (1502-55): scholar, served under Oliver Cromwell in the administration of Wales and the Marches. In 1546, he published the first book in the Welsh language: *Yn y Lhyvr Hwnn* (In this Book).

Price, Joseph Tregelles (1784-1854): iron master and Quaker philanthropist whose management of the Neath Abbey Iron Works made it an important center of Welsh industry in the early part of the 19th century. David Thomas "father of the US anthracite industry" began his career here.

Price, Kathryn: b in Gwent, she is an internationally acclaimed young cellist, debuttng at Carneie Recital Hall in June, 1998, with many works commissioned especially for her, she has played at the World's most prestigious concert halls. Her cello was made in 1706.

Price, Dame Margaret (b. 1941): internationally known soprano with a distinguished career in concert, opera, and recital. Acclaimed for her wide repertoire, debuted with the Welsh National Opera.

Price, Phillip (b. 1967): Pontypridd, rookie in the 2002 Ryder Cup who beat the world's Nr.2 golfer Phil Mickelson to help Europe defeat the U.S.

Price, Dr. Richard (1723-91): philosopher and economist from Llangeinor, Glamorgan, author of *Observations on the Nature of Civil Liberty* (1776), one of the most important contributions to the pamphlet literature of the American Revolution. Price enumerated the principle that every community has the right to govern itself, but subject to a central administration on matters that were of common concern. His attempts to resolve the differences between Britain and the Colonies came too late. In 1778, he was offered U.S. citizenship.

Price, Thomas (*Carhuanawc*, 1787-1848): a prolific author, passionate about Welsh culture, helping Lady Guest translate the *Mabinogion*. He advocated the use of Welsh in schools, an important figure in the Welsh Manuscripts Society and Welsh Minstrelsy Society.

Price, Thomas (1852-1909): b. Brymbo, near Wrexham, the first Labour Party premier of an Australian state (South Australia) in 1905. A former mason, he worked on the building in which he later acted as Premier and introduced important legislation.

Price, Dr. William (1800-93): at Cardiff Assizes in 1884, he was tried for burning the body of his infant son Iesu Grist (Jesus Christ) in a ceremony of his own invention. His acquittal established the legality of cremation in British law). A leader of the Newport Rising in 1839, he escaped to France.

Prichard, Caradog (1904-80): b. Bethesda, Caerns; poet and novelist, winner of the Crown for three successive years, much of his work deals with the effects of insanity, including *Un Nos Ola Leuad* (One Night of the Last Moon, 1961).

Prichard, Rhys (Yr Hen Ficer, 1579-1644): vicar of Llandovery; his *Canwyll y Cymry* (the Candle of the Welsh (1681) was to be recited by generations of children, earning a special place in history.

Prichard, Thomas J. (1790-1862): from Builth, acted in London under the name Mr Jerreries, returned to Wales to write *Welsh Minstrslsy* and achieved fame with *The Adventures and Vagaries of Twm Shon Catti* in 1828.

Prince of Wales: following the 1294 Statute of Rhuddlan that made Wales a province of England, Edward lst brought his bride to Caernarfon to give birth to their son Edward, given the title *Prince of Wales and Count of Chester* in 1301. Since that date, the first-born son of the English monarch has been given these titles. The German motto of the Prince of Wales, *Ich Dien* (I Serve) came from an inscription beneath the ostrich feathers on the helmet of the King of Bohemia, killed at Crecy.

Princess of Wales: see entries for Gwenllian and Spencer, Lady Diana.

Protheroe, Daniel (1866-1934): musician who left Ystradgynlais in 1885 to begin a career as a choral conductor and hymn writer at Scranton, Pa.

Pryce, Jonathan (b. 1947): from Holywell, studied at RADA, began a stage career at Nottingham, going on to the Royal Shakespeare Company. His singing roles have included Miss Saigon on Broadway; his movies, include *Evita* (where he played Peron), *Glengarry Glen Ross, Tomorrow Never Dies.*

Pryce, Tom (1949-1977): from Ruthin, Denbighshire, destined to become a great racing car driver, but killed in an accident in S. Africa two years after winning the World Race of Champions.

Pryce-Jones, Arthur Glyn: b. Penarth, contemporary choral director, began with the Welsh National Opera, worked with D'Oyly Carte Opera and founded the Noel children's choir; Musical Director of Northern Ballet since 1992.

Pryce-Jones, Pryce: founder of the world's first mail order business in 1859 at Newtown, Montgomeryshire. Many of the area's farmers lived in isolated valleys and had little time or suitable transportation to come into town. The Warehouses, packed with goods, answered their needs. It began a service that quickly attracted companies such as Montgomery Ward in the U. S, with its even greater distances and scattered population.

Prys, Edmund (1543-1623): scholar at Cambridge, parish rector, a prolific poet of debate, of thanks, of religion and morals, and even of a game of football. His metrical Psalms, *Salmau Can* remained in common use until late 18th Century.

Prys, Elis (Y Doctor Coch, 1512-94): from Ysbyty Ifan, Denbs; helped Cromwell dissolve the Welsh monasteries; was M.P. for Merioneth and Sheriff of four North Wales counties and a member of the Council of the Marches.

Prys, Tomos (1565-1634): from Plas Iolyn, Denbs. a soldier and poet who fought in Flanders and in many campaigns including defense against the Armada before becoming a pirate.

Pryse, Robert J. (Gweirydd ap Rhys, 1807-89): from Llanbadrig, Agnlesey; taught himself to read and write; a poet and historian, an authority on Welsh language and literature, important contributor to the *Welsh Dictionary*, and Eisteddfod prize winner.

Prys-Jones, Arthur G. (b. 1888): b. Denbigh; teacher and school inspector, helped found Cardiff's Little Theatre, compiler of poetry anthologies; President of English language section of *Yr Academi Gymreig* (1970).

Prys-Thomas, Lewis (1916-69): head of Wales School of Architecture, Cardiff; a consultant for many government buildings in Wales.

Puddicombe, Anne (1836-1908): from Newcastle Emlyn; her romances about the common folk of Wales that made her a best selling author and influenced a later generation of Welsh novelists and dramatists.

Puffin Island (Ynys Seiriol): S.E. coast of Anglesey, once called Priestholm, settled by St. Seiriol in the 6th century. The abundant puffins drastically declined as a result of being pickled and eaten or by an infestation of rats.

Pugh, Edward (1761-1813): b. Ruthin, Denbs: painter and writer on topography who illlustrated his own tour of North Wales that helped begin the tourist trade in that spectacular region.

Pugh, Ellis (1656-1727): b. Dolgellau, Mer. Quaker who settled in Gwynedd, Pa. in 1687 to mininster to many Welsh settlers; the author of the first book published in the Welsh language in North America (see *Anerch I'r Cymru).*

Pugh, Vernon (1945-2003): from the Amman Valley, chairman of the International Ruygby Board, former chairman of the Welsh Rugby Union Board, World Rugby Cup director, and a key figure in the professionalism of rugby union. A barrister, he played for Cardiff High School Old Boys before his work with the IRB, which included bringing Italy into the Six Nations' Championship and setting up the Heineken Cup.

Pumpsaint, Dyfed: (see Dolcothau).

***Pura Wallia*:** Welsh-controlled areas to the west of Marchia Wallia that were more or less left alone by William lst and his Marcher Lords.

Puw, Huw (1663-1743): from Tal y Llyn, Mer. athlete and priest, who deserves mention for his feat of jumping over the heads of his parishioners on their way to church one day, causing his mother to die of fright. His monument is at the Ashmolean, Oxford.

Pwnco: a wedding custom popular in West. Wales that involved the recitation of verses in competition between followers of the groom and those of the wife's family at the bride's door. The visitors would then search for the hidden bride.

Ph

Twentieth letter of the Welsh alphabet (pronounced as English "f." It is found at the beginning of words as a mutation of p (Ex. *ei phen hi* (her head). It is also found in names borrowed from English such as Philips.

Q

There is no Q in the Welsh alphabet. The same sound occurs in the Welsh combination cw (as in *Nercwys* or *cwestiwn*).

Quant, Mary (1934): born in London to Welsh parents, evacuated to Tenby during the War for a short while. Her 1960's fashions, especially her Chelsea Look and her mini skirts, broke the stranglehold of Dior and Chanel by creating styles at the working-girl level.

R

Twenty-first letter of the Welsh alphabet
(always sounded and trilled).

Radical Poets (mid-15th century): after the failure of
the Glyndwr rebellion, poets such as Lewis Glyn Cothi
prophesied the overthrow of the hated Saxons.

Radio Cymru: begun in 1977 following the B.B.C.
Welsh language programs begun at Bangor in 1935.

Radio Eireann (Irish Radio): in 1927 the station that
broadcast the only regular Welsh-language radio
programs.

Radnor: a border county created out of the old
Marcher lordships in 1536. With the smallest
population of any in Wales, it is almost entirely English
speaking. Added to Brecon and Montgomery to
become Powys in 1974.

Raglan Castle, Gwent: the last example of medieval
fortification in Britain, formerly the opulent home of
the Earls of Worcester.

Rebecca (1973-82): a magazine published periodically
in Cardiff to expose corruption in public places.

Rebecca Riots: a group of men destroyed the gates at Efailwen in May, 1839 led by Thomas Rees (*Twm Carnabwth*), disguised in women's clothes. The rioting and burning carried out by the gang ended only when a government commission advocated the reduction of tolls, especially those on lime.

Reardon, Ray (b. 1934): snooker player from South Wales, an ex coal miner who won six World Championships 1970-78.

Recorde, Robert (1510-1558): to the chagrin of schoolboys and girls ever since, mathematician and doctor of medicine Robert Recorde, of Tenby, wrote books on arithmetic and geometry (as well as medicine), including *The Whitstone of Witte* (1558) but also invented the "equals" sign. His proposal was to use "a paire of parelleles, or {twin} lines of one length because no two lines can be more equal."

Red Bandits of Mawddwy: a 16th Century band of robbers in Merionethshire of whom Thomas Pennant reported that eighty were hanged for their misdeeds, which included the murder of a Sheriff of the county. There are many popular traditions of these red-haired outlaws whose descendants are said to still live in the area.

Red Book of Hergest **(1382-1410):** in the Bodleian Library at Oxford, a book crucial to the study of medieval Welsh literature, containing the Brut

(Geoffrey of Monmouth), Brut y Tywysogyon, *The Dream of Rhonabwy,* the *Mabinogion* Collection and other priceless works.

Red Dragon (*Y Ddraig Goch*): perhaps the first

mythical beast in British heraldry. Legend has Macsen Wledig and his Romano-British soldiers carrying the Red Dragon banner to Rome on in the 4th century. Adopted in the early 5th century by the Welsh kings of Aberffraw, by the 7th century, it was known as the *Red Dragon of Cadwallader*, to be ever after associated with the people of Wales. The 9th century *historian* Nennius mentions the red dragon in his *Historia Brittonum.* It is also referred to by Geoffrey of Monmouth in his *Historia Regum Britanniae.* It was known as the British standard at the Battle of Crecy (1346), in which Welsh archers played so prominent a part. The Red Dragon was also used by the Tudor monarchs to signify their direct descent from one of the noble families of Wales. Henry Vll's standard was white over green "with the red dragon over all". During Henry VIII's reign, the red dragon appeared on many of the Royal Navy ships; it was also a favorite of Queen Elizabeth, but was replaced by a unicorn in 1807 on the orders of James lst, reappearing on the Royal Badge of Wales. In 1953, a new royal badge was officially approved for Wales containing the motto: *Y Ddraig Goch ddyry Cychwyn* (The Red Dragon

Inspires). The national flag came into prominence in the early 20th century, being used at the 1911 Investiture of Edward, the Prince of Wales. It was not officially recognized until 1959.

Red Dragon, the (1882-87): a monthly magazine published in Cardiff that explored Welsh historical figures and literary works.

Red Kite (Barcud): a British bird found solely in Wales. Nesting in the high moorlands, it is protected by bird watchers who revel in its acrobatic displays and revival from near extinction.

***Red Lady of Paviland* (c. 20,000 B.C.):** discovered in a Gower cave in 1823, the skeletal remains of a young man, stained in red ochre, wearing a necklace of wolf and reindeer teeth.

Rees, Alwyn D. (1911-74) editor of the magazines *Barn* (Opinion) for eight years and *Yr Einion* (the Anvil) for nine years; a strong champion of the fight to save the Welsh language and culture.

Rees, Angharad (b.1949): actress raised in Cardiff, trained as a teacher, famous for her role as Demelza in television's *Poldark*. After a break from acting for ten years to raise her family, she returned to television in the 1990's.

Rees ap Meredith (15th century): soldier who struck the final blow to Richard lll at the Battle of Bosworth.

Rees, Chris 1931-2001): b. Swansea to an English-speaking family; he set up the first Cwrs Wlpan (intensive Welsh learning course) at the University of Wales and received a prestigious award at the National Eisteddfod at Llanelli in 1999 for his work on behalf of Welsh learners. As Welsh patriot, he had served time in Swansea Gaol as a conscientious objector to the military draft during the 1950's.

Rees, Dai (1913-1983): b. Pontygary; great golfer who won four British PGA titles and was runner up in three British Opens. In 1957, he captained the Ryder Cup team that defeated the USA for the first time in 22 years. Awarded a CBA and Sportsman of the Year Awards, he died following a car crash.

Rees, Daniel (1855-1931): from Pembrokeshire, Liberal journalist and translator who edited *Yr Herald Cymraeg* and the *Carnarvon and Denbigh Herald*, supported Lloyd George, and founded the weekly *Papur Pawb* in 1893.

Rees, Evan (Dyfed, 1850-1923): from Pembrokeshire four-time Chair winner and the Chair at the World Fair Eisteddfod at Chicago in 1893; archdruid 1905-1923.

Rees, Goronwy (1909-79): important in journalism and academia, for a short period Principal of University

College of Wales, Aberystwyth; author of many works of literature including biographical sketches, essays, and three novels.

Rees, Gwendoline (1906-1994): b. Aberdare, Professor Rees was the first Welsh woman Fellow of the Royal Society. An expert in parasitology, the study of the life-cycle of certain organisms, her good looks often got her picture into *Vogue* Magazine.

Rees, Hopkin (19th century): from Cwmafan, began a missionary school in 1898 in China that developed into the University of Beijing.

Rees, Ioan Bowen (b. 1929): b. Dolgellau, Mer; became Chief executive of the Gwynedd Conty Council in 1980; has written a number of legal studies of Welsh and essays on politics, mountain climbing.

Rees, Sir John Frederick (1883-1967): from Milford Haven: author, university lecturer, and Principal at Bangor University with many studies in Welsh history.

Rees, Leighton: contemporary Welsh darts player who won the first ever World Championship in 1978 by defeating John Rowe of England. Another Welshman, Richie Burnett, won the title in 1995.

Rees, Richard (Dic, b. 1929): b. Ystradgynlais. Dic came to work for the DuPont Co. in Wilmington, Delaware where he was honored by the American

Chemical Society as a Hero of Chemistry for his discovery of Surlyn iononer resins, a versatile family of plastic used in high strength food packaging with airtight seal, and of enormous benefit in laminated safety glass in buildings and automobiles.

Rees, Sarah Janes (Cranogwen, 1839-1916): from Llangrannog, Card; schoolteacher, editor of the women's magazine *Y Frythones* (1879-91) and founder of the Temperance Unon of South Wales Women.

Rees, Thomas (Twm Carnabwth, 1806-76): one of the attackers of the tollgates at Efailwen in 1839in the Rebecca Riots.

Rees, Thomas Ifor (1890-1977): from Bow Street, Cards; Civil Servant who retired as British Ambassador to Bolivia in 1949 but who wrote of his work and translated novels and poetry into Welsh.

Rees, William (Gwilym Hiraethog, 1802-83): the first to receive the Medal of the Honorable Society of the Cymmodorion for writings, lots of which appeared in *Yr Amserau* (The Times 1843-59). He also adapted *Uncle Tom's Cabin* into a Welsh tale about slavery.

Rees, William (1808-73): from Llandovery, Carns; his press was one of the most celebrated in Wales printing much of *The Mabinogion* and the publications of the Welsh Manuscripts Societry.

Rees, William (1887-1978): b. Abersycir, Brecon: distinguished historian and college professor. His writings include *South Wales and the Border in the Fourteenth Century* (1933), and *An Historical Atlas of Wales* (1951).

Reese, Alfred J. Jr. (b. 1924): a Director of the St. David's Society of Schuylkill and Carbon Counties in Pa; the National Welsh American Foundation; and the Welsh National Gymanfa Ganu Association. He helped form the Pennsylvania Welsh Federation and led the effort to restore the Welsh Church at Lansford, Pa. He has served on the Board of Cymru A'r Byd (Wales International) and earned many honors for his work on behalf of Welsh Americans.

Referendum of 1997: on September 19, with the final vote cast by Carmarthen, the people of Wales voted for a democratically elected national body (see Assembly).

Renan, Ernest (1823-92): French philosopher who wrote of the distinctive characteristics of the Celtic peoples, regarding *The Mabinogion* as one of the sources of the romances to change the direction of the European imagination.

Rendel, Stuart (1834-1913): Liberal M.P. for Montgomeryshire, "the Member for Wales." He helped pass the Intermediate Education Act of 1889, which ironically did much to hasten the decline of the Welsh language by its setting up of the Central Welsh Board to organize secondary education in the English language.

Revival, The (b. 1859): a religious movement that helped promote Welsh literary and educational consciousness for a number of years.

Richard, Edward (1714-1777): from Ystrad Meurig, Cardiganshire, he founded St. John's College, a pioneering school to prepare Welsh students for Oxford and Cambridge.

Richard, Henry (1812-1888): from Tregaron, Liberal M.P. for Merthyr in 1868; religious and political leader. A keen supporter of the League of Nations, he was called "the Apostle of Peace."

Richards, Alun (1929-2004): Pontypridd-born former sailor and probation officer, novelist and critical dramatist of contemporary Wales, author of six novels and a collection of short stories, memoirs and plays, including the TV series "The Onedin Line."

Richards, Brinley (1904-81): poet from Llynfi Valley, Glam: a solicitor, Eisteddfod Chair winner and Archdruid from 1972-74.

Richards, Ceri (1903-71): a Surrealist; one of the most important British painters of the century, his work includes paintings based on the poetry of fellow-Welshmen Vernon Watkins and Dylan Thomas.

Richard, David (Dafydd Ionawr, 1751-1827): from Tywyn, Mer; his inclusion here is that he wrote one of the longest poems in the Welsh language *Cywydd y Drindod* (Verse of the Trinity: 13.000 lines). It is hardly ever read.

Richards, Melville (1910-73): Scholar and college Professor who wrote of medieval Welsh society and the Laws of Hywel Dda.

Richards, Nansi (*Telynores Maldwyn*, 1888- 1979): harpist influenced by the Welsh Romany Band, "The Original Cambrian Minstrels," formed by renowned harpist John Roberts. She passed on the knowledge of gypsy harping and their tunes to Llio Rhydderch and other prominent harpists. Nansi's playing can be heard in the movie *The Last Days of Dolwyn*. Many credit her with suggesting the logo of a rooster to Dr. Kellogg for his corn flakes, telling him that his name was similar to the Welsh *ceiliog*.

Richards, Thomas (1878-1962): b. Talybont, Cards; teacher, historian, author, and Librarian at Bangor, where he helped make the college an important center of Welsh studies. His autobiographies translate as *Memories of a Cardi* (Native of Cardiganshire).

Richards, Thomas (b. 1909): from Tywyn, Mer; journalist with *Cambrian News* and the *Western Mail* then the BBC at Swansea; wrote humorous dramas.

Robert ap Huw (1580-1665): musician linked with the Tudor family of Penmynydd; haropist to king James lst, he wrote the ony guide to Welsh harp music in medieval times, *the Penllyn Manuscript*.

Robert, Gryffydd (1532-98): master of language and grammar, moved to Italy in 1559 to write in Welsh to show its acceptability for literary works.

Roberts, Alwyn (b.1933): b. Penygroes, Gwynedd: vice-chancellor, University of Wales, Bangor 1990-97; lectured at Cambridge; also at Assam, India; and Univ. College, Swansea (vice-principal 1985-94): BBC National Governor for Wales; Chairman Broadcasting Council for Wales, President of the National Eisteddfod (1994-6).

Roberts, Arturo (b. 1928): b. Patagonia; moved to the U.S. in 1956 where he is devoted to the dissemination of Welsh culture in North America. Founder, owner and editor of *Ninnau;* past president of Argentina Medical Society; president of Andes Associates; founder of the Welsh North American Chamber of Commerce; founder and president of the Welsh-American Genealogical Society, Chairman of Cyfellion Bodiwan, dedicated to preserving the Bala home of Michael Jones, the founder of Wladfa (Patagonia). Arturo was inducted into the Gorsedd for his service to Wales and the overseas Welsh.

Roberts, Bartholemew (*Black Bart,* 1682-1722): notorious pirate from Pembrokeshire, killed by the Royal Navy, but not before he had been the first to fly the Skull and Crossbones flag.

Roberts, Brynley Francis (b. 1931): b. Aberdare; taught Welsh Language and Literature at Swansea (1978-85); Fellow of Jesus College, Oxford, Chairman Welsh Books Council (1989-94); edited *Dictionary of Welsh Biography* and books on Welsh literature.

Roberts, Caradog (1878-1935): Rhosllangerchrugog-born hymn writer best known for his tune *Rachie*, to which are sung the words "I Bob un sydd Ffydddlon" or "Onward Christian Soldiers."

Roberts, David (b. 1980): world class paralympic swimmer from Pontypridd with 4 Gold Medals at Athens Games, including two world records.

Roberts, Eigra Lewis (b. 1939): playwright, short-story writer and novelist specializing in the woman's point of view. Her major work is *Mis o Fehefin* (The Month of June), 1980.

Roberts, Eliazar (1825-1912): b. Pwllheli; musician pioneered the tonic sol-fa system in Wales, published texts in Welsh and wrote of the vibrant Liverpool Welsh community.

Roberts, Elis (d. 1789): Bala-born, known as *Y Cowper*, poet and writer of interludes.

Roberts, Ellis, (1827-95): writer and editor, specializing in stories of Church life at Bangor and the history of Wales.

Roberts, Enid (1917-2002): from Llandgadfan, Mont; teacher and author who has written extensively on the social life of the gentry of the 16th and 17th centuries, a work of literary history and an edition of poet Sion Tudor.

Roberts, Evan (1878-1951): former coalminer, apprentice blacksmith who religious leader who began *The Great Revival* in the Valleys (early 20th century) despite having no license to preach and no formal religious training. He attracted 100, 000 converts before going into seclusion and dying in obscurity.

Roberts, Sir Gareth (b.1940): taught physics at University College, Bangor; and University of Durham (Applied Physics); chief scientist and head of research (1986-90): Chancellor, Univ. of Sheffield (1991-2000). A Fellow of Univ. of Wales College of Medicine, he has written on the physics of semiconductors and molecular electronics.

Roberts, Glyn (1904-62): historian and college administrator whose writings on Medieval Welsh society are *Aspects of Welsh History* (1969).

Roberts, Gomer Morgan (1904-1993): b. Llandybie, Carms; coal miner and Calvinist Methodist minister with many publications on his religion.

Roberts, Isaac (1829-1904): B. Grows, Denbigh, astronomer who pioneered the photography of distant stars through his telescope and camera combination, producing detailed pictures of the Andromeda Nebula. The Roberts Crater on the moon is named for him.

Roberts, John (1576-1601): Catholic priest born in Trawsfynydd, active in London, who was given a great feast in his honor at Newgate Prison the night before his execution for treason.

Roberts, John (*Sion* Robert Lewis, 1731-1806): from Holyhead, hymn writer, compiler of almanacs, and the first book on arithmetic in Welsh.

Roberts, John (Ieuan Gwyllt, 1822-77): responsible for Wales's reputation as "the Land of Song," he published his *Llyfr Tonau Cynulleidfaol* (Book of Congregational Tunes) in 1859; and his Swn y Jiwbili (Sounds of the Jubilee) in 1874, both of enormous influence.

Roberts, John John (Iolo Carnarvon, 1840-1914): b. Llanllyfni, Caerns; minister; three-time Crown winner; prolific member of the "Bardd Newydd school.

Roberts, Kate (1891-1985): novelist and short-story writer, a most distinguished Welsh language author whose stories deal with life in the North Wales quarrying districts. She edited *Baner ac Amserau Cymru* (Banner and Welsh Times) at Gwasg Gee for a number of years, and wrote books for children.

Roberts, Lynette (1909-1995): born to Welsh emigrants in Argentina; after working in Buenos Aires, moved to London, married Keidrich Rhys in 1940, settled in Wales. Her "Gods with Stainless Ears" has been praised by Anthony Conran as the greatest war poem of 1939-45.

Roberts, Rachel (1927- 1980): b. Llanelli, committed suicide in Los Angeles; a gifted stage and screen actresses; began her long, alcohol and depression-filled career at the Grand Theatre Swansea in 1950 (with future stars Clifford Evans, Richard Burton, and Kenneth Williams). Her films included *Saturday Night and Sunday Morning* (1960), *This Sporting Life* (1963) and many others. For two years, a regular on the American TV series *The Tony Randall Show.*

Roberts, Richard (1789-1864): quarryman from Montgomeryshire who had remarkable mechanical ability. Working for John Wilkinson, he invented a screw-cutting lathe a machine to plane metal in 1817. He also improved weaving machines, steam engines, ships and rail cars.

Roberts, Robert (*Bob Tai'r Felin* **1870-1951**): folk singer who helped preserve traditional ballads that otherwise may have disappeared.

Roberts, Robert (*Silyn*: **1871-1930**): poet prominent in the early 20th century Welsh literary revival. An ardent Socialist, he founded the N. Wales branch of the Workers' Education Association in 1925.

Roberts, Robert Evan ((b. **1912**): b. Llanilar, Denbigh: General Secretary of National Council of YMCA's (1965-75): member of World Council of Y.M.C.A.'s.

Roberts, Samuel (*S.R.* **1800-85**): from Llanbrynmair: minister and writer who had great influence in the struggles of Welsh Nonconformity against the Establishment. His radical activities led to his emigration to the U.S. in 1857 to try to establish a Welsh community in Tennessee, but its failure meant return home.

Roberts, Selyf (1912-1995): b. Corwen, Mer; novelist and short-story writer, ex P.O.W. and Prose Medal winner who has translated Lewis Carrol into Welsh.

Robert, Thomas (1765-1841): b. Abererch, Caerns; pamphleteer who began something of a tourist trade in North Wales by bringing visitors to view Telford's suspension bridge over the Menai Straits.

Roberts, Thomas Richard (b.1948): educated St. Asaph Grammar and Univ. College, Swansea; director of Center for Ecology and Hydrology, National Government Research Council; Prof. of Botany at Toronto; vice-President, Welsh National Council, 1975. Has published works on planning and ecology.

Roberts, William Jon (Gwilym Cowlyd, 1828-1904): b. Trefriw, Caerns. Printer, bookseller and minor poet who began a short-lived assembly as a rival to the Gorsedd: *Arwest Glan Geirionydd* (1865-90.)

Roberts, Sir Wyn (b. 1930): Anglesey-born politician, a former journalist and program director with the BBC, appointed as Minister of State of the Welsh Office in 1979; first elected as Tory MP for Conwy, 1970.

Roberts-Jones, Ivor (1914-1997): Welsh sculptor whose best-known work is the huge bronze statue of Winston Churchill outside the Houses of Parliament.

***Robins, the*:** Wrexham's battling team, the only North Wales side to play in the English Football League. Has had its share of ups and downs.

Robinson, Steve (b. 1969): on April 16, 1993, featherweight boxer who became the first Welsh World boxing champion in 25 years when he defeated John Davison of Newcastle.

Rolls, Charles Stewart (1878-1910): Monmouth-born, son of Lord Llangatock, partnered Henry Royce to form Rolls-Royce Ltd in 1906. In 1910, he was the first Briton to die in a plane crash.

Roose-Evans, James (b. 1927): b. London of Welsh parents, raised in Powys: theatre director and author of children's stories and plays for broadcasting.

Rorke's Drift (1879): battle depicted in the movie *Zulu*, in which a handful of soldiers of the South Wales Borderers held off thousands of Zulu warriors.

Roscius: the sailing ship that took David Thomas and his family to the U.S. in May 1839 to make that country the number one iron producer in the world within ten years. His story is told in *From Wales to Pennsylvania*. (Peter N. Williams).

Rowland, Daniel (1713-1790): converted to Methodism in 1737, famous for his fiery sermons at Llangeitho whose publications were of enormous influence in the formation of the Calvinistic Methodist Church of Wales (now the Presbyterian Church of Wales).

Rowland, Robert David (Anthropus, 1853-1944): Corwen minister, poet, and journalist, worked on *Yr Herald Cymraeg* and literary editor of *Baner ac Amserau Cymru* (1904-14): wrote weekly articles and authored books and stories for children; edited *Trysorfa'r Plant* (Treasures for Children (1912-32).

Rowlands, Dafydd (b. 1931): poet, essayist, teacher; Eisteddfod Crown and Prose Medal winner.

Rowlands, John (b. 1938): college lecturer who has written critical studies of Dafydd ap Gwilym and several novels.

Rowlands, Robert John (*Meuryn*, 1880-1967): poet and journalist, editor *Yr Herald Cymraeg* (1921-1967), prize-winning poet and writer of children's books.

Rowlands, William (1802-65): bibliographer who collected and catalogued Welsh books, including *The Cambrian Bibliography* (1869).

Royal Harpists: include Robert ap Huw, harpist to Edward lst. Subsequent royal harpists from Wales have been William More, harpist to Henry Vlll; Lewis Willimas-Evans, harpist to James ll; Charles l, and Charles ll; Charles Evans, William Powell, for who Handel wrote his *Harp Concerto*; blind John Parry (harpist to the Prince of Wales, later George III); John Thomas (harpist to Queen Victoria) and Catrin Finch, harpist to the current Prince of Wales.

Royal Welch Fusiliers (b. 1689): unique for its right to wear the Flash of black ribbons on the collar (allowed to remain by William lV). Begun as the 23rd

Regiment of Foot formed by Lord Herbert of Cherbury at Ludlow after the Battle of the Boyne it fought on the Continent, including Blenheim. It distinguished itself in the American Revolutionary War, including the capture of Charleston and the Battle of Camden. The Regiment fought with distinction over the next two hundred years, ranging from Crimea to China to the Gulf and Bosnia. In the Boxer Rebellion, the regiment fought alongside American Marines at Peking. In 1844, the regimental goat joined the ranks, a gift from Queen Victoria.

Royal Welsh Show. Llanwelwedd, Builth: begun by a small group of farmers meeting at the Lion Royal Hotel, Aberystwyth in 1904 to form an Agricultural Society for Wales with its first show the same year. After W Wl, the show was revived under Lord Davies of Llandiman, moving from place to place each sujmer. In 1922, the show received royal patronage. In 1963, now the biggest agricultural show in Europe, (with 7.000 entries of livestock and over 1, 000 trade stands) it moved to its present, permanent site.

Rupert the Bear: a character from a story by Mary Tourtel, first appeared in the *Daily Express* in November, 1920 but made popular in 1935 as the beloved illustration of Alfred Bestal, schooled in Colwyn Bay, who spent most of his life in Beddgelert., Gwynedd.

Russell, Bertrand (1872-1970): b. Monmouthshire, philosopher and mathematician. He published many influential works, including *Principia Mathematica* (1910-13) with Alfred North Whitehead, and *History of Western Philosphy* (1945). He won the Nobel Prize for Literature in 1950.

Rush, Ian (b. 1961): b. Flint: footballer who began his professional career with Chester, but made 658 first team appearances for Liverpool where he became the club's all-time leading goal scorer; played for Wales 73 times.

Rutter, Sir Frank (1919-2003): physician and medical administrator who left Wales in 1963 for New Zealand after serving with the Royal Army Medical Corps in WWll; first chairman of the newly formed New Zealand Welsh National Gymanfa Committtee in 1991.

Rh

Twenty-second letter of the Welsh alphabet
(pr. as aspirated r).

Rhagfyr: twelfth month of the year, called December in English.

Rhees, Morgan John (1760-1804): Baptist minister who worked to oppose the slave trade, propose a missionary movement, establish Sunday schools, reform Parliament, and disestablish the Anglican Church in Wales. In 1794, he bought a large tract of land in Pennsylvania that he named *Cambria*.

Rhees, Benjamin Rush (1798-1831): Welsh-American medical doctor and pioneer in combating smallpox in Philadelphia; helped found Jefferson College, where he became Dean and chaired the Institute of Medicine and Medical Jurisprudence.

Rhees, William Jones (1830-1907): son of Benjamin; served as Chief Clerk, then Chief Executive of the Smithsonian Institution and keeper of the Archives.

Rhigymau (Rhymes): a folk tradition involving recitation of impromptu verses.

Rhodri Mawr (*Rhodri the Great*, d.877): the only Welsh King to be called Great. He unified the kingdoms of Wales into a strong state, successfully defended against both the Vikings and the English.

Rhondda, the: two valleys (Rhondda Fawr and Rhondda Fach) that epitomize the South Wales coal industry that suffered a dramatic decline after the Second World War.

Rhondda Heritage Park: commemorates the life and culture of the famous mining valley. An audio-visual display simulates a journey into a mine.

Rhosllanerchrugog, Denbs: village near Wrexham that has hung on to its Welsh character in a heavily Anglicized area; home of two Male Voice Choirs.

Rhuddlan, Flintshire: strategically placed near the estuary of the Clwyd, the mighty castle was the second of Edward 1st's chain of fortresses in North Wales. He held a parliament here to issue the Statute of Rhuddlan (*The Statute of Wales*, 1284) to govern his newly conquered territory. In reality it meant complete subjugation for the Welsh.

Rhydderch Hen (6th century): a king of Welsh Strathclyde, associated with the legends of Myrddyn (*Merlin*) found in the works of Geoffrey of Monmouth.

Rhyddarch, Rhees: (1620-1707): from Carmarthen: served as an officer under Cromwell, emigrated to US in 1701 when he was 81 years old with wife Catherine; he became a leading figure in Delaware's Welsh community at Welsh Tract Baptist Church.

Rhydderch, Llio: one of her nation's premier contemporary harpists. Taught by Nansi Richards, she is called "Queen of the Welsh Triple Harp."

Rhyd y Groes, The Battle of (1039): the invading Mercian army was defeated by Gruffudd ap Llywelyn, King of Gwynedd and Powys who later defeated the kingdom of Deheubarth.

***Rhydygroes (1*902):** one of the most popular of all Welsh hymn tunes; composed by Thomas David Edwards.

***Rhyfelgyrch Capten Morgan* (1784):** a popular tune originally a war song commemorating an ancient battle or hero now played at eisteddfodau to accompany the chairing of the Bard.

Rhygyfarch (*Ricemarchus*, 1056-99): Latin scholar at Lanbadarn Fawr, who wrote a Life of St. David as well as *The Ricemarch Psalter*.

Rhys ap Gruffydd (the Lord Rhys, 1132-1197): King of Deheubarth, whose long struggle against the Normans intent on totally eradicating all traces of "the

Britannic name," kept alive in southern Wales the idea of Welsh nationhood.

Rhys ap Tudor (1040-93): King of Deheubarth who heroically resisted the invasions of the Normans after he had gained control of Deheubarth in battle against the kings of Morgannwg and Gwynedd.

Rhys, Edward Prosser (1901-45): Eisteddfod Crown winner, and editor of *Baner ac Amserau Cymru* (Banner and Welsh Times) 1923 -1945.

Rhys, Ernest (1859-1946): poet and prose writer, a leading figure in Welsh literature and editor of Dent's *Everyman Library*, the largest library of cheaply priced books before *Penguin*.

Rhys, Jean (1894-1979): daughter of a Welsh doctor and Creole mother, she came to London from Dominica as a teenager; writer of short stories and novels, including *Wide Sargasso Sea* (1966).

Rhys, John (1840-1915): philologist, Celtic professor and Principal of Jesus College, Oxford. He placed Welsh in the context of other Indo-European Celtic Languages; edited the *Mabinogion*, and wrote on archeology and folk customs.

Rhys, Keidrych (1915-87): poet and editor, who founded the periodical *Wales* in 1937, the Druid Press in Carmarthen; worked as a columnist for the English newspaper, *The People*, and edited poetry anthologies, including *Modern Welsh Poetry* (1944).

Rhys, Morgan (1716-79): b. Cil y Cwm, Carmarthen. A school teacher and one of his century's most important Welsh hymn writers.

Rhys, Sion Dafydd (1534-1609): b. Anglesey; medical doctor who wrote an influential Welsh Grammar and defended the writings of Geoffrey of Monmouth.

Rhys-Davies, John (b. 1944): born to a Welsh family in England, a popular actor wtith many television and screen successes, including Grimli in *Lord of the Rigngs* and Priam in *Helen of Troy.*

S

Twenty -third letter of the Welsh alphabet (sounded as in English word "so" never as in "wise".

Sain (Sound): a leading Welsh record company begun by Dafydd Iwan and friends in 1969 to modernize Welsh recording industry and to introduce Welsh singers and musicians. In 1970, it moved from Cardiff to a converted cowshed in Llandwrog, Gwynedd. Its first release was *Dwr*, by Huw Jones.

St. Asaph (*Llanelwy*): Denbighshire: the little town that boasts the smallest cathedral in Britain, dating from the 6th century. The shrine holds an original Bishop Morgan Bible of 1588, of incomparable worth to the Welsh language.

St. David's (*Ty Ddewi*), Pembrokeshire: the smallest city in Britain; the cathedral and shrine of St. David is situated in Glyn Rhosyn where a monastery was founded by St. David in 55 A.D. Known in the Middle Ages as Manor Fynyw (*Minevia*), it was chosen as a place of pilgrimage by Pope Calixtus in the 12th century. Nearby are the ruins of the ancient chapel and holy well of St. Non, David's mother.

St. David's Day (March 1st): a feast day ordered by Archbishop Arundel in 1398, that became a Welsh national festival in the mid-eighteenth century. On St. David's Day, 1979, during one of the worst periods of industrial unrest in Britain, with little enthusiasm from both sides and attacked by such so-called Welshmen as Neil Kinnock, the Welsh Act of 1978 to establish an Assembly went down to a resounding defeat (see Assembly).

St. Giles, Wrexham: its enormous tower a prominent landmark, the church has an exact replica at New Haven, Connecticut because of its connection with Elihu Yale (the founder of Yale University) buried in the Wrexham churchyard.

St. Winefride's Well, Holywell (*Treffynnon*), an important site of pilgrimage for centuries. The former natural spring is housed in a shrine erected by the mother of Henry Vll in honor of Winefride (see Holywell).

St. Woolos Cathedral, Newport, Gwent: became a cathedral church in 1949 in the new diocese of Monmouth. It is named after a 5th Century Welsh nobleman, Lord Gwynllyw, who converted to Christianity.

Salem: the little chapel is the subject of the painting by Curnow Vosper that was used to advertise a popular brand of soap and is supposed to show the Devil in the old lady's shawl. A copy is found in many Welsh homes.

Salesbury, William (1520-1584): scholar; an important pioneer of publishing in Welsh; he translated the scriptures, beginning with *Kynniver Llyth a Ban*, the main text of the 1553 Prayer Book, and a translation of the New Testament (1567), thus leading to the translation of the whole Bible by Bishop Morgan.

Salmau Can **(Psalms, 1621):** published by Edmund Prys, the first printed book in Welsh to contain music.

Samhain **(Tachwedd, November lst):** All Saints Day in the Christian Church, the start of the Celtic year, one day after Samhain Eve (*Halloween*). In 1982, S4C (the Welsh Language Channel) began broadcasting on this day.

Samwell, David (Dafydd Ddu Feddyg, Black David the Doctor, 1751-98): doctor on Captain Cook's *The Discovery*, who wrote of the death of his captain and of his adventures in the South Seas. With Iolo Morganwg, he helped found the Gwyneddigion and the Gorsedd Beirdd Ynys Prydain.

Sarn Helen: a Roman road between Caernarfon and Carmarthen. Tradition tells us that it was ordered built by princess Elen, wife of Magnus Maximus.

Saunders, Erasmus (1670-1724): Anglican priest who wrote the history of his church, a primary source for 18th century Welsh religious history.

Scarlets, the: Llanelli's rugby team, whose Stradey Park has been the scene of many a famous victory, including the 9-3 win over New Zealand October 31, 1972. The team has provided many players for Wales.

Scotch Cattle: a workers' group who fought against their exploitation by the iron mastersmin thew early part of the 19th century. Named after a herd of prize cattle owned by a Monmouthshire iron magnate, they destroyed property, attacking workers who refused to go along. In 1834 their leader Edward Morgan was captured and hanged.

Scranton, Pennsylvania: by 1900, perhaps nearly 20 percent of all Welsh immigrants to the United States were living in Scranton and its neighbor Wilkes-Barre. Lloyd George came to the town in 1923 to a huge welcome. A few chapels still hold an annual Gymanfa Ganu, though most of the singing is now in English. A famous son was baritone Thomas L. Thomas.

Sealyham terrier: breed of terrier developed in Wales in the late 19th century by Captain John Edwardes for hunting on his estate.

Secombe, Sir Harry (1921-2001): one of Britain's most-loved entertainers, rising to prominence as a comedian with the famous *Goon Show* (1949-1958), Swansea-born Harry sang at the London Palladium, acted in several films, including *Oliver*, and starred in television, including *Songs of Praise*.

Second Aeon **(1966-1974):** a magazine published in Cariff with 21 issues.

Secretary of State for Wales: since 1970, the Secretaries of State for Wales have been the following: Peter Thomas (1970); John Morris (1974-5); Nicholas Edwards (1979-1985); Peter Walker (1987); David Hunt (1990-92); John Redwood (1993-94); William Hague (1995-96); Ron Davies (1997-2002); and Paul Murphy (1999-2002, and Peter Hain (2002-present).

Sefydliad (Foundation): the only All-Wales organisation of its kind. It supports a wide range of voluntary organisations and community groups concerned with improving quality of life for those experiencing in the valleys, towns and rural areas—all over Wales. All the projects have a common theme—they are well run and are addressing clearly identified needs. Sefydliad does not help the big well known national charities, it is restricted to Wales, helping small local charities that others often do not reach.

Sefydliad Mudiad Ysgolion Meithrin (f. 1971): the Welsh Nursery School Movement, set up to educate young children in the Welsh language from their very first day of schooling. They have been a great success in the anglicized parst of Wales.

Segontium, Caernarfon: only the foundations show its former importance as a Roman fort, along with an on site museum.

Seiriol, St. (6th century): saint connected with Anglesey and Ynys Seiriol (*Puffin Island*).

Seisyllwg: created in the 8th century, it became an independent kingdom under Cadell ap Rhodri; it became part of Deheubarth under Hywell Dda.

Selyf (d. 615): King of Powys killed fighting the Northumbrians at the momentous Battle of Chester.

Senghenydd, near Caerphilly (October 14, 1913): the village of the greatest mine disaster in British history when 439 miners died in a huge explosion after warnings were repeatedly ignored by the mine owners.

September 20, 1997: "in the wee small hours of the morning," a small majority of the people of Wales learned that their wishes for their own Assembly, composed of their own elected officials, to meet in their own country, had at last been realized, no matter how limited its powers.

Seren, Y (The Star, 1885-1974): a weekly Radical newspaper from Gwasg y Bala, Merionethshire.

Seren y Dwyrain (**Star of the East**): a newspaper published in Cairo for Welsh troops in the Eighth Army in the W.W.II. Under its original publisher, T. Elwyn Griffiths, it developed into *Yr Enfys*, the journal of Cymry a'r Byd (*Wales Internationa*l) for Welsh men and women all over the world.

Seren Cymru **(f. 1851, Star of Wales)**: newspaper published at Caernarfon that became a weekly in 1863; it has been a Baptist publication since 1936.

Seren Gomer **(Star of Gomer, 1814-1983):** the first newspaper in the Welsh language, published in Swansea as a general information weekly but ending its career as a Baptist quarterly.

Seven Wonders of Wales: a 19th Century anonymous rhyme probably composed to attract visitors to North Wales: "Pistyll Rhaeadr and Wrexham Steeple/ Snowdon's Mountain without its people/ Overton Yew Trees, Gresford Bells/ Llangollen Bridge, and St. Winifride's Wells."

Severn *(Hafren):* at 220 miles (354 km), beginning high up on Plynlimon in Dyfed, this is the longest river in Britain. The famous Severn Bore (a wall of water rushing upstream) results from some of the highest tides in the world.

Sewin (Sea Trout): found in most tidal rivers and estuaries in Wales.

Sharon, Pennsylvania: an iron manufacturing town where the first American rolling mill was built by David Morgan from Pontypool in 1871.

Sheen, Michael (b. 1969): from Newport, Gwent, actor who played Mozart in the Broadway production of *Amadeus* (1999).

Sheep: with a fraction over 8,000 sq m., Wales raises eleven million sheep, about 15 percent of all the sheep in the European Community.

Shimli **(Chimney***):* a custom popular in West Wales that grew out of the need to gather the harvest before it had ripened so that it would not spoil in the Autumn rains. The crop was dried in a kiln over a period of 36 hours. Being Welsh, the young people who had helped with the harvest sang and recited.

Shires of Wales, The: created by Edward lst in 1284. The surviving Marcher lordships also became shires In 1536. The thirteen Welsh shires (counties) became eight In 1972 (Gwynedd, Clwyd, Powys, Dyfed, Monmouthshire, and West, Mid and South Glamorgan). New divisions were created in 1996, based on population, creating Anglesey, Gwynedd, Conwy, Denbigh, Flint, Wrexham, Poyws, Ceredigion, Pembroke, Carmarthen, Swansea, Neath Port Talbot, Bridgend, Rhondda Cynon Faff, Merthyr Tydfil, Torfaen, Vale of Glamorgan, Cardiff, Newport, Blawenau Gwent, and Monmouthshire (also called Gwent).

Shotton, Flintshire: on land reclaimed from the Dee, former site of one of the largest steel works in Europe

(John Summers and Sons) Shotton Paper is the largest manufacturer of newsprint in Britain, producing 470,000 tonnes of newsprint each year; it is the only British mill to depend solely on UK resources. It is being converted to produce 100 percent recycled fiber.

Sianel Pedwar Cymru (Wales Channel Four,1982): a T.V. station set up after a protest movement led by Gwynfor Evans and thousands of other Welsh patriots finally persuaded the Government to enable Welsh listeners to enjoy programs in their own language.

Siddons, Sarah (1755-1833): famous actress born in a tavern in Brecon. Of her, William Hazlitt wrote "Passion emanated from her breast as from a shrine."

Silures: a tribe of southeast Wales recorded by Roman historian Tacitus. Led by Caratacus, they offered strong resistance to the Roman invaders, but were finally forcible settled in Venta Silurium (Caerwent). Their prowess in battle continued as mercenaries for English kings in campaigns against the French.

Singing to Oxen: an ancient, long-surviving folk custom of encouraging oxen to pull the plough.

Sion Cain (1575-1630): the last herald poet to travel through North Wales.

Sion Cent (15th C.): a master of satire who wrote that worldly reality is mere illusion. His literary skills greatly influenced later Welsh poets.

Sion Corn: Father Christmas (*Santa Claus*).

Sion Dafi (1441-68): b. Cemais, Montgomery; a professional soldier and favorite of Edward lV; he had a hand cut off and replaced by one of silver.

Sion Tudor (1522-1602): St. Asaph; satirical poet, one of the last poets of the Gentry.

Sioni Wynwyn (Sioni Wnions): a name given to Breton onion sellers, once common in the valleys of South Wales, with strings of onions for sale.

***Sir Briggs* (1846-1874):** a brave horse that carried Captain Godfrey Morgan to victory at Cowbridge Races after having taken part in cavalry charges at Inkerman, The Alma, and Balaclava in the Crimean War. Captain Morgan later became Lord Tredegar.

Siwan (Joan: 1195-1237): daughter of English King John and wife of Llywelyn Fawr (*Llywelyn the Great*), reconciled to her husband after an affair with a Marcher Lord (who was hanged for his part).

Skerries, the: islands off the northwest coast of Anglesey that have caused hundreds of shipwrecks over the centuries.

Skull Attack: the local name for Brain's S.A. (Strong Ale) brewed in Cardiff.

Smith, David (b. 1945): Tonypandy historian, critic, and college lecturer. Has written on Welsh industry and rugby, and produced a TV series.

Smith, Ray (1936-1991): Rhondda actor began at Swansea's Grand Theatre played a "heavy" on BBC T.V.

Snell and Sons (f. 1900): the famous Swansea Company that is the largest publisher of Welsh music. Surviving the great blitz of World War Two, it continues its catalog of traditional and popular Welsh music that is sold throughout the world. "Sending to Snell's" is a tradition in Welsh music.

Snowdonia, Gwynedd:(from the Saxon Snow Dun, the snow hill or fort): Dominated by *Yr Wyddfa* at 3,560 ft, Snowdonia National Park is overrun all-year round by tourists enjoying the hiking, climbing, orienteering, pony trekking, etc. A cog railway to the summit, begun in 1896, adds to the congestion.

Society for the Propagation of Christian Knowledge (1699): founded by Sir John Phillips of Picton to set up a network of charity schools in Wales that allowed the use of Welsh. It published many religious works.

Sospan Bach (Little Saucepan): along with the hymn *Calon Lan*, perhaps the most sung of all Welsh tunes. It is especially beloved in Llanelli, where little tin *sospans* are banged at rugby games.

South Wales Borderers (f. 1689 as Dering's Regiment of Foot): an infantry regiment now part of the Royal Regiment of Wales; has served with distinction with over 100 battle honors gained with Marlborough in Europe, in the American War for Independence, and in both World Wars. In the movie *Zulu*, they were shown winning acclaim for their heroic stand at Rorke's Drift in 1879.

South Wales Echo, Cardiff: newspaper established in 1884.

South Wales Evening Post, with nearly 20,000 readers daily, the newspaper publishes edition for Swansea and vicinity: Llanelli, Carmarthen and Ammanford; another for the Neath, Port Talbot area.

South Wales Miners' Federation (the Fed, b. 1898): following the arrival of the newspaper *Llais Llafur* (the Voice of Labour), "the Fed" began in 1898 with Mabon its first president; its quarter of a million members temporarily dominated life in the Valleys.

Southall, John Edward (1855-1928): b. Leominster, Hereford, but set up printing press in Newport where he wrote books on the Welsh language and bilingual texts for Welsh schools.

Southall, Neville (b. 1958): from Llandudno, played in goal for Everton 750 times, with 93 appearances for Wales. Voted "Footballer of the Year" in 1985.

Speed, Gary (b. 1969): from Flintshire, the most experienced footballer in the Premier League. Left Everton for Leeds to win the championship 1992; then moved to Newcastle and now at Bolton. By March, 2004 he had played for Wales over 75 times.

Spencer, Lady Diana Frances (1961-1997):

 the most well-known and best loved Princess of Wales in history, Diana came into her title upon her marriage to Prince Charles in 1981 at St. Paul's, London, in a ceremony televised world wide. Diana had lived with her divorced father, Earl Spencer, her two elder sisters, and her younger brother at Althorp. She gave birth to William in 1982 and Henry in 1984. Divorced in 1996 and throwing herself into charitable and humane causes, she was killed in a car crash in Paris.

Spinetti, Vincent (b. 1932): actor born at Cwm, Ebbw Vale to Italian parents; appeared in three Beatles films. Trained at the Welsh College of Music and Drams, he debuted on the West End in *Expresso Bongo*; received Tony Award in New York for *Oh What a Lovely War.*

Sports Council for Wales, the (1972): the main advisory body to the National Assembly on sporting matters, to develop and promote sport, it also administers the Lottery Sports Fund for Wales.

Spring, Howard (1889-1965): Cardiff born novelist whose tales set in the Welsh Valleys include *Heaven Lies about Us, O Absalom!,* and *Fame is the Spur.*

Spurrell, William (1833-89): Carmarthen printer who published works for the University of Wales and the National Library of Wales and several dictionaries. In 1957, under new ownership, it became known as the Five Arches Press.

Squires, Dorothy (1915-1998): singer from Pontyberem, Dorothy made her London debut in West End Cabaret in 1936, going on to star in theaters all over Britain. Married for a time to Roger Moore, of James Bond fame, she made a remarkable comeback at the London Palladium in 1970 after a long absence before starring at Carnegi Hall, in New York in 1971. She died in the Rhondda after long struggles with illness divorce proceedings, and bankruptcy.

Stable Loft Singing: in parts of Wales, unmarried male servants, who slept above the stables, were allowed to bring together their friends in the cold winter nights for an evening of singing. They could break away from the hymn-singing traditions of the Cymanfa and entertain themselves with more traditional ballads and folk songs. The Jew's harp and the accordion were often used to accompany the singing.

Stableford System: a system of scoring in golf invented at the Glamorganshire Golf Club by Dr. Stableford in 1898 to ensure fair competition.

Standard Welsh: see Cymraeg Byw ("living Welsh").

Stanley, Henry Morton (1841-1904): journalist, explorer, finder of Livingstone in Africa, born as John Rowlands (an illegitimate child) at Denbigh, spent his childhood in an orphanage at St. Asaph befor moving to New Orleans at age 13, where he adopted the name of a wealthy merchant. After serving in the Confederate Army, he joined the *New York Herald* as a journalist in 1867.

Stanton, Charles Butt (1873-1946): trade union leader, politician, friend and influence on Keir Hardie, whom he succeeded as Inedpendent Labour Party M.P. for Merthyr in 1915.

***Statute of Rhuddlan* (the Statute of Wales, 1284):** created the counties of Anglesey, Caernarfon, and Merioneth, to be governed by the Justice of North Wales; the county of Flint, to be placed under the Justice of Chester; and the counties of Carmarthen and

Cardigan, to be left under the Justice of South Wales. In the new counties the English pattern of courts was firmly set in place.

Steadman, Ralph (b. 1936): brought up in Abergele, N. Wales; a prolific cartoonist and illustrator who has worked for *Punch, Private Eye, The New Statemsman,* and the *Daily Telegraph* and many books.

Steer, Irene: at Stockhom in 1912, she was the first Welsh woman to win an Olympic Gold Medal (4x100 metre relay in swimming.)

Stephens, Evan (1854-1930): b. Pencader, Carmarthen, went to Salt Lake City, to become first Director of the Salt Lake Choral Society in 1889.

Stephens, Meic (b. 1938): writer, editor, prolific author on the culture of Wales, founder of the Triskel Press, the magazine *Poetry Wales*, and the literary director of the Welsh Arts Council.

Stephens, Thomas (1821-75): antiquary and critic, eisteddfod winner and judge who set high literary standards, and author of *The Literature of the Kymry* (1849. He helped improve social conditions in Merthyr in a long, distinguished public career.

Stereophonics, the: popular rock group from Cwmaman whose road to success began with the release of *Word Gets Around* in August, 1997.

Stevens, Matthew (b. 1977): from Carmarthen, a world-class snooker player; voted Young Player of the Year in 1998; won U.K. championship in 2003.

Strata Florida (*Ystrad Fflur*) Cardiganshire: Cistercian abbey; political, religious and educational center in the 12th and 13th centuries. Reputed to be the burial ground of many Welsh princes as well as poet Dafydd ap Gwilym.

Stringer, Sir Howard (b.1942): b. Cardiff; Chief Executive Officer of Sony Corporation of America, previously Chairman of Tele-TV following a career as journalist, producer, and chief executive at CBS, 1988-1995. Coming to the US in 1965, he served in the U.S. Army in Vietnam. With many awards for his achievements and leadership in journalism, knighted in 2000, and appointed head of Sony in 2005, the first foreigner to head the Japanese Company.

Studia Celtica (*f. 1966*): periodical important in the field of Celtic linguistics.

Sul y Blodau (Flowering Sunday): a custom of dressing graves with flowers on Palm Sunday: also the name of a well-known Welsh lament.

Sulien (1010-91): associated with Llanbadarn, where he set up a center of learning; and with St. David's, where he was twice Bishop.

Sullivan, Jim (1903): the most dominant player in the English Rugby League, kicking a hundred or more goals in each of 18 consecutive seasons, scoring a total of 2,959 goals, 96 tries, and a grand total of 6,206 points. His record 204 goals in 1931-4 stood for 24 years. In one game alone, he kicked 24 goals.

Summer Birch, The: an ancient tradition that involved the erection and decoration of the birch tree, a fertility symbol.

Sunday Closing Act (1881): one of the very first pieces of legislation passed by Parliament that was specifically designed for Wales, conferring upon it a much belated status as a distinct national unit.

Sunday Schools (f. late 18th C.): following the success of the schools set up by the SPCK, free Sunday Schools established under the leadership of Thomas Charles of Bala to play an important part in the growth of literacy and the survival of the language.

Super Furry Animals: a music group (playing "acid-tinged fuzz-rock" that surfaced in Wales in the 90's). Based in Cardiff and enjoying a phenomenal success, the eccentric group will not perform on St. David's Day and has released albums entirely in Welsh.

***Super Ted* (b. 1982):** with his friend Smotyn, one of Welsh television's most popular characters.

Swansea (*Abertawe*): the second largest city in Wales (pop: c. 200,000) named for Swain, a Viking chieftain, it has managed to shake off the relics of its industrial past and is now an important tourist center for the unspoiled Gower Peninsular and a summer resort. The Royal Institute of South Wales, its eclectic "museum of a museum" has a wonderful collection. The Glyn Vivian Art gallery shows off its famous Swansea China; the Guildhall is home to Sir Frank Brangwyn's murals; and the restored dock area is now an attractive marina, where the Maritime and Industrial Museum is neighbor to the Dylan Thomas Theatre, many new hotels and restaurants. The University College is located in Singleton Park. Clyne Castle has a splendid botanical garden.

Swansea Jack (1930's): a retriever that lived down at the Swansea Docks who became famous for saving the lives of people and other dogs. He is commemorated by a carved stone and by a pub near the waterfront.

Sycharth, Denbighshire: site of the splendid mansion of Owain Glyndwr, the Welsh leader and most famous patron of poet Iolo Goch (1320-1398) to whom we owe the description of its former glory.

T

Twenty-fourth letter of the Welsh alphabet. In many words beginning with t, the letter is mutated to d, nh, or th. (ex: *dy deulu, yn Nhreorchy, a theulu)*.

Tachwedd: eleventh month (November in English).

Taff (*Taf*): the 41-mile long river at the estuary of which is Cardiff.

Taffy: a Welshman (from Dafydd): Some 17th century English writers referred to Wales as "Taffydom." The corrupt few in contemporary high places and political circles are now known as "The Taffia."

Taffy (1953-1980): a Welsh collie that held the record for Europe's oldest dog.

Taffy: name of the mascot of the Royal Welch Fusiliers, a Kashmiri billy goat.

Taff Vale Railway Company Dispute, 1900: when judgement was given in favor of the company and against the striking workers of the Amalgamated Society of Railway Servants, the unions saw that they had to have legislation to protect their rights. To promote their interests, the Labour Representative

Committee was founded in London that was the forerunner of the Labour Party.

Talgarth, Powys: little town where Hywel Harris experienced a religious awakening. A converted barn, Maesyronnen Chapel (1696-7) is the oldest unaltered nonconformist meeting place still in use in Wales.

Taliesin (6th Century): a poet of Strathclyde, part of the *Old North* (now Western Scotland) mentioned by Nennius. His poetry was collected in the 14th century *Book of Taliesin*. Praising Urien Rheged's success in defeating the Germanic invaders, it survives as the oldest in the Welsh language.

Taliesin (1859-61): a quarterly magazine with eight issues, containing prose, poetry, and essays.

Taliesin **(f. 1951)**: a literary magazine with poems, short stories, essays, reviews and translations published by Yr Academi Cymreig as an important platform for the work of writers in Welsh.

Talyllyn Railway, Gwynedd: the first of the Welsh narrow-gauge railways to be saved for posterity and the enjoyment of visitors, a former slate quarryman's line from Abergynolwen to Tywyn.

Tann, Hilary (b. 1947): accomplished composer, born in a South Wales Valley, Chair of the Dept of Performing Arts at Union College, Schenectady, New

York, she has composed for many internationally-famed orchestras, including the Royal Liverpool Philharmonic for the last night of the Welsh Proms at Cardiff.

Tanner, Phil (*The Gower Nightingale*, 1862-1950): considered the greatest of all the English speaking folk performers of Wales. His vast repertoire of Gower songs and dances arc being re-discovered by modern performers and recommitted to recordings.

Tanwedd: a fiery streak of light in the sky that is a promonition of death.

Taplas: an old musical event with dancing, singing and game-playing on Saturday evenings between Easter Monday and Winter's Eve.

***Tarian y Gweithiwr* (1875-1934):** "the Shield of the Worker," a weekly paper published in Welsh at Aberdare with local news, mostly dealing with the interests of workers but also literary and political articles.

Taylor, Alison: from an Anglesey family, novelist and journalist with a career in probation and social work recognized for her work in child care and ethics. She received Arts Council of Wales Disabled Writers' Award in 1994; has novels published in many countries.

Teilo, St. (6th Century): influential church leader, contemporary of St. David; founder of Llandeilo Fawr, who became venerated in Wales and Brittany.

Tegeingl: (see Englefield).

Teisen Lap (*plate cake*): a Welsh favorite, made on an iron skillet or in a fry pan with butter, flour, lard, eggs, currants, sugar, spices and milk.

Telyn (Welsh harp): triple-stringed instrument probably introduced into Wales from Italy in the 18th Century. It is played by a tenynor (male) or telynores (female) some of whom play it in Gypsy (style over the left shoulder).

 **Terfel, Bryn (Bryn Jones b. 1965):** internationally acclaimed opera star from Pwllglas, Snowdonia; after early successes in local eisteddfodau, he studied at London's Guildhall School of Music, debuted as baritone with the Welsh National Opera Company in 1990. With a a voice and command of his art compared to that of Fischer-Dieskau in his prime after appearing at Salzburg in 1992, he is in demand at the world's leading opera houses as well as concert halls and sporting venues in his native Wales.

Teulu Abram Wood: (see Wood family).

Tewdrig (6 th C.): prince mortally wounded while leading the people of Glamorgan to victory against Saxon invasers.

Tilsley, Gwilym Richard (*Tilsli*, 1911-1997): Archdruid of Wales; Chair-winning poet whose popular verses deal with the plight of Welsh industrial workers.

Tintern Abbey, Gwent (f. 1131): after 400 prospcrous years, the Cistercians left the Abbey at its dissolution in 1536, at which time all articles of value were catalogued, weighed, and sent to King Henry VIII's treasury.   In 1782, the Reverend William Gilpin's *Observations on the River* Wye began a trickle of visitors that became a flood after the paintings of William Turner and the writings of William Wordsworth praised the hallowed spot.

Tir Newydd **(New Ground, 1935-39):** a quarterly magazine dealing with the arts of contemporary Wales.

Tithe War: began in the 1880's in Clwyd as a tenants' protest against tithes due the Established (Anglican) Church, ended when the Tithe Act of 1891 transferred obligation to the landowner.

Tlysau Hen Oesoedd **(Treasures of the Ancient Ages, 1735):** published by William Morris, it was the first Welsh periodical (but only one issue).

Toili (teulu, "family"): the phantom funeral that is a premonition of death.

Tolkien, Royd (b. 1969): from Sychdyn, near Mold, Flintshre, a cast member of the film *Lord of the Rings: Return of the King.* And grandson of J.R.R. Tolkien.

Tonypandy, Rhondda Valley: after rapid industrial growth in the early 20th century, it was the scene of a major strike, a lock out, and a riot in 1910. Policemen and soldiers sent by Home Secretary Winston Churchill left a legacy of bitterness (though their relations with the workers were mostly amicable).

Tower Colliery, Hirwaun, Mid-Glam: the only worker owned mine in Europe, it began as a drift mine in 1864, the main shaft was dug in 1941. Closed by British Coal in April 1994, it was bought out by the workforce and re-opened in January, 1995 as Goitre Tower Anthracite.

***Traethodydd, Y* (the Essayist f. 1845):** published by Thomas Gee, a magazine of essays on various topics.

***Treachery of the Blue Books*:** a satirical expression from the play *Brad y Llyfrau Gleision* by R.J. Derfel (1854) to describe the government report of 1847 that blamed the Welsh language and Nonconformity for "the sad state of education" and for "dirtiness, laziness, ignorance, superstition, promiscuity, and immorality."

Treachery of the Long Knives*:* in Nennius, elaborated by Geoffrey of Monmouth, about the slaughter of British leaders invited to a banquet by the Saxons.

Trefechan Bridge, Aberystwyth: the site of a demonstration in 1962 that blocked the way in and out of town and began the movement to give Welsh legal status.

Trefor, Sion (d. 1410): Bishop of St. Asaph, partner in the deposition of Richard ll; a staunch supporter of Owain Glyndwr whose cause he unsuccessfully represented in Parliament.

Trelew, Patagonia: a bustling town, now mostly Spanish speaking, formed when Moriah Chapel was built by Welsh immigrants in 1880. It was connected by rail to Port Madryn in 1888.

Treí'r Ceiri (*Home of the Giants)*, Gwynedd: the impressive remains of an Iron Age village still used in Roman times high on *Yr Eifl* (The Forks) Mountain.

Tretower Castle and Court, Breconshire: home of the 15th century Vaughan family set in the grounds of a 13th century round castle keep.

Tri Brenin o Gwlen, **Y** (The Three Kings of Cologne, 16th C.): one of only two surviving Welsh miracle plays (with *Y Dioddeaint a 'r Atgyfodiad*).

Tri Thlws ar Ddeg Ynys Prydain: *(*see Thirteen Treasures of the Isle of Britain).

Triads of the Isle of Britain (13th and 14th centuries): stories of the heroes and heroines of Medieval Wales that served as source material for centuries of poets and historians.

Triban: the three-green triangle emblem of Plaid Cymru, the Party of Wales. It was also the name of a popular form of medieval poetry particularly associated with folk customs in Glamorganshire.

Tribes of Wales: at the time of the Roman invasions, the four main tribes of Wales were the Silures, Demetae, Ordovices, and Decangli.

Trinity College (*Coleg y Drindod*), Carmarthen (f. 1848): an Anglican Teachers' College.

Trioedd y Meirch: (see Triads of Horses).

Trioedd Ynys Prydain (*see Triads of the Isle of Britain*).

Tripp, John (b. 1927): journalist and poet, former literary editor of *Planet*, whose subject has mainly been the history of modern Wales.

Tristan and Iseult: the doomed lovers of the medieval romances linked to the Arthurian cycle.

Troelus a Chresyd (**Troilus and Cressida**): an anonymous 17th century work derived from Chaucer's poem, it is the first ful-length play written in Welsh.

Trywerin (d. 1957): a Welsh-speaking community in a Merionethshire valley displaced by a reservoir to provide a water supply for Liverpool Corporation. "Cofiwch Drywerin" ("Remember Trywerin") became a rallying cry for Welsh youth in the late 1960's.

Tudful, St. (6th Century): daughter of Brychan, she was killed by Saxons; commemorated at Merthyr Tydfil, where she had founded a church.

Tudor (*Tudur*): a prominent Anglesey family, centered at Penmynydd, one of whom, Owain, married Catherine of Valois, widow of Henry V, thus beginning the royal dynasty that began with the reign of Henry Vl in 1485.

Tudor Aled (1465-1525): from Llansannan, a master craftsman, a poet of the Gentry, and a valuable source for the history of leading Welsh families.

Twenty-four Metres (**14th century**): a classification of poetic meters that differed from the ancient metrical tradition.

Twm Siôn Cati (**Jones, Thomas, 1530-1609):** character pardoned by Elizabeth lst for his misdemeanors. His exploits, real or otherwise, were made famous through a novel, *The Adventures and Vagaries of Twm Sion Cati*

(1828), and through George Borrow's *Wild Wales* (1862).

Twmpath: originally a "tump" of ground upon which young people danced, sang and played. Now revived as an evening of folk dancing and merriment.

Tyler, Bonnie (Gaynor Hopkins, b. 1953): b. Skewen, Swansea, Bonnie sang began a recording career in 1975 following surgery that left her voice husky. She has won platinum and gold records, touring Europe in sell-out concerts.

Tylwyth Teg (*fairy folk*): the name first appeared in a 15th century poem. Particularly active at night or around lakes and bogs, they appear in many folk tales. Also known as *Mamau* (mothers).

***Tynged yr Iaith (Fate of the language,* 1962)**: a radio talk by Saunders Lewis attacking the government's lack of effort in preserving the Welsh language and appealing for civil disobedience. It served as a catalyst to the activities of newly formed Cymdeithas yr Iaith Gymraeg (*Society for the Welsh Language*).

Tysilio, St. (7th century): son of a Prince of Powys, founder of the church at Llandysilio.

Ty Mawr, Gwynedd: near Penmachno, the home of Bishop William Morgan, translator of the Bible into Welsh.

Ty Un Nos (*House of One Night*): many unemployed families had no homes. The story is that if they could build a home from local stone overnight and have smoke escaping from the chimney, they could claim legal ownership.

Tywyn, Merionethshire: home to an ancient church containing St. Cadfan's Stone, with inscriptions in 8th century Welsh, the oldest surviving example. The Talyllyn Railway is a narrow-gauge line preserved since 1950, the first in the world to be restored and operated by volunteers.

Th

Twenty-fifth letter of the Welsh alphabet.
(pronounced as in English words *think*, never as in
than. Borrowings from English include *Thomas* and
most of the list that follows)

Thirteen Treasures of the Island of Britain, the (**Tri
Thlws ar Deg Ynys Prydain**): a 15th century list of the
treasures of Welsh heroes. The number varies in
different documents; they include the sword of
Rhydderch Hen, the horn of Bran Galed, the chessboard
of Gwenddolau, the hamper of Gwyddno Garanhir, the
cauldron of Diwrnach the Giant, the mantle of Tegau
Eurfron, and the stone and ring of Eluned.

Thomas, Alan (b. 1936): director of music in various
schools in Britain, active with the National Youth
Orchestra of Wales; moved to Canada in 1974; Director
of Music at Ashbury College, Ottowa; conductor of the
Parkdale Symphony and a celebrated organ
accompanist.

Thomas, Dafydd Elis (b. 1946): Carmarthen born,
after early career as lecturer, writer and broadcaster,
elected for Plaid, Meirionydd Nant Conwy in 1993.

Thomas, David (*Dafydd Ddu Eryri*, 1759-1822): *Black David of Snowdon*, poet who established literary societies, teaching the traditional meters.

Thomas, David (*Dai y Stiward*, 1794-1882): Neath-born David emigrated with his family from Ystradgynlais in 1839, setting up blast furnaces at Allentown, Pennsylvania, utilizing the hot blast to smelt iron ore with anthracite (a process he had used at Ynyscedwyn Iron Works). Within ten years of his arrival, the Lehigh Valley had become the world's leading iron producer. His story is told in *From Wales to Pennsylvania* (Red Dragon Press).

Thomas, David Alfred (1856-1918): the first Viscount Rhondda; a wealthy coal owner and Liberal MP for Merthyr Tydfil; controller of British food production during W.W.I.

Thomas, Dylan (1914-1953): a major lyric poet profoundly influenced by his native Wales, though he wrote in English. His three volumes of poetry, published before the Second World War, were followed by *Deaths and Entrances* (1946), by which time his reputation as a great literary craftsman had been well established. A wonderful evocation of childhood on a Welsh farm is "Fern Hill." He died in New York City.

Thomas, Ebenezer (*Eben Fardd*, 1802-63): poet and critic whose school at Clynnog Fawr trained candidates for the ministry and whose work has been praised as heralding the golden age of the epic in Wales.

Thomas, Edward (1878-1917): London-born poet to Welsh parents; preferred to call himself Welsh. His major theme was the loss of innocence in the heady rush of "progress." In 1905, he published *Beautiful Wales*. Much of his poetry was published after his death as a soldier in the First World War; it influenced later poets, especially Dylan Thomas.

Thomas, Edward Morley (Ned Thomas, b. 1936): writer and editor; taught Welsh literature at Aberystwyth in 1970. Published *The Welsh Extremist* in 1971, a year after he had helped found *Planet*. Ned's most ambitious project is to found a Welsh-language newspaper, *Y Byd (The World)* to begin in 2005.

Thomas, Ernest Lewis (Richard Vaughan, 1904-83): b. Llanddeusant, Carms; novelist and journalist who wrote of the farming communites of his region.

Thomas, Gareth (b. 1974) from Bridgend, rugby player with 77 appearances for Wales, in July 2004 he beat Ieuan Evan's record by scoring his 34th try.

Thomas, George, Viscount Tonypandy (1909-1997): miner's son from Port Talbot, known to millions of radio listeners for his role as the Speaker of the House of Commons from February 1976 to June, 1983. Entered Parliament in 1945, as Labour M.P. for Cardiff Central; succeeded Cledwyn Hughes as Secretary of State for Wales in 1968. One of the old school of Welsh Labour politicians, fiercely antagonistic to any ideas of Welsh independence, he vigorously opposed the creation of a National Assembly for Wales.

Thomas, Gwyn (1913-1981): Rhonda-born socialist novelist and dramatist whose characters desperately and often hilariously survive in the harshest of conditions. The author was an uncompromising critic of the Welsh language and those who wrote in it.

Thomas, Gwyn (b. 1936): scholar, poet and dramatist who specialized in the work of Ellis Wynne and the earliest Welsh poetry. His many volumes of poetry have made him one of the most widely read of modern Welsh language poets.

Thomas, Helen Wynne (1966-89): from Newcastle Emlyn, a member of the Greenham Common Women's Peace Camp in late summer, 1981, protesting Britain's policies on nuclear armament, she was killed by a police horse box.

Thomas, Hugh Owen (1833-91): from Anglesey, a leading specialist in orthopedic surgery at Liverpool who created many modern medical appliances.

Thomas, Islyn (d. 2002): b. Maesteg; came to the US at age eleven. As the founder of the Thomas Manufacturing Company and Thomas International, his contribution of parts for the Rolls Royce aircraft engines brought him the OBE from Queen Elizabeth. He was a founder member of N.W.A.F. and the author of *Our Welsh Heritage.*

Thomas, Jennie (1898-1979): author who introduced the popular animal characters *Sion Blewyn Coch* and *Wil Cwac Cwac* to Welsh children in her *Llyfr Mawr y Plant* (Big Book for Children) 1931.

Thomas, John (*Ieuan Ddu*: Black John, 1795-1871): b. Carmarthenshire; patriotic musician, poet and influential choir director and singer who published his collection of tunes, *Y Caniedydd Cymreig* (Welsh Song Book), 1845.

Thomas, John (1795-1871): from Bridgend; *Pencerdd Gwalia* (Chief Musician of Wales), harpist to Queen Victoria; an instructor at the Royal College and the Guildhall School of Music, his work is collected as *Welsh Melodies* (1862-1874).

Thomas, John (1886-1933: b. Flint, raised in Harlech, he left the Nobel explosives factory in Scotland to become chief chemist at Solway Dyes Company, pioneering in research and edevelopment of dyes; later became Director of the Dyes Division of Imperial Chemical Industries (ICI).

Thomas, John (*Eifionydd*, 1848-1922): editor *Y Geninen* (The Leek, 1883-1922), valuable for information about Welsh cultural life.

Thomas, Sir John Meurig (b. 1932): b. Gwendraeth Valley, Carms. Professor of chemistry at the Davy Faraday Research Laboratory, The Royal Institution of Great Britain whicn he directed 1985-1991; head of chemistry at Abcrystwyth, later King's College, Cambridge. For his contributions to catalysis, solid state chemistry of materials and surface science, he has been given numerous honours, including the Davy Medal, the Rutherford Lectureship of the Royal Society, the Messel Gold Medal of the Society of the Chemical Industry and so on. He is a Fellow of many internationally recognized societies, including the Royal Society and an Honorary Fellow of the American Academy of Arts and Science, and the U.K. Institute of Physics. A member of the Gorsedd, Dr. Thomas has written many influential science texts.

Thomas, Lucy (1781-1847): "the Mam" of the Welsh coal industry, remembered for opening the first level at Waunwyllt colliery, near Merthyr, for the mining of coal for household use.

Thomas, Mansel (1909-1986): one of the most influential musicians of his generation, famous as a composer, conductor and adjudicator. For many years, he was the BBC's principal music representative for Wales; he wrote a large and varied range of music, vocal, choral, and instrumental. He won the Rhondda Scholarship to the Royal Academy of Music at age 16, joined the BBC in 1936, eventually becoming the principal conductor of the BBC Welsh Orchestra. He retired in 1965 to devote himself to composition.

Thomas, Margaret Haig, Viscountess Rhondda (1883-1953): early suffragette kept out of the House of Lords on legal grounds after the death of her father. She founded *Time and Tide*, a weekly journal of politics and literature in 1920. In 1915 she survived the sinking of the *Lusitania*.

Thomas, Mark (b. 1956): from Penclawdd, near Swansea; musician, graduated from University of Wales, led the Royal Ballet Orchestra (1981-83): played with London Symphony and Royal Philharmonic Orchestras; composed music for *Highlander, Superman, License to Kill, Twin Town,* and many other major films and T.V. programs.

Thomas, Mickey (b. 1954): b. Mochdre, footballer with Wrexham before moving to Manchester United and Everton; he returned to help Wrexham beat Arsenal in the F.A. Clup contest in 1993, scoring the winning goal. He played for Wales 51 times, helping them defeat England 4-1.

Thomas, Rachel (1905-1995): from the Swansea Valley, actress who epitomized the indomitable Welsh *Mam*, she made her last appearance aged 97 (with

Emlyn Williams in the B.B.C. film *Caring*). Beginning with local eisteddfodau, she began with the BBC in the early 1930's, she appeared in many movies, including *Tiger Bay* (1959) and *How Green Was My Valley* (on B.B.C, television 1959-1960).

Thomas, Richard (1838-1916): steel magnate, founder of Richard Thomas and Sons in 1884: merged with Baldwin's in 1945 and with Guest Keen in 1947 to form the Steel Company of Wales, prosperous up to the late 1950's.

Thomas, Richard James (1908-76): lexicographer, his *Enwau Afonydd a Nentydd Cymru* (Names of Welsh Rivers and Streams, 1938), is still the standard.

Thomas, Robert (Ap Vychan, 1809-80): from Llanuwchllyn, Mer., minister, preacher, Professor of Divinity at Bala Independent College (1873); co-editor of Y Dysgedydd, Eisteddfod Chair winner.

Thomas, R.S. (1913 -2000): Cardiff-born Anglican priest and poet who learned Welsh as an adult, inspired by rural Wales with its partisanship and growing sense of national consciousness as a defense against the encroachments of an unfeeling, materialistic, English-speaking world. Wrote over 1500 poems in a 50-year period. Awarded the Queen's Gold Medal in 1964.

Thomas, Robert Jermain (1839-1866): b. Llandovery; the first Protestant martyr of Korea, killed in

Pyongyand after his capture with the crew of the American schooner *General Sherman*.

Thomas, Stanley (b. 1942): from Merthyr, a billonaire who began acquiring airports through his company TBI which he began after amassing a fortune selling met pies to fish and chip shops (Pete's Savoury Products). He supports numerous charities in Wales where he is president of the Boys and Girls Clubs and is building a children's hospital.

Thomas, Sydney Gilchrist (1850-85): born in London to Cardiganshire parents; at Blaenavon, with Percy, his cousin, he discovered a method of taking phosphorus out of the pig iron in the manufacture of steel that was to have enormous impact on the making of steel throughout the world.

Thomas, Thomas L: born in Pennsylvania to a Welsh family, one of America's greatest baritones, star of opera and concert hall and a favorite on American T.V. in the 1950's.

Thomas, William (*Islwyn*, 1832-78): poet whose greatest work Y Storm reflects his emotional and spiritual torment following the death of his love, Ann Bowen.

Thompson, David (1770-1857): born in London of Welsh parents, known as "that Welshman" and "the man who measured Canada," he surveyed most of the

Canadian-U.S. border in the late 18th century.
Covering 80,000 miles on foot, dog sled, horseback and
canoe, discovering the Columbia River, Thompson
defined one-fifth of the North American continent. His
77 volumes of his studies in geography, biology and
ethnography make him one of the world's greatest
geographers.

Thrale, Hester (Hester Lynch Piozzi, 1741-1821):
author and letter writer, a Salusbury of Tremeirchion,
Flintshire. As wife of wealthy brewer Henry Thrale,
she was acquainted with the leading literary figures in
London. As a widow, she was courted by Dr. Johnson
but married music teacher Count Piozzi.

Three Tries for a Welshman: an expression with
multiple meanings that dates back to 19th century.

U

Twenty-sixth letter of the Welsh alphabet pronounced as "ee" in pita or "I "in pin.
(Cymru is *Kumree;* Llandudno is *Thlan-did-no*).

*Un Nos Ola Leuad (***One Moonlit Night, 1961)**: by Caradog Prichard, one of the most popular novels in Wales. It has been made into a movie.

Undeb Awduron Cymru **(Union of Welsh Writers):** begun in 1973 to promote writings in Welsh.

Undeb Cymru Fydd **(Union of a Future Wales, 1941)**: an organization committed to the culture and language of Wales. Through its publications and active lobbying at Westminster, it planted the seeds that grew into the formation of Cymdeithas yr Iaith Cymraeg and a quasi-Parliament for Wales.

Unification of Wales (1200-1240): under Prince Llywelyn ap Iorwerth, Wales was united as a single unit enjoying peace and prosperity.

Union, Acts of: (see Acts of Union).

University of Wales: founded by Royal Charter on 30 November, 1893. The colleges of the University are Aberystwyth (1872); Cardiff (1883); Bangor (1884);

Swansea (1920); the Welsh National School of Medicine (Cardiff, 1931); Newport (1996, formerly Newport Mechanics Institute (1841) and Gwent College of Further Education (1975). The former Institute of Science and Technology (1967) merged with Cardiff in 1988. In the new category of University colleges, formally incorporated into the University of Wales in 1996, are the University of Wales Institute, Cardiff, and University College, Lampeter (formerly St. David's College, 1827).

Unofficial Reform Committee, f. 1911: established at Tonypandy to try to settle a disagreement about pay, but which led to a series of strikes that affected the whole South Wales coal field. Demands for legislation to ensure a fair wage and the spread of the strike led to the passing of the Minimum Wage Bill in 1912.

Urban (12th C.): Bishop of Glamorgan who helped Llandaff to become an important ecclesiastical center; he was the first Welsh bishop to swear allegiance to Canterbury.

***Urdd Gobaith Cymru* (League of the Hope of Wales, 1922):** founded by Ifan ab Owen Edwards through his magazine *Cymru'r Plant* (the Children of Wales). Its support of the National Eisteddfod, promotion of Welsh-language schools, summer camping activities and so on have contributed immensely to the survival of Welsh language and culture. Its first national eisteddfod was held at Corwen, Merioneth, in 1929.

Urien Rheged (6th century): a king of Rheged, in the Old Northern kingdom, who, according to Nennius, resisted the Anglo-Saxon invaders, and who is praised by Taliesin.

Utica, New York State: the chief town of Oneida County, the heart of what was once the largest Welsh settlement in the United States.

V

There is no v in the Welsh alphabet.
In many Welsh names, the beginning letter f has been
been anglicized to v. (as in *Vaughan*, from Fychan).

Vale of Rheidol Railway: a narrow gauge line that
began in 1902 to carry lead ore from local mines, ti runs
from Aberystwyth to Devil's Bridge (Pont y Mynach).

Valentine, Lewis, Rev (1893-1986): b. Llanddulas,
Denbighshire: a minister at Llandudno and
Rhosllanerchrugog, one of the "PenyberthThree," Plaid
Cymru's first President, and its first Parliamentary
candidate in 1929 (his 609 votes became known as the
"Gallant Six Hundred." He expressed his nationalistic
views as editor of *Seren Gomer*.

Valentine's Day: (see St. Dwynwen).

Valle Crucis, Llangollen (f. 1201): a wind swept ruin
subject of many poetical works in the Middle Ages.
The Abbot once told Owain Glyndwr that he had
arrived a hundred years too early.

Valleys, the: the Taff, Rhondda, Rhymney, Ebbw and
Cynon, former industrial region where up to 250,000
miners produced over 57 million tons of coal each year.
With the rapid decline in iron, steel, tinplate, and coal,

the Valleys are starting to bloom again as tourist venues (or dormitories for Cardiff commuters)

Vaughan, Aled (b. 1920): journalist, short-story writer, and radio and television producer; he helped establish Harlech Television.

Vaughan, Gruffudd (1417-47): a Montomeryshire gentleman, helped capture Sir John Oldcastle and fought in France. The most famous jouster of the day, he killed his master. Forced to become and outlaw, he was caught and executed.

Vaughan, Henry (*the Silurist,* 1621-95): from Tretower, near Brecon, he wrote intensely emotional, religious poetry. The title of one of his Welsh poems is "Y Cerbyd" (the Chariot), a term also used by the Ministry of Transport to denote traffic on the M4 in South Wales.

Vaughan, Philip (18th Century): iron master at Carmarthen who patented radial ball-bearings for the axle bearings of carriages in 1794, many years ahead of the precise grinding machines that would accurately produce perfectly spherical metal balls.

Vaughan, Robert (1592-1667): antiquary and translator whose library at Hengwrt, Merionethshire helped save the priceless collection of manuscripts that includes *The Black Book of Carmarthen, The White Book of Rhydderch*, and *The Book of Taliesin.*

Vaughan, Rowland (1587-1667): translator and poet, his many translations (mainly of English religious works) show his mastery of Welsh prose.

Vaughan, Thomas (1621-66): metaphysician, soldier and alchemist, a twin brother of the more famous Henry; wrote some Latin and English poems before blowing himself up accidentally in his laboratory.

Vaughan-Thomas, Wynford (1908-87): popular writer and broadcaster began a distinguished career in broadcasting as a war correspondent, progressing to Director of Programs at HTV. He also wrote books on Wales that deal with history and landscape.

Vendotia: the Latin name for the ancient Kingdom of Gwynedd.

Vicari, Andrew (b. 1938): from Port Talbot, he is the highest paid living artist, the official painter for Interpol and the King and Government of Saudi Arabia. His first success was at the National Eisteddfod (gold medal at age 12); he chronicled the Gulf War and has been awarded a 25 million pound commission to paint the world's biggest oil painting *The Parable of Majesty*, to be colleted in 2005.

Vikings: sea-raiders whose place names survive in coastal Wales from Great Orme in the North to Swansea in the South.

Vivian: a family whose copper smelting made them millionaires, bought them a seat in the House of Commons, built Singleton Abbey and Park in Swansea, and poisoned the Tawe Valley for generations.

Vorderman, Carol (b. 1960): Denbigh-born Carol has become one of Britain's highest paid performers. Her "brains and beauty" first got her a job at Yorkshire Television, later made her the star of *Countdown* and numerous other television series.

Vortigern (*Gwrtheyrn*): British chieftain blamed for inviting the Saxons to settle in Britain. Mentioned by English historian Bede (8th Century), and by Welsh historian Nennius (9th century), he was named *Gwrtheyrn* by Gildas (6th Century). Nant Gwrtheyrn is home to the Welsh National Language Center.

Vulliamy, Clwyn Edward (*Twm Teg*, 1886-1971): a prolific writer from Radnorshire who began with anthropology and archeology in the 1920's, completed biographies of Voltaire and Rousseau, and other historical characters, and wrote novels under his pen-name *Anthony Rolls* and satirical prose and verse.

W

The twenty-seventh letter of the Welsh alphabet, mostly pronounced as the English U (as in *Bws*: Bus) or English OO (as in Welsh *Cwm*: Koom).

Wade-Evans, Arthur (1875-1964): b. Fishguard, Pembs; church vicar and distinguished scholar who counteracted the prevailing view of English historians regarding the early Welsh (mainly from Gildas), claiming that they were not displaced Britons but descendants of the Roman culture.

Waddington, Augusta: (see Lady Llanover).

Waithman, Robert (1764-1833): from Wrexham, became a successful draper in London, where he rose to become M.P., Sheriff, and Lord Mayor.

Wales: (see Cymru).

Wales **(1937-60):** an English-language magazine founded by Keidrych Rhys with works by many important Welsh writers, including the early Dylan Thomas, Vernon Watkins, R.S. Thomas, Emyr Humphries and others.

Wales and Berwick Act (1746): legislation that provided that all references made in Parliament to

England automatically included Wales (from then on it was common to find encyclopedia entries such as "For Wales, see England."

Wales Books Council, the (f.1961): to promote the writing and marketing of books for adults in Welsh.

Wales Craft Council (*Crefft Cymru*): begun in 1977 as an independent, non-political membership organization of full-time professional producers working Wales. With head office at Welshpool, it has over 120 craftsmen and women with skills ranging from wood carving to candlestick making.

Wales Gas Board (1947): when nationalization of British industry began, only the Wales Gas Board was recognized as a distinct, national entity.

Wales Gene Park (f. 2004): being developed in Cardiff, a multi-million pound virtual genetics knowledge park for Wales that came from collaboration between the University of Wales College of Medicine and other partners to establishe the biosciences sector as a major contributor to the Welsh economy.

Wales International Centre (f. March 15, 2004**):** an office at the Chrysler Building, New York. founded to promote Wales in North America.

Wales Millenium Centre, Cardiff: opened in the Fall of 2004, the new Centre is home to seven diverse cultural organizations including the Welsh National Opera, Urdd Gobaith Cymru, and The Touch Trust (to use movement, massage and music to aid people with profound disabilities). Built of Welsh materials and housed in Cardiff Bay, the Centre will be an icon for the resurgence of a re-emerging nation.

Wales on the Web (f.2002): based at the National Library of Wales, the primary access point to access information and services associated with Wales; an online guide to quality, validated websites with dependable information of Wales and Welsh life.

Wales, Prince of: (see Windsor, Charles).

Wales, Princess of: (see Spencer, Lady Diana).

Wales Tourist Board: set up in 1969 to encourage visitors to Wales and to provide and improve tourist facilities and amenities.

Wallace, Alfred Russell (1823-1913 b. Usk, Monmouth, the famous naturalist and author came to his opinions based on his own research into the processes of evolution independently of Darwin.

Walter, Lucy (1630-58): Pembrokeshire born, the mistress of Charles II when he was the Prince of Wales. Their son James, Duke of Monmouth, was executed after his rebellion against James II.

Walters, John (1721-97): lexicographer; compiled an English-Welsh dictionary and books on Welsh language.

Ward, John Powell (b. 1937): university lecturer, poet and critic, also editor of *Poetry Wales,* 1975 to 1980.

Watkins, David (b. 1942): captain of Great Britain in Rugby Union and Rugby League, a feat he duplicated for Wales before retiring to become Chairman of Newport Rugby Club.

Watkin, Morgan (1878-1970): scholar many of whose works deal with French influence on the literature and language of medieval Wales.

Watkins, Vernon (1906-1967): b. Swansea; contemporary of Dylan Thomas, Watkins lived a quiet life, with much of his poetry dealing with life's perplexing problems and the innocent memories of youth. Inspired by the beauty of the Gower, he is regarded as one of the greatest of Welsh poets in English.

Wat's Dyke (Flintshire, 8th Century): attributed to Aethelbald, King of Mercia as a boundary between Welsh and Saxon, it was a precursor of Offa's Dyke.

Webb, Harry (1920-1996): Swansea-born prolific poet, journalist, essayist, television writer, and political activist who used both Welsh and English to express his main themes, which he called "unrepentantly nationalistic." His first collection of poems is *The Green Desert* (1969).

Welsh Alphabet (Y Wyddor): seven vowels: a, e, i, o, u, w, y; twenty one consonants: b, c, ch, d, dd, f, ff, g, ng, h, l, ll, m, n, p, ph, r, rh, s, t, th; and eleven diphthongs: ae, ai, au, ew, iw, yw, oe, ow, oi, yw, and aw.

Welsh Americans: a group of Welsh Baptists under John Myles founded a church at Swanzey, Mass. in 1662. The Quakers found a home in Pennsylvania where the original Welsh Tract, granted by William Penn, still retains Welsh names such as Bryn Mawr, Bala Cynwyd, Tredyffryn and so on. The Welsh who came to Delaware in 1703 named their tract Pencader where they built two churches, both still standing. The Welsh Society of Philadelphia, founded in 1729, is the oldest ethnic society of its kind in the U.S. Large numbers of Welsh men and women moved to Pennsylvania, where they made up large numbers of the population of Scranton, Pittston, and Wilkes-Barre in the late 19th century. Others came from the quarrying districts of North Wales to settle in Bangor, Delta, and Cardiff on the Maryland-Pennsylvania border. Others moved out West, to Minnesota, Oregon, and California. The largest percentage of Welsh is found in Utah, where Welsh Mormons began the famous Tabernacle Choir.

Welsh American Genealogical Society (f. 1990): Poulntey, Vt, provides a link for Welsh genealogical researchers anywhere throughout the Welsh world.

***Welsh Anvil, The* (Yr Einion, 1949-1958):** an annual journal of the Guild of Graduates of the University of Wales that served as a forum for many up and coming Welsh writers on a variety of topics.

Welsh Arts Council (f. 1967): a committee of the Arts Council of Britain that supports the many activities connected with the arts in Wales. Its Literature Department helps provide funding for the Welsh Books Council, the Welsh Academy, and other societies.

Welsh Australians: four Welsh men and women arrived in Austalia as convicts on the *First Fleet* of 1788 followed by many rioters from Merthyr and by Chartist leaders in mid 19th century. Gold and coal attracted thousands more. William Meirion Evans of Llanfrothen, Merioneth, held the first Welsh religious services in 1849 at Burra. David Jones from Barmouth owned the largest drapery story in Victoria. David John Thomas of Carmarthen, an eminent surgeon, founded the Melbourne Hospital. Edgeworth David discovered and developed major coal seams in New South Wales. Lewis Thomas of Talybont became known as the "King of the Queensland Coalfields." Sir Samuel Walker Griffith, from Merthyr, was the principal architect of the federal constitution. William Morris Hughes, "the little digger," was the Prime Minister of Australia

(1915-1923).   Thomas Price was elected the first
Labour Premier of South Australia (1905).

Welsh Barony, Pennsylvania (17th Century): an area
chosen by William Penn to the wet of Philadelphia
(now called Main Line) where Welsh settlers (mainly
Merionethshire Quakers) could practice their own form
of government and religion; the verbal treaty was later
set aside by Pcnn and the Barony abolished by the
colonial government in 1690.

Welsh Black: cattle native to Wales that can survive in
harsh, mountain country. Mentioned in early literature,
originally bred for milk but now only for quality beef.

Welsh Books Council: an independent organization
with charitable status. funded by the national Assembly
and local authorities to promote all sectors of the
publishing industry in Wales, in both languages in
conjunction with libraries, schools, and publishers.

Welsh Cake (pice ar y maen): a small baked pancake,
with raisins and sprinkled with sugar (originally baked
on a stone).

**Welsh Cambrian Society of Canterbury, N.Z. (f.
1890):** to preserve and promote Welsh traditions in
music, literature and history and to give assistance to
members and new immigrants.

Welsh Canadians: The first Welshman to arrive in Canada is believed to have been Sir Thomas Button, who led an expedition to find the Northwest Passage in 1612. Other early Welsh in Canada came after the signing of the Treaty of Paris in 1763 and following the aftermath of the American Revolution (1775-1783). One of the first efforts to encourage Welsh emigration to Canada began in 1812 when John Matthews settled in the township of Southwald, near what is now London, Ontario. By 1817 he had brought over more relatives who built homes on the 100-acre lots granted to them by Colonel Thomas Talbot. The colony attracted 385 Welsh settlers by 1850. Early Welsh immigration to Canada was also spurred on by the Cariboo gold rush in British Columbia in 1858. The development of mining provided employment for many skilled Welsh miners who remained in the area. In 1902 Welsh immigrants arrived in Saskatchewan from Patagonia, which had been incorporated into Argentina. Many Welsh came to Alberta from their home country during the peak homesteading years after the turn of the century to become active in the trade union movement. David Milwyn Duggan, a Welshman, was the mayor of Edmonton from 1921 to 1923. Many other states have active Welsh societies, mainly in the larger cities, such as Vancouver, Ottawa, and Toronto.

Welsh Cavalry: name given affectionately to the lst Queen's Dragoon Guards (f. 1685), mostly made up of solders from Wales. For their bravery in Iraq, the Welshmen of the Dragoons, nicknamed "the commando light horse cavalry" were made honorary Royal Marines in April, 2003.

Welsh Countryside Council (Cyngor Cefn Gwlad): the natural wildlife conseration authority, that is the government's statutory advisor on sustaining natural beauty and wildlife and providing the opportunity for outdoor recreation in Wales and its inshore waters.

Welsh Development Agency (W.D.A.): set up in 1975 by Act of Parliament to further the economic development of Wales, promote business efficiency and international competitiveness, and to improve the physical environment. Since Devolution, it has taken over many functions of the Welsh Office, but in 2004, it came under the umbrella of the Assembly.

Welsh Fairies: (see Tylwyth Teg).

Welsh Family Names: last names (surnames) were unknown among the Welsh until the mid-16th century when the Acts of Union changed the way the country was administered. The Welsh patronymic system of using *ap* or *ab* for t *son of* was abandoned, the spelling of Welsh baptismal names was anglicized, and many old names were replaces by biblical or royal names such as John, David, Richard, and Henry. The Welsh were also obliged to adopt a system of fixed surnames as in England. (eg. Sion ap Dafydd became John Davies; John became Jones, Wiliam became Williams and so on).

Welsh Folk Dance Society (Cymdeithas Ddawns Werin Gymru, f.1953): founded to co-ordinate the activities of the many folk dance groups in Wales.

Welsh, Freddie (Frederick Hall Thomas, 1886-1927): b. Pontypridd; he went to the U.S. as a teenager. He defeated Willie Ritchie in 1914 to win the World Lightweight title, retained it for three years and was elected to the International Boxing Hall of Fame in 1997.

Welsh Folk Museum (*Amgueddfa Werin Cymru*: the Museum of Welsh Life, Cardiff): part of the National Museum of Wales. Its spacious grounds, centered on the former home of Lord Plymouth, contain chapels, farmhouses, mills, shops, miners' cottages etc.; the spacious interior is devoted to agriculture, costume, music and folklore.

Welsh Harp: 10th century sources mention the small Welsh or Breton harp but the name is usually given to the large triple harp of the 18th century that came from Italy as a baroque harp.

Welsh Heroes: in a poll conducted by *Culturenet. Cymru* in 2004 to determine the 100 greatest Welsh men and women, Aneurin Bevan topped the list, just beating out Owain Glyndwr, with Tom Jones coming in at third place. Three and a half million visitors to the website sent in 85,000 votes. Fourth was Gwynfor Evans; fifth, Richard Burton; sixth, Gareth Edwards;

seventh, Dylan Thomas; eighth, David Loyd George; ninth, Robert Owen; and coming in at number 10, Saunders Lewis. John Charles, who died a few days after the poll ended on March lst, came in at number 19. Top Welsh women were Catherine Zeta Jones at number 13 and Tanni Grey-Thompson at number 25.

Welsh Imperial Singers: "the Gentlemen of Song," toured Britain and overseas, including the U.S. and Canada, 1926 and 1939. Led by R. Festyn Davies from Trawsfynydd, the all-male choir gave its first concert in Anglesey in October, 1926. The outbreak of war in 1939 ended this glorious choir.

Welsh Language, the: a branch of Brythonic, derived from Celtic, spoken in the British Isles for three millenia, now restricted to about 500,000 speakers in Wales and probably that many in England and overseas.

***Welsh Language Act* (1967):** formally dissolved the legislation that had stood since the infamous *Wales and Berwick Act* of 1746 that provided that references made in Parliament to England automatically included Wales.

Welsh Language Board (f. 1988), a statutory body reconstituted in 1993 by the National Assembly to promote the use of the Welsh language and to ensure its equal treatment by public bodies in Wales.

Welsh Language Society: (see Cymdeithas yr Iaith Gymraeg).

Welsh Love Spoons: a tradition dating back to the 16th century by which a young man would carve a spoon for his beloved from a single piece of wood employing symbols as the wheel (I will work for you), the ball and cage (a soul imprisoned by love) and so on. They are now sold as tourist items.

Welsh National Gymanfa Ganu Association (W.N.G.G.A): an organization that began at Goat Island, Niagara Falls in 1929, it holds a national North American Gymanfa in a different location in the U.S. and Canada each Labor Day weekend (including Wales on two occasions). The Gymanfa has evolved into a four-day cultural event to be known as the North American Festival of Wales.

Welsh National Opera Company: begun as an idea at the home of a London Welshman in 1943, the company debuted with *Cavalleria Rusticana* at Cardiff's Prince of Wales Theatre in 1946. In 1970 the Welsh Philharmonic was formed that later became the Orchestra of Welsh National Opera. The Chorus became fully professional in 1973 one year after Carl Rizzi had become Musical Director, leading the company to international fame.

Welsh Nightingale, the (see Wynne, Edith).

Welsh Not: sometimes called the *Welsh Knot* or *Welsh Lump*, a heavy board placed around the neck of any pupil caught speaking Welsh in his school during the latter part of the 19th and early part of the 20th Century.

Welsh Office: (est. 1965): a government department responsible to the Secretary of State for Wales. It replaced various departments that had dealt specifically with Welsh issues including education, ancient monuments, health insurance, agriculture and fisheries. Further additions included housing and local government, transport, and forestry. In 1969 the use of Welsh in the registration of births, marriages and deaths was assigned to the Sec. of State for Wales; additional functions came in the 1970's in education and teachersí training and the establishment of the Develpt Board for Rural Wales. In 1997, the government published a *Voice for Wales* that proposed the transfer of most of the powers of the Office to an elected Assembly to take effect in July 1999. Since 1970, the Secretaries of State for Wales have been: Peter Thomas (1970); John Morris (1974-5); Nicholas Edwards (1979-85); Peter Walker (1987); David Hunt (1990-92); John Redwood (1993-4); William Hague (1995-96); Ron Davies (1997-99), Paul Murphy (1999-2002) and Peter Hain (2002-present).

Welsh Pony: acknowledged as the world's most beautiful pony, the breed became officially recognized in 1901 with the formation of the Welsh Pony and Cob Society. The Mountain pony is easily tamed and bred. A Welsh cob named *Fronaeth Cymraes Ddu* was bought for 4000 pounds in 2004 in Ceredigion.

Welsh Rarebit (or Welsh Rabbit): a delicious toasted dish made of cheese, butter, and beer.

Welsh Regiment: formed in 1990 by combining 3d Battalion, Royal Welch Fusiliers and 2d Battalion the Royal Regiment of Wales.

***Welsh Review, the* (f. 1939):** a magazine begun as a monthly, suspended during WWll, and began again as a quarterly until 1948, publishing works by Anglo-Welsh writers, including short stories, reviews, and poetry.

Welsh School of Medicine (f. 1931): part of the University of Wales at Cardiff.

Welsh Society of Philadelphia (St. David's Society): founded in 1729, the oldest ethnic society of its kind in the United States, members of which have made significant contributions to American history: in politics, agriculture, industry, and justice.

Welsh Sunday Closing Act (1881): the first piece of legislation passed by the British government specifically designed for the people of Wales, thus granting it the status of a distinct national unit.

Welsh Television (see Sianel Pedwar Cymru)

Welsh Terrier: formerly known as the black -and -tan wirehaired terrier, bred breed for centuries to hunt badgers, otters, and foxes.

Welsh Tract (see entries for New Wales and Welsh Barony).

Welsh Trust, The (f. 1674): a fund to provide the means to educate Welsh children in English and to provide adults with devotional books in Welsh, a predecessor of the S.P.C.K. (see above entry).

Welsh Voices **(1967):** an anthology introducing Anglo-Welsh poets.

Welsh Wars of Independence: two wars fought from 1276-7 and 1282-3 by Llywelyn ap Gruffuddd against Edward lst's designs to conquer and subdue all Wales. The first war ended with Llywelyn's defeat and the Treaty of Aberconwy. The second war begun by Dafydd ap Gruffuddd, ended when Llwyelyn was slain at Cilmeri and Dafydd was executed.

Welshtown, Nova Scotia: settled by Welsh immigrants who crossed the Atlantic on the ship *Fanny* in 1819.

Wenglish: called "the official voice of the Anglo-Welsh—a mixture of Welsh and English spoken by inhabitants of the South Wales Valleys.

Western Mail, the (f. 1869): one of the very few daily newspapers published in Wales, begun in Cardiff to promote the interests of the third Marquis of Bute (the owner of Cardiff Castle). Practically unheard of in much of North Wales, it thinks of itself as the national newspaper of Wales. With the revival of all things Welsh beginning in the 1960's, it became more sympathetic to the aims of Welsh Nationalists, to the drive to establish a Welsh Assembly, and to the Welsh language (Dafydd Iwan once sang that his favorite meal was fish and chips wrapped in the paper).

Westgate Square, Newport: site of the massacre of 1839 when a Chartist march was met by a volley of gunfire from a troop of Highlanders stationed inside the Westgate Hotel (demolished in 2004 for a shopping centre).

Weston, Simon (b. 1961): from Nelson, Treharris, joined the Welsh Guards in 1978, was horribly burned in the Falklands War aboard the *Sir Galahad.* He set up the Weston Spirit in 1988, to promote the personal and social development of disadvantaged young people. He was awarded the OBE in 1992.

Wheldon, Sir Huw (b. 1916): from Prestatyn, began in Office for Wales of the Arts Council, moved to t BBC as TV publicity officer in 1952, producing many outstanding programs and series, and becoming Managing Director in 1968.

White, Baroness Eirene (1909-1999): daughter of Tom Jones (deputy cabinet secretary to four P.M.'s), began a career as political journalist with Manchester Evening News in 1945, the year she was elected as Labour MP for East Flint. A tireless worker, she held many important offices, and was the first woman MP from Wales to become a minister; Chairman of the Labour Party in 1968-9.

***White Book of Hergest* (Llyfr Gwyn Hergest, mid 15th Century)** destroyed in the early 19th century, it contained many important texts: some transcripts have been preserved in the National Library of Wales.

***White Book of Rhydderch* (*Llyfr Gwyn Rhydderch*, mid-14th Century):** a two-volume collection of medieval Welsh prose that is the source of many tales in the *Mabinogion* and religious writings.

White Cattle of Dynevor: a rare breed descended from the "White Kine of Dynefawr" mentioned in the Laws of Hywel Dda.

White, Rawlins (1485-1555): one of three Welsh Protestants who were burned at the stake during the reign of Bloody Mary (see entries for Robert Ferrar and William Nichol).

Whitford, Richard (1495-1542): religious writer and priest from Flintshire, a friend of Erasmus and Sir Thomas More, and translator of Thomas a Kempis.

Whitland, Carmarthenshire: a small market town where a few fragments survive of the Cistercian abbey once known as *Ty Gwyn ar Dafi* (The White House on the Taf), the Mother house of Strata Florida and Strata

Marcella where Hywel Dda established his code of laws for entire Wales.

Whittaker, Thomas W. (b. 1919): from Blaenau Ffestiniog, served in India and Burma in WWll in Royal Welch Fusiliers, was instrumental in having the regimental museum located in Caernarfon Caslte.

Whittaker, Thomas (b. 1948): mountaineer, trainer and coroporate speaker, son of Thomas W, he became the first disabled person to climb Everset (1998). Having learned mountain climbing in Snowdonia, he is now a US citizen.

Wigley, Dafydd (b. 1943): M.P. for Caernarfon in 1974, led Plaid Cymru to succeed Gwynfor Evans in 1991, has a long and distinguished political career, particularly interested in the rights of the disabled. His majority at Caernarfon increased in each of five subsequent elections. A patriotic and tireless worker, he transferred his considerable talents and energy from Westminster to Cardiff as an Assembly Member. Dafydd is married to harpist Elinor Bennett.

Wil Friendly (*Gwilym Dawel)*: member of the London Welsh in the late 18th century who edited poetry, produced a Welsh dictionary, and published a *Cambrian Register* and a *Cambrian Biography*.

***Wild Wales* (1862):** an account of travels in Wales by English writer George Borrow whose friendship with local characters and knowledge of Welsh helped him present a fascinating contemporary picture.

Wilde, Jimmy (*the Mighty Atom,* 1892-1969): boxer began in fairgrounds Tylerstown, Rhondda, taking on all challengers. He had over 500 fights from age 16, winning the World Flyweight Championship in 1916, keeping it for seven years, the longest reign in history. Rated by Nat Fleischer and Charley Rose as the number one all-time flyweight champion of all time, Jimmy was elected to the International Boxing Hall of Fame in 1997.

Wiliam ap Tomas (1406-46): of Berth-hir, Mon; *Y Marchog Glas o Went* (The Blue Knight of Gwent) fought at Aginourt, prominent gentleman of Raglan and public officer in Gwent and Glamorgan; he married the daughter of the infamous Dafydd Gam).

Wiliam Llyn (1534-80): from Llyn, Caerns; one of the last of the poets to enjoy the patronage of the native aristocracy of Wales.

Wiliam, Urien (b. 1929): b. Swansea; playwrite, and novelist (son of Stephen J. Williams). A Senior Lecturer at the Polytechnic of Wales, he has written six novels, a number of plays and two-time Drama Medal winner at the National.

Wilkins, Charles (1831-1913): English writer closely identified with Wales, publisher of a number of historical works dealing with Welsh industry; editor of *The Red Dragon* and prolific contributor to south Wales weekly newspapers.

Wilkinson, "Iron Mad" John (1728-1808): iron manufacturer at Bersham (and nearby Brymbo), who once led the world in the production of iron cannon and cylinders for the new steam engines.

William de Braose (1150-1211): a Norman Marcher Lord who massacred his Welsh guests at a banquet. He was the grandfather of the equally notorious William de Braose hanged by Llywelyn ap Iorwerth.

William Cantrell Ashley: last sailing lifeboat in Great Britain, taken out of service in 1948 at New Quay, Dyfed.

William, Dafydd (1720-94): preacher and author of some 120 hymns, one of which is "Yn y dyfroedd mawr a'r tonnau" (often sung to the tune *Ebenezer*).

Williams, Alice (Alys, b. 1925); from Brynrefail, Llanberis; distinguished teacher and adjudicator of Welsh Folk Dancing, working tirelessly to ensure high standards of the craft in Wales and America.

Williams, Alice M.L. (Alis Mallet Williams, 1867-1950): novelist and early supporter of Plaid Cymru as well as efforts to revive the Breton language.

Williams, Anna (d. Dec 1987): at the time of her death at Swansea, Anna was 114 yrs old—the oldest lady in the world. She had seven siblings who reached 90 years; one sister was 101.

Williams, Dafydd (1720-94): Carmarthenshire preacher and hymn writer; convert to the Baptists, whose 121 Welsh hymns include the popular "Yn y dyfrocdd mawr a'r tonnau" (to the tune *Ebenezer*).

Williams, David (1738-1816): philosopher, whose works on religious freedom, universal education and the need for voting rights put him way ahead of his time; his 1782 *Letters on Political Liberty* was praised by Benjamin Franklin and also greatly influenced the Chartist movement of the next century. In 1790, Williams established the Royal Literary Fund, a benevolent society.

Williams, David (1900-78): historian and college Professor, whose *History of Wales* 1485-1931, *A History of Modern Wales,* and his writings on the social unrest of the 19th century are invaluable.

Williams, David John (D.J. 1885-1970): patriot, poet, teacher and short-story writer. A founder of Plaid Cymru and participant in "the Fire at Penyberth." His masterly descriptions of people and places are best seen in *Hen Dy Ffarm* (The Old Farmhouse) and *Hen Wynebau* (Old Faces).

Williams, David John (1896-1950): writer of childrens' stories; he founded the comic magazine *Hwyl* in 1949.

Williams, Dafydd Rhys (b. 1954): b. Canada to parents from Bargoed; proud of his Welsh background, he obtained his Doctorate in Medicine and Master of Surgery at McGill University. With many honors for his clinical research in emergency medicine, he joined the Canadian Space Agency in 1992 to become Director of the Space and Life Sciences Directorate. A Manager of the Missions and Space Medicine Group in the Astronaut Program, as an astronaut, he took the Red Dragon of Wales Flag into space. In November 2002.

Williams, Edward (Iolo Morganwg, 1747-1826): a patriotic London Welshman who brought about a revival of the study of Celtic literature and of what he considered to be Celtic customs. A stonemason from the Vale of Glamorgan, he helped create the *Gorsedd* that plans the elaborate ceremonies of the National Eisteddfod of Wales.

Williams, Eliseus (*Eifion Wyn*, 1867-1926): school teacher and poet whose *Telynegion Maes a Mor* (lyrics of Field and Sea, 1906) is still popular.

Williams, Emlyn (1905-1992): from a Welsh-speaking area in Flintshire, dramatist Williams toured the world portraying Charles Dickens and Dylan Thomas on the stage. His autobiographical novel *The Corn is Green* has been filmed by Hollywood twice and staged countless times. Williams also acted in many of his own plays, including *Night Must Fall, The Wind of Heaven, Druid's Rest,* and others. He appeared in a number of British and American movies.

Williams, Eric Idwal (1923-2001) from St. Clears, Carmarthen, a member of the Royal College of Veterinary Surgeons at age 21. His diagnostic test for Hardware Disease in cattle became known as the Williams Test. In 1961, he moved to Oklahoma to teach and research at Oklahoma State University. He received many honors for his work in science and on behalf of Welsh Americans; he reported in Welsh to the BBC Welsh Region, and wrote several books about his work.

William, Evan James (1903-1945): b. Llanwenog, Carms; a Fellow of the Royal Society, brilliant physicist and explorer of quantum mechanics who predicted the existence of a new particle, the meson. In WWll, his analytical mind helped produce the device that defeated German submarines, up until then playing havoc with Atlantic shipoing.

Williams, Gerald (b. 1949): from Ebbw Vale, he won the Mr. Universe contest (in the 65 kilo category) at Philadelphia in December, 2004) despite his relatively advance years.

Williams, Sir Glanmor (1920-2005): Dowlais-born, distinguished professor at Swansea 1945-1982; for ten years vice-president at Aberystwyth University; BBC's National Governor for Walwes 1965-71; general editor of Glamorgan County History, author of *Language, Religion and Nationality in Wales* (1979), and many other works of history; a leading Welsh historian and authority on modern Wales.

Williams, Grace (1906-1977): Barry composer with BBC, many of whose works are concerned with Welsh themes, especially the folk songs: *Fantasia on Welsh Nursery Tunes* (1940), *Sea Sketches (1944)* and *Penillion (1955).*

Williams, Griffith John (1892-1963): from Cellan, Cardigan, literary historian named by Meic Stephens as "perhaps the most versatile Welsh scholar of all time." Professor of Welsh at Cardiff, he specialized in the work of Iolo Morganwg, founded the scholarly magazine *Llen Cymru* (Welsh Literature), and was the first President of Yr Academi Gymreig (the Welsh Academy).

Williams, Gwyn (1904-90): b. Port Talbot, a prolific author and translator whose works include *An Introduction to Welsh Poetry* (1953), *The Burning Tree* (1956), and *Presenting Welsh Poetry* (1959). He also wrote novels and travel books of the Middle East and a collection of poetry.

Williams, Gwyn Alfred (1925-1995): b. Dowlais; historian, television personality and public speaker; among his books are *The Merthyr Rising* (1978); *Madoc: the Making of a Myth* (1979), and *When was Wales* (1985). With Vaughan Thomas, he produced *The Dragon has Two Tongues* for BBC television (1985).

Williams, Gwyn L.: arts and Music producer for the BBC in Wales, a lecturer at Bangor and Associate of the Royal Academy of Music.

Williams, Harri (1913-83): b. Liverpool, scholar, theologian and novelist, Prose Medal winner; a prolific author on a variety of subjects.

Williams, Hayden (1903-1965): Rhosllanerchrugog, nr. Wrexham; nationalist and promoter of the Welsh language, Director of Education for Flintshire who fought hard with eventual success to establish high schools where the language of instruction would be Welsh. He also lobbied for the setting up of a Welsh television station in areas of Northeast Wales unable to receive Welsh language programs.

Williams, Hugh (1796-1874): from Machynlleth, a prominent Chartist, he may have masterminded the Rebecca Riots of 1839-42.

Williams, Ifor (1881-1965): b. Bethesda, professor and scholar, editor of many books on early Welsh poetry, including *Pedeir Keinc y Mabinogi* (The Four Branches of the Mabinogi, 1930); publisher of works by poets of the Gentry, including Dafydd ap Gwilym. A lecturer with BBC, he served as editor of the Language and Literature section of the *Bulletin of the Board of Celtic Studies*.

Williams, Islwyn (1903-57): b. Ystalyfera, author of short stories that deal with life in the Valleys in all its colorful aspects.

Williams, Jac Lewis (1918-77): Cardiganshire-born; short story writer, professor; an authority on bilingual education and Anglo-Welsh literature.

Williams, Jane (Ysgafell, 1806-85): b. London; lived in Talgarth, learned Welsh and wrote a number of books on Wales including a biography of Beti Cadwaladr, the real nursing heroine of the Crimea War.

Williams, Jeremy Huw (b. 1969): Cardiff-born baritone, renowned for his Lieder, who began with the Welsh National Opera and has gone on sing with the world's leading opera companies.

Williams, John (1582-1650): a member of the illustrious Wynn family of Gwydir. Archbishop of York and supporter of Charles 1st. As his family seal is similar to that displayed over the monument to Shakespeare at Stratford on Avon, some scholars believe he may have written some or part of the plays.

Williams, John (ab Ithel, 1811-62): Denbighshire-born churchman, editor and antiquary, he helped revive Welsh culture in the early nineteenth century; founder and editor of *The Cambrian Journal* in 1853, and editor of many texts for the Welsh Manuscripts Society.

Williams, John (1840-1926): Carmarthenshire-born surgeon and physician to Queen Victoria, collector of the *Llanstephan Manuscripts*, an important source for medieval and later Welsh literature, including *The Red Book of Talgarth,* and poems of Dafydd ap Gwilym, Tudor Aled and others. He helped establish the National Museum of Wales and Library (he donated his collection on condition it be set up in Aberystwyth).

Williams, John Ellis (1901-75): born at Penmachno, Caernarfon; schoolmaster, prolific writer of plays, detective novels and children's books.

Williams, John Ellis Caerwyn (1912-1999): from Gwaencaegurwen, Swansea, Director of the Centre for Welsh and Celtic Studies who specialized in the literary traditions of Wales and Ireland.

Williams, John James (1869-1954): Talybont short story writer and poet, ex-miner, Congregational minister; Chair winner, and Archdruid (1936-39).

Williams, John Owen (Pedrog, 1853-1932); raised at Llanbedrog, Caerns; Archdruid (1928-32): Chairman of Union of Welsh Independents in 1927 and editor of *Y*

Dysgedydd (1922-28). A prolific contributor to the periodical presss, he is the all-time leader in number of eisteddfod prizes.

Williams, J.P.R. (b. 1949): b. Cardiff, a Welsh rugby great, with over 55 caps from 1969-1981. A medical doctor, he also won a junior tennis championship at Wimbledon. In 1997, he was elected to the International Rugby Hall of Fame.

Williams, John Roberts (John Aelod Jones, b. 1914): b. Llangybi, Caernarfon; journalist and broadcaster; edited *Y Cymro,* 1945-1962), the tv news magazine *Heddiw* (Today); became head of the BBC North Wales in 1970; with many short stories and a volume of essays, *Annwyl Gyfeillion* (Dear Friends, 1970).

Williams, Kyffin (b. 1918); Anglesey-born, one of his country's most known painters, specializing in Gwynedd landscapes exhibited in many prestigious museums and art galleries.

Williams, Llewellyn (1867-1922): b. Llansadwrn, Tywi Valley, he went from Llandovery College to Oxford University where he was influenced by the Dafydd ap Gwilym Society to work for Wales, especially for religious freedom from control by Canterbury. Liberal M.P. for Carmarthen Boroughs, he was a staunch nationalist, opposed to Lloyd George's abandonment of self-government for Wales and Ireland.

Author of *The Making of Modern Wales,* he also completed two novels. and a collection of short stories.

Williams, Mark (b. 1975): from Cwm, nr. Ebbw Vale, he earned the title of worlds' number one professional pool champion. Still playing at the Emporium, Bargoed, he turned pro in 1992 ten years before winning the Embassy World championship when he became thc first left-handed champion.

Williams, Morris (Nicander 1809-74): b. Llangybi, Caerns. Prominent in the Oxford Movement, he provided hymns for the use of Anglican congregations in Wales and is second only to William Williams in the number of hymns he contributed to the Church hymnal.

Williams, Moses (1685-1742): b. Llandysul, Carms., librarian and Parish rector, who translated English devotional works, helped edit *Leges Wallicae* (Welsh Laws 1730), and who left an important collection of old Welsh manuscripts.

Williams, Peter (1723-96): from Carmarthenshire; a leader of the influential Methodist Movement in the 18th century; the author of many religious books and hymns and the publisher of an annotated edition of the *Welsh Bible* in 1770. The first one to be published in Wales; it remained popular for over a century.

Williams, Phil (1939-2003): from Tredegar, outstanding professor of Physics at the University of

Wales, Aberystwyth, he was elected to the Welsh Assembly for Plaid Cymru (South East) in 1999. He was Shadow Secretary on Economic Develoment until his untimely sudden death.

Williams, Raymond (1921-1988); from Pandy, Monmouth; scholar, university tutor, Fellow, and professor, a leading cultural historian, author of books that include *Culture and Society* (1958), *The Long Revolution* (1966), *Marxism and Literature* (1977), and novels on contemporary Wales.

Williams, Rhydwen (1916-1997): Rhondda Valley-born writer of 5 volumes of poetry (two have won the Crown at the National Eisteddfod), novelist, television actor, and editor of *Barn* (Opinion).

Williams, Rhys (1892-1969): actor and Hollywood regular born in a mining valley in South Wales; appeared in over 60 films, stealing the show as boxer Dai Bando in *How Green was my Valley* after he had been hired to teach Welsh accents to the mostly Irish cast.

Williams, Richard (Dic Dywyll, 1790-1862): blind balladeer, "King of the Balladeers" singing of the Merthyr Uprising and the Rebecca Riots.

Williams, Richard (*Gwydderig*, 1842-1917): eisteddfod winner, a native of Brynamman who came home to Wales after some years as a miner in the U.S.

Williams, Richard Bryn (1902-81): b. Blaenau Ffestiniog, librarian, eisteddfod winner, and chronicler of the Welsh settlements in Patagonia where he was raised. Author of *Cymry Patagonia* (1942), *Y Wladfa* (1962), *Gwladfa Patagonia* (1865-1965, and children's novels, stories, and poems about life in Patagonia.

Williams, Richard Hughes (D*ic Tryfan*, 1878-1919): short story writer and journalist from Rhosgadfan, Caernarfon, whose hundreds of stories mostly deal with the lives of the North Wales quarrymen.

Williams, Richard Tecwyn (1909-1979): from Abertillery, Fellow of the Royal Society. Through a systematic analysis of drug metabolism, he explored the chemistry of how drugs affect the human body. Almost alone in doing vivo studies with the living body, as opposed to vitro studies in test tubes, his pioneering work forms an established part of pharmacology and toxicology.

Williams, Richard Hughes (Dic Tryfan, 1878-1919): b. Rhosgadfan, Gwynedd; short story writer and journalist whose hundreds of stories mostly deal with the lives of the North Wales quarrymen.

Williams, Robert (R*obert ap Gwilym Ddu*, 1766-1850): Caernarfonshire-born author of some moving religious poetry and hymn writer, whose "Mae'r gwaed a redodd ar y groes" is usually sung to the tune *Deemster*.

Williams, Robert (Trebor Mai, 1830-77): poet from Llanrhychwyn, Caerns. Whos claim to fame is his bardic name "I am Robert" in reverse.

Williams, Robin (1924-2004): from Pencaerau, Eifionydd, author, broadcaster, and popular preacher for many years; presented the Welsh hymn singing program *Dechrau Canu Dechrau Canmol* on television and chaired the Welsh *Natural History Brains Trust* as well as many radio programs.

Williams, Roger (1540-95): from Penrhos, Monmouth, author of books on military tactics, as a soldier famed for his bravery and skill in battle, perhaps the model for Fluellen in Shakespeare's *Henry V.*

Williams, Ronnie (d. 1997): actor in the T.V. series *Ryan and Ronnie* with fellow comedian Ryan Davies. They split in 1975 after a long partnership, Ronnie moving to Bangor to direct Theatr Gwynedd and appear in Welsh language TV programs. He committed suicide after business failings.

Williams, Rowan Douglas (b. 1950): from Swansea; elected as 104th Archbishop of Canterbury in 2002 (enthroned in February, 2003) after service as Archbishop of Wales.Former Professor of Theology at Oxford (the college's youngest professor at age 36), he is the first Welsh speaker at Canterbury in at least 1, 000 years. Author of a numnber of books on the history of theology and spirituality, he is a poet and a Fellow of the British Academy; a staunch patriot.

Williams, Prof. Stephen J. (1896-1992): from Ystradgynlais; after army service in India, he became lecturer (from 1924) then Professor of Welsh at University College, Swansea (from 1953), he has written and edited on Welsh subjects including grammar books for Welsh learners.

Williams, Thomas (*Twm Chawrae Teg*, "Fair Play Tom", 1737-1802): owner of the Parys Mines at Amlwch, which produced half the copper of late 18th C. Britain and set world prices.

Williams, Thomas Arfon (b. 1935): from Treherbert, Rhondda; dental officer with the Welsh Office Cardiff, prominent member of *Cymdeithas Cerdd Dafod*; a master of the englyn.

Williams, Thomas Marchant (1845-1914): from Aberdare; editor and writer, active in London Welsh societies, author of critical sketches (that gave him his nickname "Tom the Acid Drop"); edited *The Nationalist.*

Williams, Waldo (1904-71): teacher poet born in Haverfordwest. His anger at what was happening to Wales (by the government at Westminster), his commitment to Pacifism, his political activities with Plaid Cymru, and his struggle with personal demons is reflected in much of his work, called by Meic Stephens as "the most astonishingly original in the Welsh language."

Williams, Watkin Hezekiah (Watcyn Wyn, 1844-1905): from Brynaman, Carms. He worked underground at age eight; became a Congregational minister and Principal of Ysgol y Gwynfryn, Ammanford. Published several volumes of poetry and translated the hymns of Sankey and Moody into Welsh.

Williams, William (Pantycelyn, 1717-1791): Carmarthenshire-born, known as *Y Per Caniedydd* (The Sweet Singer), the most important hymn writer in Welsh history, a preacher and organizer of Methodist societies (along with Daniel Rowland and Howel Harris). His most popular hymn, beginning with "Lead me, O thou great Jehovah," is sung to *Cwm Rhondda*.

Williams, William (1781-1840): from Llanfachreth, Mer., an outstanding preacher who founded new chapels and attracted many to the cause.

Williams, William (1788-1865: from Llanpumpsaint, industrialist and radical M.P. Concerned that Welsh children should have more opportunity to learn English, his commission looked at the state of education in Wales (see the "Blue Books of 1847"); helped found the University of Wales.

Williams, William (Crwys, 1875-1968): Glamorganshire-born poet and eisteddfod winner, Archdruid of Wales (1939-47): noted for four volumes of verse.

Williams, William (b. 1909): from Denbigh, North Wales, where at the age of 95 (in 2004) he celebrated working over 70 years as a volunteer paperboy.

Williams, William Aubrey (Gwilym Gwent, 1834-91): from Tredegar, popular composer of Yr Haf and many other musical works, he emmigrated to Pennsylvania in 1872 where he is memorialized at Wilkes Barre.

Williams, William Llewelyn (1867-1922): from Llansadwrn, Carmarthen, journalist, lawyer, politician and historian. Editor of the first *South Wales Post,* M.P. for Caernarfon Boroughs (1906-18); he bravely opposed the war policies of David Lloyd George, and advocated Home Rule for Wales.

Williams-Ellis, Clough (1883-1978): distinguished architect and author, born of Welsh parents; creator of Port Meirion, a dream village on the Llyn Peninsula that was the setting for the cult T.V. series *The Prisoner* in the 1960's.

Williams-Wynn family, The: "the Uncrowned Kings of North Wales; by far the greatest landed family in Wales in 150, 000 acres in three counties. William

Williams (1634-1700) was Speaker of the House of Commns and AttorneyGeneral Watkin Williams (1693-1749) was a leading Jacobite; he took the surname Wynn and changed the family mansion from Wattstay to Wynnstay. The Watkin Williams Wynns represented Denbighshire in Parliament from 1716-1885. After the deat of the tenth baronet (1904-51), the Glanllyn mansion ner Bala became a center for *Urddd Gobaith Cymru*, and Wynnstay is the home of Lindisfarne College.

Wilson, Richard (1713-82): Penygroes-born, known as "the father of British landscape painting," known for his English and Welsh landscapes as well as scenes of Italy (where he was trained). He had a great influence on Turner, Conpstable and others. In 1769 he helped found the Royal Academy. The sign at the Loggerheads Inn near Mold is said to have been painted by Wilson to pay for his lodging.

Wilson-Roberts, Maimie Noel (1913-2003): from Felinheli, Caernarfon: an accomplished musician who worked in the 1930's with Gustav Holst; she became popular for her work on Welsh radio, for accompanying tenor David Lloyd, and at the International Eisteddfod, Llangollen for many years, where she was also a three-time winner.

Windsor, Charles Philip Arthur George (b. 1948): heir to the British throne; invested with the title Prince of Wales in an elaborate ceremony at Caernarfon in

1969, following a custom begun in 1284 by Edward lst to pacify the Welsh. Educated in England, Scotland, and Australia, he spent a few weeks in Aberystwyth early in 1969 to prepare for speeches he was scheduled to give in the Welsh language. Known to many nationalists in Wales as *Carlo*, he has spent little time there.

Winefride (Gwenffrewi, 7th century): the saint who has given her name to the holy shrine at Holywell, a place of pilgrimage for many centuries.

Winstone, Howard (1939-2000): from Merthyr, lost three fingers on his right hand as a child; won the British featherweight title, 1961; undefeated as British and European champion; won the World Championship, 1968.

Wladfa, Y: the name given to the Welsh settlements in Patagonia, Argentina. Nearly 200 Welshmen and women sailed from Liverpool on the *Mimosa* in late May, 1865 arriving at Puerto Madryn on the 27th day of July. They set up their own administration with a president, twelve councilors, a justice of the peace, a secretary, a treasurer and a registrar. Efforts to keep the Welsh language alive have seen the borrowing of teachers from Wales. For her work in fostering the preservation of the Welsh heritage of Yr Wladfa, Tegai Roberts was admitted to the Gorsedd in 1999.

Wlpan: a method of teaching Welsh through total immersion in the language that was adopted from Israel where Hebrew is taught to all newcomers.

Wogan, Thomas (1648-69): from Wiston, Pembs; a leading Welsh Parliamentarian, he fought at St. Fagans, was M.P. for Cardigan and was one of the two Welshmen who signed the death warrant of Charles lst. At the Restoration he was imprisoned, escaped and fled to Holland.

Wood family (Teulu Abram Wood): a gypsy family who arrived in Wales in the early 18th century speaking a form of old Romany, who introduced the fiddle to Wales. One member, John Roberts of Newtown, was known as *Telynor Cymru (*harpist of Wales). The last of the family was harpist Eldra Jarman.

Wooller, Wilfred (1912-1977): all-round sportsman playing rugby for Wales and cricket for Glamorgan. His rugby career cut short by internment in a Japanese POW camp, he captained Glamorgan in cricket, became President of the Glamorgan Cricket Club, and began a new career with BBC.

Woosnam, Ian (b. 1958): from a Welsh family at Oswestry, world class golfer Ian won the Swiss Open in 1982, and the U.S. Masters in 1991. In 2001, he won the World Matchplay Championship for the third time.

Woulds, James: Theatre manager at Swansea during the summer seasons from 1831 to 1839, who hired many of Britain's leading actors.

Wrexham (North Wales Electoral Region): parliamentary constituency, area 504 sq. km; pop. 125.2 thousand, with 15.4 Welsh speaking.

Wrexham: the largest town in North Wales, it serves a wide area as a market, industrial, sporting center and center of high technology. Outstanding is St. Giles Church where Elihu Yale is buried.

***Wrexham Leader, The* (f. 1920):** has missed only one day, due to a storm in 1969. In the General Strike of 1926, it published a one-page edition. In 1934, it received national recognition for its coverage of the disaster at Gresford. In 1975, it began the *Evening Leader* to blend local and national news.

Wright, Frank Lloyd (1869-1959): one of the 20th century's most influential architects. Proud of his Welsh ancestry, he designed the Jonson Wax Company Building at Racine, Wisconsin; the Guggenheim Museum in New York, *Taliesin* at Scottsdale, Arizona and many others.

Writers of Wales (f. 1970): a series of monographs on Welsh and Anglo-Welsh writers published by the University of Wales Press for the Welsh Arts Council.

Wroth, William (1576-1641): from Abergavenny, Mon, influential Puritan leader who began the first Independent church in Wales at Llanfaches, Gwent.

Wyddor, y: (see Welsh alphabet).

Wye (*Gwy*): scenic river beginning in the hills of Plynlimon, Ceredigion, travelling 130 miles (209 km) to the Severn Estuary.

Wyn, Eirug (1951-2004): from popular novelist and satirist, literary prize winner and editor and publisher of *Lol.*

Wyn Davies, Geraint (b. 1957): from Swansea, went to Canada, aged seven to become one of his new country's most popular TV and stage stars in such prouductions as *DOA, Deadly Harvest* and *Forever Knight.*

Wynne, Edith (1842-97): b. Northop, Flints, soprano who became famous in the U.S. as "The Welsh Nightingale."

Wynne, Ellis (1671-1734): N. Wales clergyman; his *Gweledigaetheu y Bardd Cwsg* (Vision of the Sleeping Bard (1703), became an enduring Welsh classic.

Wynne family, The: of Peniarth, Mer: William Watkin Edward Wynne (1801-80), M.P. for Merioneth in 1852, was a distinguished historian and genealogist who inherited the great library at Hengwrt; his son William Wynne Vll (1840-1900) was MP for Merioneth in 1865.

Wynne, Ellis (1671-1734): Merionethshire, Anglican priest remembered for his influential *Vision of the sleeping Bard* (*Gweledigaetheu y Bardd Cwsc*), 1703.

X

There is no letter X in the Welsh alphabet. A similar sound comes from the use of cs, as in *Wrecsam*: the Welsh spelling of Wrexham.

Y

The twenty-eighth and last letter of the Welsh alphabet, pronounced as in English y in *myrrh* or *Betty*. Both pronunciations are found in *y ty* (the house).

Yale: a distinguished family one of whom (Elihu) helped establish the University in New Haven, Connecticut. His tomb is in Wrexham churchyard.

Young, David (*Dai,* b. 1967): from Aberdare, played rugby league at Salford, with 14 international appearances; then union at Cardiff, with 51 caps.

Y Byd (The World): national Welsh-language newspaper, to begin in 2005 (see Thomas, Edward Morley).

Y Gymraes (the Welsh Woman): begun in 1850 by Ieuan Gwynedd, it was the first Welsh language weekly for women.

*Ymadawiad Arthur (*The Departure of Arthur, 1902):** a poem by T. Gwynn Jones that won the Chair and helped spark a renaissance in Welsh literature.

Yn y Llyvr Hwnn (In this Book): by John Prys of Brecon in 1546, the first book published in the Welsh language.

Ynys Afallon (Avalon): the island where mortally wounded Arthur rested after the Battle of Camlan.

Ynyscedwyn, Ystradgynlais: a foremost iron-producing center in the early 19th century where David Thomas used a hot blast to smelt iron ore with anthracite. The works produced iron until 1871 and tin until 1947.

Yorath, Terry (b. 1950): footballer at Leeds, Coventry, and Spurs, managed Swansea in 1986. Won 59 caps for Wales, appointed manager in 1991.

Yorke, Philip (1743-1804): from Erddig, Wrexham, antiquary who wrote *Royal Tribes of Wales* (1799): his descendant Philip was the last owner of Erddig.

Z

There is no Z in the Welsh alphabet
(but see entry for Catherine Zeta Jones, of Hollywood
fame).

Zito, Jayne (b. 1964): from Rhondda, Jayne married
Jonathan Zito who was stabbed to death in Dec, 1992
by a man with a history of violence and psychiatric
problems. Jayne set up the Zito Trust to campaign for
better support and treatment of the mentally ill. In
2001, she was awarded the OBE for her outstanding
work.

About the Author

Peter N. Williams was born in Mancot, a little village in Flintshire, North Wales, just inside the border with England. Brought up in the industrial town of Flint, he was educated at King's School, Chester, England and at the University College, Swansea, South Wales.

Peter came to the United States in 1957. Following his military service with the U.S. Army in Germany, he taught high school in Delaware for a number of years before completing his M.A. and Ph.D. at the University of Delaware. He then taught English at the University before becoming chairman of the English Department at Delaware Technical and Community College. Peter is the editor of *Celticinfo.com, Celtic_Worlds.com,* and *The Eagle and Dragon* (the official publication of the National Welsh American Foundation).

Founder of the Welsh Society of Delaware, and a director of the National Welsh American Foundation, Peter was honored for his work on behalf of Wales and Welsh Americans by being made a member of the

Gorsedd of Bards at the National Eisteddfod of Wales in 1999. He is the author of *The Sacred Places of Wales; From Wales to the Lehigh: the David Thomas Story; the Seven Wonders of Wales: a New look; The History of Wales in Verse; Wales from A to Y; The Book of Wales,* and the *editor of 38 Hymns in Welsh and English.*